Southern New Hampshire Trail Guide

Hiking trails in Southern New Hampshire

Compiled and edited by Jon Burroughs and Gene Daniell

APPALACHIAN MOUNTAIN CLUB
BOSTON, MASSACHUSETTS

Cover Photograph: Robert Kozlow
Book Design: Carol Bast Tyler

Library of Congress Cataloging-in-Publication Data
Southern New Hampshire trail guide: hiking trails in
southern New Hampshire / compiled and edited by Jon Burroughs and Gene Daniell.
p. cm.
Includes index
ISBN 1-878239-73-2 (alk.paper)
1. Hiking—New Hampshire Guidebooks. 2. Trails—New Hampshire Guidebooks.
3. New Hampshire Guidebooks. I. Burroughs, Jon. II. Daniell, Gene.
VGV199.42.N4S68   1999
917.4204'43—dc21   99-22411
                                                      CIP

The paper used in this publication meets the minimum requirements of the American National Standard for Information Sciences—Permanence of Paper for Printed Library Materials, ANSI Z39.48-1984. ∞

**Due to changes in conditions, use of the information
in this book is at the sole risk of the user.**

Printed in the United States of America.

Printed on recycled paper using soy-based inks.

10 9 8 7 6 5 4 3 2   00 01 02 03 04

Contents

List of Maps

Folded, in pocket:

1. Monadnock

2. Cardigan

Page maps:

Key to Maps

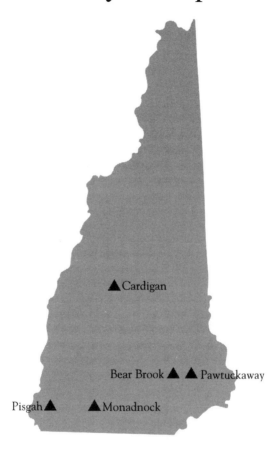

PULL-OUT MAPS
Mt. Monadnock, map 1
Mt. Cardigan, map 2

IN-TEXT MAPS
Pisgah State Park, p. 24
Bear Brook State Park, p. 118
Pawtuckaway State Park,
p. 194

Introduction

During the past two decades there has been a spectacular growth in the number and variety of trails available in New Hampshire south of the White Mountains. Recognizing that our *White Mountain Guide* could afford the space for only a small fraction of these trails, we decided to inaugurate a guide to trails in southern and central New Hampshire. Even this book cannot include every trail that exists in this region, but we have attempted to give complete coverage to the trails on Mt. Monadnock, Mt. Cardigan, and Mt. Kearsarge—the three most prominent peaks in the region—as well as the trail systems of the three largest state parks, Pisgah, Bear Brook, and Pawtuckaway. In other areas we have not applied any arbitrary criteria of length or strenuousness, but have attempted to choose trails that seem to offer those qualities that most appeal to the hiker: views, climbs, summits, and interesting natural features, giving particular weight to the comparative importance of a given trail or feature relative to others in its vicinity. In general we have avoided what might be described as nature walks, except when they visit hilly ground with views or unusually significant natural features. For nature walks, see *Nature Walks in Southern New Hampshire* and *Nature Walks in the New Hampshire Lakes Region,* both written by Julia Older and Steve Sherman and published by AMC Books.

Many trails that could not be included in this first edition merit consideration for inclusion in future editions. Some of these trails could not be included because agreements with landowners for their permanent routes have not been completed, while others have been excluded by time and space considerations. The editors of this book will gratefully accept suggestions from our readers concerning trails that should be considered for inclusion in future editions.

This book is intended to be used primarily in the snowless season, which can vary considerably from year to year; higher elevations have much shorter snowless seasons. Trails in general are much harder to follow when there is snow on the ground, and deep snow requires ski or snowshoes and the skill to use them efficiently (although popular trails may be broken out through most of the winter). When ice is present, there is particular danger on mountains with steep open ledges, such as Monadnock, Cardigan, and Mt. Major. Accidents, some of them serious, are common on such lesser mountains when winter conditions prevail because of the ease of access for people who are unequipped and unprepared for the hazards they encounter. Do not underestimate the difficulty of these small mountains in adverse cold-weather conditions. Monadnock and Cardigan, especially, are high enough to have severe weather conditions. In spring, deep snowdrifts may remain on northern slopes even at lower elevations after all snow is gone on southern exposures. At this time of year, in order to avoid encountering deep drifts, hikers should be particularly wary of northern slopes as well as higher elevations.

Plan your trip schedule with safety in mind. Consider the strength of your party and the general strenuousness of the trip: the overall distance, the amount of climbing, and the roughness of the terrain. Get a weather report, but be aware of the fact that most forecasts are not intended to apply to the mountain region; a day that is sunny and pleasant in the lowlands may well be inclement in the mountains. The National Weather Service in Gray ME issues a forecast for New Hampshire that includes a recreational forecast for the White Mountain region; it is broadcast on its short-wave radio station each morning and also carried on the National Weather Service telephone line (603-225-5191). Mountain weather information is also available on the AMC website (www.outdoors.org). Conditions on even the highest peaks of southern New Hampshire are usually considerably less severe than those in the high peaks of the White Mountains, but the recreational forecast may help to suggest lesser but still serious weather problems that may occur elsewhere in the state.

Plan to finish your hike with daylight to spare (remember that days grow shorter rapidly in late summer and fall). Hiking after dark, even with flashlights (which frequently fail), makes finding trails more difficult and crossing streams hazardous. Let someone else know where you will be hiking, and do not let inexperienced people get separated from the group. Many unpaved roads are not plowed in winter or are not passable during the spring mud season (which varies from place to place), so access to some trails may be much more difficult at these times.

Most of the trails in this book are located in public parks and forests or in the reservations of conservation organizations such as the New Hampshire Audubon Society and the Society for the Protection of New Hampshire Forests (SPNHF). Others—most prominently the Monadnock-Sunapee Greenway, the Wapack Trail, and the Meta-comet-Monadnock Trail—lie mostly on private land, but with the protection of formal agreements with landowners. On such trails hikers should exercise care to observe regulations that have been designed to protect the land itself and the rights of landowners. There are in addition a number of trails that cross private land with no formal permission from the landowner; the existence of such trails is supported only by a long tradition of public use. Some of these trails are among the most popular in southern New Hampshire—the trail to Mt. Major from NH 11 is an example—and despite many decades of public use and enjoyment these trails are subject to closure at the will of the landowner, so hikers should be particularly careful to respect the lands these trails pass over so as not to give the owners cause to consider closing them.

Many trails in the three largest state parks—Pisgah, Bear Brook, and Pawtuckaway—are multi-use trails, open to mountain bikes in summer and snowmobiles in winter. In most cases they have been much more heavily used for these purposes than for hiking in the past. Hikers, skiers, and snowshoers should be aware that they will be sharing the trails and should be prepared to extend trail courtesies to these other users.

With a very few exceptions (as noted in individual descriptions), trailside camping (backpacking) is not permitted along the trails described in this book. In state parks, camping is allowed only in vehicle-accessible campgrounds. On private lands (including those owned by organizations such as the Audubon Society and the SPNHF) camping is permitted only with the permission of the landowner, which is very rarely given. Hikers also should never kindle wood campfires, even in places where others have obviously done so. Illegal camping and campfires are among the most common practices that may cause landowners to close trails.

Litter is frequently a problem, particularly in areas where vehicle access is permitted (or unauthorized vehicular access is easy). Hikers should be scrupulous about never contributing to this problem, and picking up litter left by thoughtless others improves the beauty of the woods and contributes to goodwill with landowners—just as the presence of litter antagonizes landowners.

Hikers should be aware that some trails in this book (as noted in descriptions) are far less easy to follow than others; the presence of signs and blazes varies, and some trails are too new to have a well-beaten footway while others have received very little use. Inexperienced hikers should avoid trails that are described as being difficult to follow, and all trail users should observe and follow trail markings carefully. It cannot be emphasized too strongly that there is almost no trail that might not be closed unexpectedly or suddenly become obscure or hazardous under certain conditions. Trails can be rerouted or abandoned or closed by landowners. Signs are stolen or fall from their posts. Storms may cause blowdowns or landslides, which can obliterate a trail for an entire climbing season or longer. Trails may not be cleared of fallen trees and brush until late summer, and not all trails are cleared every year. Logging operations can cover trails with slash and add a bewildering network of new roads. In addition, even momentary inattention to trail markers, particularly arrows at sharp turns or signs at junctions, or misinterpretation of signs or guidebook descriptions can cause hikers to become separated from all but the most heavily traveled paths—or at least lead them into what may be a much longer or more difficult route. So please remember that this book is an aid to planning, not a substitute for observation and judgment.

As a consequence, all the trail-maintaining organizations, including the AMC, reserve the right to discontinue any trail without notice and expressly disclaim any legal responsibility for the condition of any trail. Most organizations give priority to heavily used trails, so lightly used trails quite often do not receive their share of attention and following them may require great care.

The mountains themselves may seem virtually changeless, but the lands of the New Hampshire mountains and forests are constantly subjected to the powerful forces of nature and the pervasive effects of contacts with human visitors and their management policies. Since change is therefore the rule, no source of information can be perfectly trustworthy, and a guidebook to this region can never be more than a record of the way things were at a given moment in time. Though great care has been taken to make this book as accurate as possible, it will be a useful tool only if its owner employs constant good judgment and vigilance. In the woods, we are visitors who must accept that this environment can be only partly adapted to our convenience—and in fact most of us prefer to visit a backcountry relatively undisturbed by human interference—so we must make up the difference by adapting our behavior as circumstances demand.

No attempt is made to cover any kind of skiing (alpine, downhill, or cross-country), although several cross-country (ski-touring) trails are mentioned where they are open to hiking use in summer or happen to intersect hiking trails. Rock climbs are not described in this book, since they require special techniques and equipment and should be undertaken only by roped parties under qualified leaders, due to the high degree of danger to inexperienced or insufficiently equipped climbers or groups.

We request your help in keeping this guide accurate. New editions are published at intervals of about four or five years. This book belongs to the entire hiking community, not just to the AMC and the people who produce it. If you encounter a problem with a trail, or with a map or description in this book, please let us know. The comments of a person who is inexperienced or unfamiliar with a trail are often particularly useful. Any comments or corrections can be sent to the *Southern New Hampshire Trail Guide,* AMC, 5 Joy St., Boston, MA 02108.

Following Trails

Hikers should always carry a map and compass and carefully keep track of their approximate location on the map. The Cardigan and Monadnock maps included with this guide are topographic maps (maps with the shape of the terrain represented by contour lines). Maps to all parts of New Hampshire, including the areas not covered by our Cardigan and Monadnock maps, are available from the United States Geological Survey (USGS). They are published in rectangles of several standard sizes called quadrangles ("quads"). All areas in the regions described in this guide are now covered by the recent, more detailed 7.5-minute quads—some in metric format—which have largely replaced the old 15-minute quads. Although topography on the newer maps is excellent, some recent maps are very inaccurate in showing the locations of trails. USGS maps can be obtained at a number of local outlets and from USGS Map Sales, Federal Center, Box 25286, Denver, CO 80225 (800-USA-MAPS). Index maps showing the available USGS quads in any state (specify states) and an informative pamphlet entitled "Topographic Maps" are available free on request from the USGS. USGS maps are now also available on compact disk from a number of sources; it is possible to obtain 7.5-minute quads for the entire state of New Hampshire on one compact disk, allowing one to print a map for any desired location.

This guide features two new maps that were designed on a computer, using a variety of digital data. The most valuable source of data comes from global positioning system (GPS) technology. Every mile of trail on these maps was hiked and electronically recorded with GPS technology. The resulting maps accurately depict trail locations. Many previous maps, including USGS quadrangle maps, relied on less precise techniques to determine a trail's location. Universal Transverse Mercator (UTM) grid coordinates are included on the map sheets to facilitate the use of GPS receivers in the field. Additionally, a mileage scale runs around the outer frame of each map to help users estimate distance.

Although the original GPS data is very exact, certain features (including roads, streams, and trails) may have been approximated and/or exaggerated in order to show their proper relationships at map scale. We would appreciate your assistance by reporting corrections to: *Southern New Hampshire Trail Guide,* Appalachian Mountain Club, 5 Joy St., Boston, MA 02108.

Extra copies of AMC maps may be purchased at the AMC's Boston and Pinkham Notch offices and at some book and outdoor-equipment stores. Other maps of specific areas are mentioned in the relevant individual sections of this guide. Many of these are also available from the AMC.

The best compass for hiking is the protractor type: a circular, liquid-filled compass that turns on a rectangular base made of clear plastic. Excellent compasses of this type, with leaflets that give ample instructions for their use, are available for less than $10. Such a compass is easily set to the bearing you wish to follow, and then it is a simple matter of keeping the compass needle aligned to north and following the arrow on the base. More sophisticated and expensive compasses have features designed for special applications that are often not useful in the woods; they are normally harder to use and apt to cause confusion in an emergency situation. Directions of the compass given in the text are based on true north instead of magnetic north, unless otherwise specified. There is a deviation of approximately 16° between true north and magnetic north in the southern half of New Hampshire. This means that true north will be about 16° to the right of (clockwise from) the compass's north needle. If you take a bearing from a map, you should add 16° to the bearing when you set your compass. On the maps included with this guide, the black lines that run from bottom to top are aligned with true north and south.

In general, trails are maintained to provide a clear pathway while protecting the environment by minimizing erosion and other damage. Some may offer rough and difficult passage. Most hiking trails are marked with paint on trees or rocks, though a few still only have axe blazes cut into trees. In general, the color of blazing has no significance and may change without notice; therefore blazing color is sometimes not a reliable means of distinguishing particular trails from intersecting ones. Above timberline, cairns (piles of rocks) mark the trails. Where hikers have trodden out the vegetation, the footway is usually visible except when it is covered by snow or fallen leaves. In winter, signs at trailheads and intersections and blazes also are often covered by snow. Trails following or crossing logging roads require special care at intersections in order to distinguish the trail from diverging roads, particularly since blazing is usually very sparse while the trail follows the road. Around shelters or campsites, beaten paths may lead in all directions, so look for signs and paint blazes.

If you lose a trail and it is not visible to either side, it is usually best to backtrack right away to the last mark seen and look again from there; this will be made much easier if you carefully note each trail marking and keep track of where and how long ago you saw the most recent one. Even when the trail cannot be immediately found, it is a serious but not desperate situation. Few people become truly lost in the New Hampshire woods; a moment's reflection and five minutes with the map will show that you probably know at least your approximate location and the direction to the nearest road, if nothing else. Most cases in which a person has become lost for any length of time involve panic and aimless wandering, so the most important first step is to stop and take a break, make an inventory of useful information, decide on a course of action, and stick to it. (The caution against allowing inexperienced persons to become separated from a group should be emphasized here, since they are most likely to panic and wander aimlessly. Make sure also that all party members are familiar with the route of the trip and the names of the trails to be used, so that if they do become separated they will have some prospect of rejoining the group.) If you have carefully kept track of your location on the map, it will usually be possible to find a nearby trail or road to which a compass course may be followed. Most distances are short enough that it is possible, in the absence of alternatives, to reach a highway in half a day, or at most in a whole day, simply by going downhill, carefully avoiding any dangerous cliffs (which will normally be found in areas where the map's contour lines are unusually close together), following a rough compass course—particularly in relatively flat areas—to avoid going in circles.

What to Carry

Adequate equipment for a hike in the New Hampshire hills and forests varies greatly according to the length of the trip and the difficulty of getting to the nearest trailhead if trouble arises. If you are only strolling in to a pond or waterfall a mile or so from the road in good weather, then perhaps a light jacket, a candy bar, and a bottle of water will suffice. If, however, you are going above treeline and are not inclined to turn back at the first sign of questionable weather, you will need a good pack filled with plenty of warm clothing and food for emergency use, and other equipment. No determination of what one needs to take along can be made without considering the length of a trip and the hazards of the terrain it will cross.

Good things to have in your pack for an ordinary summer day hike include guidebook, maps, water bottle (ordinary plastic soft-drink bottles, with or without original contents, work well), compass, knife (good-quality stainless steel, since ordinary steel rusts very quickly), rain gear, windbreaker, wool sweater(s), wool hat and mittens, waterproof matches, enough food for your usual needs plus extra high-energy foods in reserve (such as dried fruit or candy), first-aid supplies (including personal medicines, a non-prescription painkiller such as aspirin, acetaminophen, or ibuprofen, and adhesive bandages, gauze, and antiseptic), needle and thread, safety pins, nylon cord, trash bag, toilet paper, and a (small) flashlight with extra batteries and a spare bulb.

Wear comfortable hiking boots. Lightweight boots, somewhat more sturdy than sneakers, are popular these days. Experienced hikers can often wear sneakers quite safely and comfortably on easy to moderate hikes. Unfortunately, most of the people who actually do wear sneakers on the trails are inexperienced and not accustomed to walking on rough trails, and have legs and ankles that are not trail-toughened. As a result, many leg injuries occur on short, relatively easy trails because of the large numbers of inexperienced hikers who wear sneakers when they need the support of boots.

Blue jeans, sweatshirts, and other cotton clothes are popular but, once wet, dry very slowly and may be uncomfortable; in adverse weather conditions they often seriously drain a cold and tired hiker's heat reserves. While such clothes are worn by most hikers on most summer trips, people who are planning to travel to remote places or above treeline should seriously consider wearing (or at least carrying) wool or synthetics instead. Wool keeps much of its insulating value even when wet, and it (or one of several modern synthetic materials) is indispensable for hikers who want to visit places from which return to civilization might require substantial time and effort if conditions turn bad. Not only do hats, mittens, and other such gear provide safety in adverse conditions, but they also allow one to enjoy the summits in comfort on those occasional crisp, clear days when the views are particularly fine and the other hikers who snickered at one's bulging pack are driven from the magnificent vistas with terse greetings forced through chattering teeth.

Backcountry Hazards

In emergencies call the toll-free New Hampshire State Police number (800-852-3411).

Hypothermia, the most serious danger to hikers in the New Hampshire woods, is the loss of ability to preserve body heat because of injury, exhaustion, lack of sufficient food, and inadequate or wet clothing. For example, most of the dozens of deaths on Mt. Washington have resulted from hypothermia. It is important to understand that the victim does not "freeze to death," since death occurs at a body temperature of about 80° F. Many cases occur in temperatures above freezing; the most dangerous weather conditions involve rain, with wind, with temperatures below 50° F. The symptoms include uncontrolled shivering, impaired speech and movement, lowered body temperature, and drowsiness. The result is death, unless the victim (who will not understand the situation, due to impaired mental function) is rewarmed. In mild cases the victim should be given dry clothing and placed in a sleeping bag (perhaps with someone else in it to provide body heat), then quick-energy food and something warm (not hot) to drink. In severe cases only prompt hospitalization offers reasonable hope for recovery. It is not unusual for a victim to resist treatment and even combat rescuers. It should therefore be obvious that prevention of hypothermia is the only truly practical course. Uncontrollable shivering should be regarded as a sure sign of hypothermia; this shivering will eventually cease on its own, but that is merely the sign that the body has given up the struggle and is sinking toward death.

Much has been written about hypothermia, and some of the advice has been confusing, largely because a victim in an advanced state of hypothermia requires radically different treatment from one in the early stages of the illness. Basically, *chronic hypothermia*—the form usually encountered in hiking situations—develops over the course of several hours when a person loses body heat faster than it can be generated. The body uses a number of means to prevent the temperature of vital organs from dropping to a level where proper functioning will be impaired; most important of these is the withdrawal of blood supply from the extremities of the body into the core. This is the reason that poor coordination of hands and legs is an important sign of a developing problem.

As the situation becomes more serious, the body goes into violent shivering, which produces a substantial amount of heat but consumes the body's last remaining energy reserves very rapidly. At this point rapid and decisive application of the treatments mentioned above may still save the victim's life. (Unfortunately, an exhausted hiker, or one who has not been eating or drinking properly, may not possess the energy reserves for violent shivering.) Violent shivering is the body's last response; once the shivering ceases the body has no more weapons to use and the descent toward death is quite rapid. This is *profound hypothermia;* and profound hypothermia cannot be treated in the field, since it requires advanced techniques such as circulating warm water through the abdominal cavity to rewarm the victim from the body core outward. Any attempt to rewarm such a person in the field will cause cold blood from the extremities to return to the heart, almost certainly causing death from heart failure. Extreme care also must be used in attempting to transport such a person to a trailhead, since even a slight jar can bring on heart failure. Since successful rescue of a profoundly hypothermic person from the backcountry is so difficult, the need for prevention or early detection must be obvious. In almost all cases, the advent of hypothermia is fairly slow, and in cold weather all members of a hiking group must be aware of the signs of developing hypothermia and pay constant attention to the first appearance of such signs—which may be fairly subtle—in all fellow party members, so as to detect the condition in one of their companions well before it becomes a serious matter. Those who do not pay attention to the well-being of their companions may well have the experience of standing by helplessly while a friend dies.

In sum, a person who is shivering violently must be treated for hypothermia immediately and aggressively. Since victims do not always exhibit violent shivering, as a general rule it is safe to render this sort of treatment to anyone who is able to eat or drink voluntarily, perhaps with minor assistance. Once violent shivering has ceased, or when a victim is unable to eat or drink without exceptional assistance, the existence of a state of profound hypothermia must be assumed. The victim should be protected from further heat loss as much as possible and handled with extreme gentleness, and trained rescue personnel should be called for assistance unless the party is capable of providing an advanced litter evacuation themselves.

For those interested in more information, a thorough treatment of the subject is contained in *The Basic Essentials of Hypothermia* by William W. Forgey, M.D., published by The Basic Essentials Series, ICS Books, One Tower Plaza, Merrillville, IN 46410.

Lightning is another serious hazard on any bare ridge or summit. In other mountain ranges throughout the world, where thunderstorms are more common and shelter often much farther away, fairly elaborate advice is often provided for finding the least unsafe place to sit out a storm. In the areas covered in this guide, the best course of action is to avoid the dangerous places when thunderstorms are likely, and to go down the mountain to shelter in thick woods as quickly as possible if an unexpected "thumper" is detected. Most thunderstorms occur when a cold front passes or on very warm days; those produced by cold fronts are typically more sudden and violent. Weather forecasts that mention cold fronts or predict temperatures much above 80° in the lowlands and valleys should arouse concern.

The most risky part of hiking in the New Hampshire woods, in the opinion of many people, has always been the drive to the trailhead, and the recent rapid increase in New Hampshire's moose population has added a significant new hazard. During the first nine months of one recent year, for example, collisions between moose and automobiles caused the deaths of four people and more than 160 moose. The great majority of these collisions occurs in the period from early May to the middle of July, when the moose leave the woods to avoid the black flies and seek out the road salt that has accumulated in ditches near highways. Motorists need to be aware of the seriousness of the problem, particularly at night when these huge, dark-colored animals are both active and very difficult to see. Instinct often causes them to face an auto rather than run from it, and they are also apt to cross the road unpredictably as a car approaches. It is thus safest to assume that moose will behave in the most inconvenient manner possible. Otherwise they probably constitute little threat to hikers on foot, though it would be wise to give bulls a wide berth during the fall mating season.

Bears are common but tend to keep well out of sight. The last known case of a human killed by a bear in New Hampshire was in

1784—a 10-year-old boy in the town of Londonderry—and since that time many thousands of bears have perished from attacks by humans or their automobiles. Nevertheless, the bear is a large and unpredictable animal that must be treated with respect, though not fear. Several recent serious incidents have been unnecessarily provoked by deliberate feeding of bears, or by harassment by a dog leading to an attack on people nearby. Bears live mostly on nuts, berries, and other plants, and on dead animals, and rarely kill anything larger than a mouse. Since the closing of many of the town dumps in New Hampshire, where some bears routinely foraged for food, bears have become a nuisance and even a hazard at some popular campsites; any bear that has lost its natural fear of humans and gotten used to living off us is extremely dangerous.

The philosophy of dealing with bears has undergone some modification in recent years. Formerly the usual advice was that, if approached by a bear, one should throw down one's pack and back away slowly. This advice works, but unfortunately it teaches the bear that people have food and that very little effort and risk is required to make them part with it. The result is a bear that is likely to be more aggressive toward the next visitor, which may result in injury to the human (who may be you) and frequently results in a death sentence for the bear. Most hikers regard bears as an indispensable feature of wild country in New England, and preservation of the bears requires us to make sure that they remain wild, so feeding them either deliberately or through carelessness should be regarded as tantamount to bringing about their execution. Thus the current advice is that a hiker confronted by a bear should attempt to appear neither threatening nor frightened, and should back off slowly but not abandon food unless the bear appears irresistibly aggressive. A loud noise, such as one made by a whistle or by banging metal pots, is often useful. Careful protection of food at campsites is mandatory; it must never be kept overnight in a tent, but should be hung between trees well off the ground.

Deer-hunting season (with rifles) is in November, when you'll probably see many more hunters than deer. Seasons involving muzzle-loader and bow-and-arrow hunters extend from mid-October through mid-December. Most hunters usually stay fairly close to roads, and, in general, the harder it would be to haul a deer out of a given area, the lower the probability that a hiker will encounter hunters there. In any case, avoid wearing brown or anything that might give a hunter the impression of the white flash of a white-tailed deer running away. Wearing hunter's-orange clothing is strongly recommended.

There are probably very few poisonous snakes in the southern half of New Hampshire. Mosquitoes and black flies are the woodland residents most frequently encountered by hikers. Mosquitoes are worst throughout the summer in low, wet areas, and black flies are most bloodthirsty from mid-May through early July; at times these winged pests can make life in the woods virtually unbearable. Fishermen's head-nets can be useful. The most effective repellents are based on the active ingredient diethyl-meta-toluamide, generally known as "DEET," but there are growing doubts about its safety. Hikers should probably apply repellents with DEET to clothing rather than skin where possible, and avoid using them on small children. Other effective repellents are available, and there is also a good deal of folklore and tradition on the subject: people who seek true solitude in the woods often employ the traditional creosote-scented recipes, reasoning that anything that repels fellow humans might have the same effect on insects.

Cars parked at trailheads are frequently targets of break-ins, so valuables or expensive equipment should never be left in cars while you are off hiking, particularly overnight.

Brook Crossings

Rivers and brooks are often crossed without bridges, and it is usually possible to jump from rock to rock; a hiking staff or stick is a great aid to balance. Use caution; several fatalities have resulted from hikers (particularly solo hikers) falling on slippery rocks and suffering an injury that rendered them unconscious, causing them to drown in relatively shallow streams. If you need to wade across a stream (often the safer course), wearing boots, but not necessarily socks, is recommended. Note that many crossings that may be only a nuisance in summer may be a serious obstacle in cold weather when one's feet and boots must be kept dry. Higher waters, which can turn innocuous brooks into virtually uncrossable torrents, come in the spring as snow melts, or after heavy rainstorms, particularly in the fall when trees drop their leaves and take up less water. Avoid trails with potentially dangerous stream crossings during these high-water periods. If you are cut off from roads by swollen streams, it is better to make a long detour, even if you need to wait and spend a night in the woods. Rushing current can make wading extremely hazardous, and several deaths have resulted. Flood waters may subside within a few hours, especially in small brooks. It is particularly important not to camp on the far side of a brook from your exit point if the crossing is difficult and heavy rain is predicted.

Drinking Water

The pleasure of quaffing a cup of water fresh from a pure mountain spring is one of the traditional attractions of the mountains. Unfortunately, the presence of cysts of the intestinal parasite *Giardia lamblia* in water sources is thought to be common, though difficult to prove. It is impossible to be sure whether a given source is safe, and all water sources in the southern half of New Hampshire should probably be regarded as contaminated, no matter how clear the water seems or remote the location. The safest course is for day hikers to carry their own water, and for those who use sources in the woods to filter the water before drinking it. The symptoms of giardiasis are severe intestinal distress and diarrhea, but such discomforts can have many other causes, making the disease difficult to diagnose accurately. The principal cause of the spread of this noxious ailment in the woods is probably careless disposal of human waste. Keep it at least 200 ft. away from water sources. If there are no toilets nearby, dig a hole 6 to 8 in. deep (but not below the organic layer of the soil) for a latrine and cover it completely after use. The bacteria in the organic layer of the soil will then decompose the waste naturally. Many people unknowingly carry the *Giardia* parasites, which have sometimes been present in municipal water supplies and frequently do not produce symptoms. Some authorities feel that the disease is more likely to be spread by party members to each other than by contaminated water. For this reason it would be advisable to be scrupulous about washing hands after answering calls of nature.

Distances, Times, and Elevation Gains

The distances, times, and elevation gains that appear in the tables at the end of trail descriptions are cumulative from the starting point at the head of each table. Elevation gains are given for the reverse direction only when they are significant, *and are not cumulative*—they apply only to the interval between the current entry and the next one (which will be the entry *before* the current one in the list). Elevation gains are not given for trails that are essentially level. Most of the trails in this book have been measured with a surveyor's wheel within the past few years. Minor inconsistencies sometimes occur when measured distances are rounded, and the distances given often differ from those on trail signs. Elevation gains are estimated and rounded to the nearest 50 ft.; some elevation gains can be determined almost to the foot, while others (such as where several minor ups and downs are traversed) are only roughly accurate. Elevations of places are estimated as closely as possible when not given precisely by our source maps. The USGS maps are used as the basis for all such information.

There is no reliable method for predicting how much time a particular hiker or group of hikers will actually take to complete a particular hike on a particular day. The factors that influence the speed of an individual hiker or hiking group are simply too numerous and too complex. Most hikers will observe that their own individual speed varies from day to day, often by a significant amount, depending on a number of factors, many of which—such as fatigue, weight of pack, and weather conditions—are fairly easy to identify. Hikers often forget to consider that a given segment of trail will usually require more time—perhaps much more—when encountered at the end of a strenuous day compared to what it might have required if encountered at the start of the day.

However, in order to give inexperienced hikers a rough basis for planning, estimated times have been calculated for this book by allowing a half-hour for each mile of distance or 1000 ft. of climbing. No attempt has been made to adjust these times for the difficulties of specific trails, since fine-tuning an inherently limited method would probably only lead to greater unjustified reliance on it. In many cases, as hikers gain experience, they find that they usually require a fairly predictable percentage of book time to hike most trails, but eventually they are almost certain to encounter a significant exception. Therefore, all hikers using this book should be well aware of the limitations of the time-estimating formula, and should always regard book times with a critical eye and check each trail description thoroughly for trail conditions that might render the given times misleading; these times may be very inadequate for steep or rough trails, for hikers with heavy packs, or for large groups, particularly those including inexperienced hikers. Average descent times vary even more greatly, with agility and the condition of the hiker's knees being the principal factors; times for descending are given in this book only for segments of ridgecrest trails that have substantial descents in both directions. In winter, times are even less predictable: on a packed trail travel may be faster than in summer, but with heavy packs or in deep snow it may take two or three times the summer estimate.

A Final Note

Hiking is a sport of self-reliance. Its high potential for adventure and relatively low level of regulation have been made possible by the dedication of most hikers to the values of prudence and independence. This tradition of self-reliance imposes an obligation on each of us: at any time we may have to rely on our own ingenuity and judgment, aided by map and compass, to reach our goals or even make a timely exit from the woods. While the penalty for error rarely exceeds an unplanned and uncomfortable night in the woods, more serious consequences are possible. Most hikers find a high degree of satisfaction in obtaining the knowledge and skills that free them from blind dependence on the next blaze or trail sign and enable them to walk in the woods with confidence and assurance. Those who learn the skills of getting about in the woods, the habits of studious acquisition of information before the trip and careful observation while in the woods, soon find that they have earned "the Freedom of the Hills."

The trails that we use and enjoy are only in part the product of government agencies and public non-profit organizations; there is ultimately no "they" responsible for providing the hiking public with a full variety of interesting, convenient, well-maintained trails. Many trails are cared for by one dedicated person or a small group. Funds for trail work are scarce, and unless hikers contribute both time and money to the maintenance of trails, the diversity of trails available to the public is almost certain to experience a sad decline. Every hiker can make some contribution to the improvement of the trails, if nothing more than pushing a blowdown off the trail rather than walking around it. They are our trails, and without our participation in their care they will languish. Write to AMC Trails, Pinkham Notch Camp, PO Box 298, Gorham, NH 03581, for more information regarding volunteer trail-maintenance activities, or see the AMC website, www.outdoors.org. Another group that is very active in trail maintenance in the southern half of New Hampshire is Trailwrights, PO Box 1945, Hillsboro, NH 03244; email: trailwrights@pobox.com.

Acknowledgments

A book like the *Southern New Hampshire Trail Guide* is the product of the efforts of many people, including those who contributed to the previous 25 editions of its forerunner, the *White Mountain Guide,* over the period of 90 years since it was first brought into being. The editors constantly have in mind the enthusiastic mountain-walkers who trod the trails before us and created and preserved this magnificent tradition which is now our cherished responsibility. Properly recognizing everyone, past and present, who made some contribution to this book would require a small book of its own, but the editors would like to recognize a few people whose contributions were especially indispensable.

First, we would like to thank our families, and particularly our wives, Anita Burroughs and Debi Clark. Their contributions to this book, though not outwardly visible, were immense. Without their constant assistance, encouragement, and support, as well as companionship on many hikes—and tolerance for two husbands who are obsessed by the project of maintaining this book and could argue for half an hour the question of whether a particular trail segment is steep or merely rather steep—we would never have been able to give this book the time and energy we feel it deserves. Therefore we dedicate our part of the life of this venerable book to them, with love and gratitude.

Among the others who made unusually important contributions to this book, we wish to recognize the following:

First, we want to thank the publications staff of the AMC, including Gordon Hardy, Mark Russell, and Elisabeth Brady. Not only did they assume all the myriad (and frequently tedious) professional responsibilities of publishing this book so that we could concentrate on preparing the text, they managed to cope with the eccentricities and frailties of the editors without complaint, giving generous support and assistance even when we made their jobs harder.

Also, we want to thank Larry Garland, who turned our fantasy of bright, beautiful new computer-generated maps into a reality. His obsession with making things right is at least equal to our own, and as a result he has managed to digest a staggering amount of detail and overcome many difficulties inherent to such a pioneering effort in order to produce maps that will actually help hikers plan their trips and complete them successfully. Larry deserves more appreciation than we will ever be able to give him. Larry, in turn, would like to thank the following individuals and concerns that contributed to this immense effort: Sarah Giffen and Steve Piotrow for logging many hours and many more miles field-mapping the trails with GPS equipment; Scott Smalley, Pat Burr, and Craig Sandborn for facilitating trail mapping at Cardigan Lodge and providing their first-hand knowledge of the area in reviewing draft maps; Ben Haubrich and Tom Mattson of NH State Parks for providing support and reviewing draft maps of Pisgah, Bear Brook, Pawtuckaway State Parks, and the Monadnock Reservation; John Mesko of FMC CADD Drafting Services for providing professional services for digitizing contours; and Jim McLaughlin of NH Office of State Planning for providing the mylar separates for digitizing.

Then, we want to thank those who made other contributions to this book. For helping review sections of the manuscript or making numerous suggestions for improvements in details of both fact and style, we want to thank Rick Blanchette, Hal and Peggy Graham, Craig Sanborn, Roioli Schweiker, and Roy Schweiker, as well as the others too numerous to mention who helped in some way to make this a better, more accurate book. We also want to thank numerous personnel of the New Hampshire Division of Parks and Recreation, including Ben Haubrich and Bob Spoerl, as well as the supervisors and chief rangers of the individual state parks: Michael Walsh of Monadnock State Park, Jim Bearce of Pisgah State Park, Jim Lane of Bear Brook State Park, and Jeff Bouchard of Pawtuckaway State Park.

Section 1

Monadnock and Southwestern New Hampshire

This section covers the southern part of the western New Hampshire hill country. Mt. Monadnock is by far the best known and most popular peak in the area. The Metacomet-Monadnock Trail runs from Meriden CT to Mt. Monadnock, passing over Little Monadnock Mtn. and Gap Mtn. The Monadnock-Sunapee Greenway runs from Monadnock to Sunapee Mtn., passing over Pitcher Mtn. and Lovewell Mtn. The Wapack Trail follows the ridgecrest of the Wapack Range, including the Pack Monadnocks, Temple Mtn., and Barrett Mtn. Pisgah State Park in Chesterfield, Hinsdale, and Winchester, a relatively undeveloped park containing 13,000 acres, has a trail network of more than 60 miles.

Other mountains covered in this section include Wantastiquet Mtn. in Hinsdale, Hyland Hill in Westmoreland, Crotched Mtn. in Francestown, Skatutakee Mtn. and Thumb Mtn. in Hancock, and Sunapee Mtn. in Newbury. Other areas containing significant trails include Fox State Forest in Hillsborough, the Pierce Reservation in Stoddard, the dePierrefeu–Willard Pond Wildlife Sanctuary in Antrim, and the Saint-Gaudens National Historical Site in Cornish.

Mount Monadnock

1

Mount Monadnock (cont.)

Metacomet–Monadnock Trail

Wantastiquet Mountain   *21*

Pisgah State Park

Pisgah State Park (cont.)

Hyland Hill *59*

Wapack Trail *60*

Crotched Mountain *66*

Fox State Forest *67*

Skatutakee and Thumb Mountains

Skatutakee and Thumb Mountains (cont.)

Pierce Reservation

DePeirrefeu–Willard Pond Wildlife Sanctuary

Monadnock-Sunapee Greenway

Sunapee Mountain

Saint-Gaudens National Historical Site

MOUNT MONADNOCK

Mt. Monadnock (3159 ft.), also called Grand Monadnock, rises in the towns of Jaffrey and Dublin, about 10 mi. north of the New Hampshire–Massachusetts border. It is an isolated mountain that towers 1500 to 2000 ft. above the surrounding country, visible from most of the prominent viewpoints in central New England. Its summit commands exceptionally extensive and distant views; Mt. Washington is sometimes visible when it has snow cover. Two prominent southern crags are worthy of note: Monte Rosa (2510 ft.) on the southwest ridge, and Bald Rock (2628 ft.), signed as Kiasticuticus (literally "Skinhead") Peak, on the south ridge. Combining extremely rugged mountain scenery, a relatively short and easy ascent, and convenient access from the population centers of southern New England, Monadnock is reputedly (after Mt. Fuji in Japan) the second most frequently climbed mountain in the world; on one Columbus Day in the late 1970s, it was ascended by throngs estimated at nearly 10,000 people. It would be wise to regard *any* water source on this mountain with extreme suspicion.

There are several major trails to the summit and a network of connecting and secondary trails on the east, south, and west sides of the main peak. This network deteriorated badly after a fire in 1954 destroyed the old hotel called the Halfway House, where many amateur trail builders had their base of operations, but most of these trails have been restored by the dedicated efforts of state park personnel. It is possible to ascend Monadnock in relative solitude on these attractive trails, particularly if you avoid weekends. The White Arrow Trail—the most direct route to the summit on this side—and many other trails begin near the Halfway House site, a starting point for many attractive circuit trips that is located on the west flank of Monadnock's south ridge at about 2100 ft. Direct routes to this site are provided by a foot trail—the Old Halfway House Trail—and by a former toll road, now closed to public vehicular use but open for hikers. The trail and road both leave a parking area on NH 124 near the height-of-land, 5.0 mi. west of Jaffrey and about 4 mi. east of Troy; the road climbs 1.2 mi. to the old hotel site.

The upper 500 ft. of the mountain is open ledge, bared by a series of forest fires. Farmers frequently set fires to clear the lower slopes for pasture, and around 1800 a major fire of unknown origin burned for about two weeks, greatly damaging the forests on the upper part of the mountain. Subsequent fires and windstorms completed the devastation, creating an impenetrable maze of blown-down trees that was a natural lair for wolves who preyed on the sheep in the pastures. (During the first half of the nineteenth century, sheep were probably the most important agricultural product in the western New Hampshire hill country.) Sometime between 1810 and 1820, a fire set by farmers attempting to oust the wolves got out of control and burned with an intensity that consumed even the soil, reducing the upper part of the mountain to bare, sterile rock. Since then small plants, shrubs, and trees have lodged themselves in various cracks and crannies, creating small pockets of soil and beginning the process that, if left undisturbed, will restore the mountain forest in a few millennia.

Visitors from outside the immediate vicinity of the mountain began to arrive at about the same time as the last of the great fires, and by 1850 Monadnock was established as a major attraction for New Englanders. Due to the proximity of the mountain to Concord MA, where the Transcendentalist literary movement with its deep interest in nature developed around the figures of Ralph Waldo Emerson and Henry David Thoreau, Mt. Monadnock attained the status of something like a sacred mountain and was immortalized in the works of these notable writers and others. Monadnock's slopes probably bear more historic trails, former trails, ruins, and named minor features than any other mountain in New England, including Mt. Washington. The *Monadnock Guide*, published by the SPNHF, provides details of much of this history as well as extensive information about the natural history of the mountain.

The public reservation on the mountain now comprises about 5000 contiguous acres cooperatively administered by the state, the town of Jaffrey, the Association to Protect Mt. Monadnock, and the

SPNHF. At Monadnock State Park, just off Memorial Rd., the state maintains picnic grounds, a parking lot, and a public campground (fees charged for each). Camping is not permitted anywhere on the mountain, except at the state park campground. Dogs (or other pets) are not allowed anywhere in the state park. The Monadnock trail system is shown on the AMC Monadnock Map included with this book, and Monadnock is covered by the USGS Monadnock Mtn. and Marlborough quadrangles.

Old Halfway House Trail

This recently reopened trail parallels the western side of the Old Toll Road and provides a more attractive, less heavily used approach to the Halfway House Site from the Old Toll Road parking area on NH 124. Although not blazed, it is easy to follow.

The trail bears left off the Old Toll Road just above the parking area, trail kiosk, and gate, and parallels the road next to an old stone wall. It soon ascends a short distance away from the road, follows a long level section, and at 1.1 mi. crosses the Cart Path just below a house to the right. It passes through an overgrown field, swings right, and ascends a short distance to the Old Toll Road less than 0.1 mi. below the Halfway House Site clearing.

Old Halfway House Trail (AMC Monadnock Map)
Distance from the Old Toll Road parking area (1490')

   to Halfway House Site (2090'): 1.3 mi. (2.1 km.), 600 ft., 55 min.

White Arrow Trail

One of the oldest and most heavily used routes to the summit, this trail continues along the north end of the toll road from the site of the Halfway House, where numerous far less heavily used side trails also originate. It is marked by painted white arrows. It follows the road, which soon ends at the old picnic area on the left, where the Royce Trail (Metacomet-Monadnock Trail), Monte Rosa Trail, and Fairy

Spring Trail begin. From this point to the summit the White Arrow Trail is part of the Metacomet-Monadnock Trail. It immediately begins to climb rather steeply through the woods on a broad, rocky path past Quarter-Way Spring. At 0.6 mi. the Amphitheater Trail enters from the right and continues across the White Arrow Trail toward the Smith Summit Trail. The upper end of the Sidefoot Trail is about 100 yd. to the right (east) on the Amphitheater Trail. The White Arrow Trail soon reaches the treeline, where it bears left and starts to ascend the ledges in the open. Just below the summit a side path on the right makes an interesting scramble up a narrow gully. The main trail soon gains the summit plateau, where it meets the Dublin Trail, and turns right in company with this trail to reach the summit in another 75 yd.

White Arrow Trail (AMC Monadnock Map)

Distance from Halfway House site (2090')

   to Mt. Monadnock summit (3159'): 1.1 mi. (1.7 km.), 1050 ft., 1 hr. 5 min.

Distance from Old Toll Road parking area (1490')

   to Mt. Monadnock summit (3159') via Old Halfway House Trail or Old Toll Road and White Arrow Trail: 2.3 mi. (3.7 km.), 1700 ft., 2 hr.

Dublin Trail

This trail ascends Monadnock from the north; it is a link in the Monadnock-Sunapee Greenway. From the flagpole in Dublin village, go west on NH 101 (Main St.). At 0.4 mi. bear left on East Lake Rd., which becomes Old Marlboro Rd. At 2.5 mi. go left downhill on Old Troy Rd., pass through a crossroads, and continue to a small clearing on the right at 4.0 mi., where there is parking space. (Beyond the houses at 3.4 mi. the road becomes narrow and poor; it may be impassable when muddy.) The trail, marked with white Ds, starts opposite the clearing and climbs to the tip of the ridge, passing an unreliable spring at 1.0 mi. It follows the ledgy ridge with occasional good views, passes another unreliable spring at the foot of a rock at 1.8 mi., and emerges above timberline. The Marlboro Trail enters on the right at 2.0 mi., just beyond a prominent cap of rock, a false summit. The Dublin Trail continues upward to meet the White Arrow Trail 75 yd. below the true summit.

Dublin Trail (AMC Monadnock Map)
Distance from Old Troy Rd. (1460')

> *to* Mt. Monadnock summit (3159'): 2.2 mi. (3.5 km.), 1700 ft., 1 hr. 55 min.

Pumpelly Trail

This is the longest, most strenuous, and most scenic direct route to the summit of Monadnock. Follow NH 101 (Main St.) west from the flagpole in Dublin village for 0.4 mi., then turn left on East Lake Rd. (sign). The trail (no sign) leaves the road left at 0.4 mi., opposite a log cabin on the pond and 75 yd. east of where the road reaches the shore.

The trail follows a woods road for 120 yd., turns right into a narrow path through a stone wall (small cairn and sign), then turns left onto a woods road again at 0.2 mi. It crosses Oak Hill at 0.7 mi. and continues with gradual ups and downs, becoming a footpath. At 1.8 mi. it turns sharp left and begins the rather steep and rough ascent of the north end of the Dublin Ridge. The trail zigzags up and emerges on the first semi-open ledges on the shoulder of the mountain at 2.2 mi., almost exactly halfway to the summit. From here the trail is rough and rocky, running near the ridgecrest with many minor ups and downs, but offers many excellent views from bare ledges. At 3.0 mi. the Cascade Link enters on the left, ascending from the Monadnock State Park trail network on the eastern slopes, and at 3.7 mi. the Spellman Trail also enters on the left just below the Sarcophagus, a huge rectangular boulder in plain view. From here onward the trail, marked by large cairns, runs mostly on open ledge where many glacial striations are plainly visible. It soon passes a small alpine meadow, and at

4.0 mi. the Red Spot Trail enters left. (This trail connects the Pumpelly Trail with the Cascade Link on the lower east slope of the mountain, and with the Smith Connecting Link on the upper east slope. The Smith Connecting Link runs across the White Dot and White Cross trails to Bald Rock, linking the Pumpelly Trail with the complex of trails that radiate from the Halfway House site.) The Pumpelly Trail soon passes through a little col with steep, ledgy walls, then comes completely into the open in another 80 yd. and continues over the ledges to the summit.

Descending, the trail runs nearly due east; look for a summit rock with "Pumpelly Trail" and a large white arrow painted on it. There are few cairns for the first 200 yd. and care must be taken to locate the first one. In several cases the cairns are rather small.

Pumpelly Trail (AMC Monadnock Map)
Distances from Old Marlboro Rd. (1530')

- *to* Cascade Link (2700'): 3.0 mi., 1300 ft., 2 hr. 10 min.
- *to* Mt. Monadnock summit (3159'): 4.4 mi. (7.1 km.), 1800 ft., 3 hr. 5 min.

White Dot Trail

This trail starts at the parking area near the Monadnock State Park headquarters at the west end of Poole Memorial Rd. in Monadnock State Park. It begins on a broad woods road, descends slightly, and crosses a small brook. At 0.5 mi. the Spruce Link leaves left; this is a cutoff path 0.3 mi. long that joins the White Cross Trail above Falcon Spring. The White Dot Trail then climbs gradually through woods to a junction with the Cascade Link and White Cross Trail at Falcon Spring at 0.7 mi. The White Cross and White Dot trails run roughly parallel from here and rejoin high up on the mountain; the White Dot Trail is steeper, but only 0.2 mi. shorter than the White Cross, while views from the White Cross are more interesting.

The White Dot Trail goes straight at the junction just above Falcon Spring, ascends the steep ridge, and emerges at 1.1 mi. on the semi-open plateau near treeline. It passes the Old Ski Path, which runs right (north) 0.2 mi. to the Red Spot Trail, then climbs on ledges through meager evergreens. At 1.6 mi. the White Dot Trail crosses the Smith Connecting Link, which circles the east side of the summit cone from Bald Rock to the Red Spot Trail, connecting the Halfway House site to the Pumpelly Trail. The White Cross Trail rejoins on the left at 1.7 mi., and the White Dot Trail continues up slanting ledges to the summit.

White Dot Trail (AMC Monadnock Map)

Distance from Poole Memorial Rd. (1380')

> *to* Mt. Monadnock summit (3159'): 2.0 mi. (3.2 km.), 1800 ft., 1 hr. 45 min.

White Cross Trail

This trail provides a less steep and more scenic alternative to the middle section of the White Dot Trail. Trail distances given below are from the state park parking area via the White Dot Trail. The White Cross Trail diverges left from the White Dot Trail at the junction just above Falcon Spring and angles gradually uphill. At 0.9 mi. the Spruce Link enters on the left, and the White Cross Trail turns sharp right and starts to climb at moderate grades over boulders left by an old slide. It passes through an old burn (good views back to the east and south across a ravine called Dingle Dell) and finally reaches the flat southeast shoulder. It soon emerges from sparse evergreens on the ledges. The Smith Connecting Link crosses at 1.8 mi., and the White Cross Trail rejoins the White Dot Trail at 1.9 mi., following the latter trail to the summit.

White Cross Trail (AMC Monadnock Map)

Distance from lower junction with White Dot Trail (1850')

> *to* upper junction with White Dot Trail (2850'): 1.2 mi. (2.0 km.), 1000 ft., 1 hr. 5 min.

Distance from Poole Memorial Rd. (1380')

> *to* Mt. Monadnock summit (3159') via White Dot Trail, White Cross Trail, and White Dot Trail: 2.2 mi. (3.5 km.), 1800 ft., 2 hr.

Harling Trail

The Harling Trail is reached from Poole Memorial Rd. 0.2 mi. east of the entrance to Monadnock State Park; follow the Hinkley Trail, a connecting trail 0.6 mi. long, to its end, then take Cross-Country Ski Trail #18, which is the Harling Trail but has no specific trail sign. The trail runs west on an old woods road and reaches the Cascade Link a short distance north of the Falcon Spring junction. From here, follow the Cascade Link right for the Red Spot, Spellman, and Pumpelly trails.

Harling Trail (AMC Monadnock Map)
Distance from Poole Memorial Rd. (1300')

   to Cascade Link (1950') via Hinkley Trail: 1.3 mi. (2.1 km.), 550 ft., 55 min.

Cascade Link

This trail runs between Falcon Spring junction and the Pumpelly Trail, angling upward, south to north. Combined with the Pumpelly Trail, it is an interesting descent route from the summit to the state park. With either the Spellman Trail or the Red Spot Trail, it offers the most varied ascents from the east side of the mountain.

The Cascade Link starts at the Falcon Spring junction, reached by the White Dot Trail. It runs northeast, descends slightly, passes the Harling Trail on the right, and continues through spruce woods to a brook and the little cascades for which this trail is named. At 0.3 mi. it crosses the brook and climbs gradually along its east side, rising about 300 ft. before it leaves the brook and winds over ledges in thick woods. The Birchtoft Trail enters on the right at 0.5 mi., and the Red Spot Trail leaves left for Dublin Ridge and the Pumpelly Trail in another 30 yd., just before an old east-west stone wall. At 0.7 mi. the Spellman Trail leaves left, and the Cascade Link climbs close to the east bank of a small brook to where the brook rises, close to the boundary between Dublin and Jaffrey. From there, prominent cairns mark the Cascade Link over open ledges to a saddle on the Dublin Ridge (2700 ft.), where it ends at the Pumpelly Trail. (The Pumpelly

Trail is a scenic route to the summit with many outlooks, marked with yellow paint blazes.)

Cascade Link (AMC Monadnock Map)
Distance from Falcon Spring (1850')

> *to* Pumpelly Trail (2700'): 1.4 mi. (2.3 km.), 850 ft., 1 hr. 10 min.

Spellman Trail

This trail leaves the Cascade Link 0.7 mi. from Falcon Spring and makes the steepest climb (700 ft. in about 0.6 mi.) on the mountain, up to the Pumpelly Trail just north of the Sarcophagus. The Spellman Trail is a good scramble in its middle section, with excellent views back to the east, including the skyline of Boston on a clear day. This trail is difficult to follow when snow covers the white dots that mark the route on the rocks because, in winding about to avoid the worst ledges, the trail does not always follow a clear line.

Spellman Trail (AMC Monadnock Map)
Distance from Cascade Link (2150')

> *to* Pumpelly Trail (2850'): 0.6 mi. (0.9 km.), 700 ft., 40 min.

Red Spot Trail

This trail, much less challenging than the Spellman Trail, provides a scenic alternative to the more heavily used trails on the east side of the mountain. It leaves the Cascade Link 0.5 mi. from Falcon Spring, 30 yd. beyond the Birchtoft Trail, and ascends somewhat roughly via long switchbacks. At 0.4 mi. the Old Ski Path leaves left for the White Dot Trail. At 0.7 mi. the Red Spot Trail emerges on ledges with good views, then passes the northern end of the Smith Connecting Link at 0.9 mi. and soon ends at the Pumpelly Trail 0.4 mi. below the summit.

Red Spot Trail (AMC Monadnock Map)
Distance from Cascade Link (2150')

> *to* Pumpelly Trail (2950'): 1.0 mi. (1.7 km.), 800 ft., 55 min.

Birchtoft Trail

This trail begins near the privately owned Monadnock Recreation Area (campground), located on Dublin Rd. 1 mi. north of Poole Memorial Rd. Follow the recreation area entrance road a short distance, then turn left on the first driveway and follow it 100 yd. to the shore of Gilson Pond (parking). The trail (sign) skirts the east and south shores of the pond. At 0.1 mi. the east end of the Gilson Pond Trail continues straight ahead as the Birchtoft Trail turns left, and at 0.2 mi. the west end of the Gilson Pond Trail diverges to the right (north). (The Gilson Pond Trail is a loop path 0.8 mi. long that runs around Gilson Pond, passing a spur path 0.3 mi. long, called the Ravine Trail, that leads into a hemlock ravine.) The Birchtoft Trail ascends by easy grades to end at the Cascade Link 0.5 mi. from Falcon Spring.

Birchtoft Trail (AMC Monadnock Map)
Distance from Gilson Pond (1210')

   to Cascade Link (2150'): 2.1 mi. (3.3 km.), 950 ft., 1 hr. 30 min.

Marlboro Trail

This is one of the oldest trails to the summit, dating to 1850 or earlier. Follow NH 124 west from Jaffrey, past the roads leading to Monadnock State Park and the Halfway House site. Take Shaker Farm Rd., the first dirt road on the right north of the Troy-Marlboro town line, 0.6 mi. north of Perkins Pond. Follow this road 0.7 mi. to a clearing on the left and an old cellar hole (parking). The trail follows a woods road for 0.9 mi. to a wall that runs east and west, then climbs up the nose of the ridge to the open ledges, marked with cairns and white Ms. At 1.3 mi. the Marian Trail leaves the Marlboro Trail on the right at the ledges known as the Rock House or Stone House (about 2450 ft.). The Marlboro Trail climbs to a shoulder where it ends at the junction with the Dublin Trail, which comes up from the left and continues 0.2 mi. to the summit.

Marlboro Trail (AMC Monadnock Map)

Distances from parking area, road west of Perkins Pond (1320')

- *to* Dublin Trail (2950'): 1.9 mi. (3.1 km.), 1650 ft., 1 hr. 45 min.
- *to* Mt. Monadnock summit (3159') via Dublin Trail: 2.2 mi. (3.5 km.), 1850 ft., 2 hr.

Halfway House Site Region Paths

An almost unlimited variety of good walks can be made starting at the old Halfway House site, reached from the Old Toll Road parking area in 1.2 mi. by either the Old Halfway House Trail or the Old Toll Road. A particularly rewarding round trip to the summit combines an ascent over Bald Rock via the Cliff Walk and the Smith Connecting, Red Spot, and Pumpelly trails with a descent on the Smith Summit Trail and one of the trails that lead down from Monte Rosa.

One of the finest scenic trails on Mt. Monadnock is the *Cliff Walk,* marked with white Cs, which begins on the Parker Trail 0.4 mi. from the Old Toll Road and runs 1.5 mi. along the south and east edge of the south ridge, from Hello Rock to Bald Rock, past splendid viewpoints—notably Thoreau's Seat, Emerson's Seat, and What Cheer Point—and historical points such as the Graphite Mine (left), which was operated around 1850. Several paths lead up to the Cliff Walk from the Halfway House site. Three such trails are the Hello Rock Trail, the Point Surprise Trail, and the Thoreau Trail, which leave the Halfway House clearing at the southeast corner between the road and Moses Spring. The *Hello Rock Trail* ascends gradually 0.4 mi. through a fine forest to the Cliff Walk at Hello Rock. At 80 yd. above the Halfway House site, the *Point Surprise Trail* diverges left and ascends 0.3 mi. to the Cliff Walk, and the *Thoreau Trail* diverges farther left and climbs 0.4 mi. to the Cliff Walk at Thoreau's Seat.

Bald Rock is the bare peak on the south ridge of Monadnock; its highest point is a pointed boulder inscribed Kiasticuticus Peak. From Bald Rock, the *Smith Connecting Link,* marked with yellow Ss, descends a short distance, soon passes Coffee Pot Corner, and shortly reaches the Four Spots, a trail junction. The Smith Connecting Link goes right at this junction and eventually crosses the White Cross Trail, then the White Dot Trail; it ends at the Red Spot Trail just below the Pumpelly Trail, a total of 0.7 mi. The trail that forks left at the Four Spots junction is the eastern end of the *Amphitheater Trail;* it climbs with little grade to join the Sidefoot Trail, which soon reaches the White Arrow Trail, after which the Amphitheater Trail continues west (no sign) to the Smith Summit Trail.

The *Sidefoot Trail* is an excellent alternative to the lower part of the White Arrow Trail and avoids much of the very heavy traffic on that trail. To reach the Sidefoot Trail, climb the bank at the left of the Halfway House clearing and follow a path a few yards into the woods to a trail junction. The Sidefoot Trail leaves left and climbs 0.7 mi. to join the White Arrow Trail at Halfway Spring. Three trails in close succession—the *Do Drop Trail* (0.2 mi.), the *Noble Trail* (0.3 mi.), and the unsigned *Hedgehog Trail* (0.3 mi.)—leave to the right of the Sidefoot Trail and climb steeply to the Cliff Walk.

The *Monte Rosa Trail* leaves the tiny clearing of the former picnic grounds just past the north end of the Halfway House clearing, where the Royce Trail (a segment of the Metacomet-Monadnock Trail) enters from NH 124. The Monte Rosa Trail climbs to a junction at 0.3 mi. where the *Fairy Spring Trail,* an alternate path that runs 0.3 mi. from the picnic grounds past the foundation of Fassett's Mountain House and Fairy Spring, enters on the right. In a few steps above this junction, the Monte Rosa Trail bears left (right is the *Smith Bypass,* leading directly to the Tooth), and ascends to the summit of Monte Rosa at 0.4 mi. The *Great Pasture Trail* leaves the junction of the Marian and Mossy Brook trails, ascends to the summit of Monte Rosa and the Monte Rosa Trail at 0.3 mi. The *Smith Summit Trail* (marked by white dots) starts at the summit of Monte Rosa, descends steeply to the Tooth, a large pointed boulder, then circles gradually up the west side of the mountain 0.7 mi. to the White Arrow and Dublin trails just below the summit. The *Amphitheater Trail,* 0.4 mi. long, leaves the Smith Summit Trail on the right a short distance beyond the base of Monte Rosa and runs across the top of the Black Precipice, giving views into the ravine called the Amphitheater, then continues across the White Arrow and Sidefoot trails to the Smith Connecting Link. The *Cart Path* leads west from the toll road about 0.3 mi. below the Halfway House site, crosses the Old Halfway House Trail and the Royce (Metacomet-Monadnock) Trail, and ends abruptly at 0.5 mi. at the junction with the Mossy Brook Trail. *The Mossy Brook Trail* continues 0.3 mi. to the junction with the Marian and Great Pasture trails. The *Marian Trail* leaves this junction, then turns sharp right near the Bear Pit, a depression to the west so named because a bear was once reputedly trapped in the quagmire, and continues 0.6 mi. to the Marlboro Trail at the Rock House (also known as the Stone House).

Parker Trail

The Parker Trail begins at the picnic area at Monadnock State Park, on the west side of the outlet brook from the reservoir, and heads west across the south slope of the mountain to the old toll road. It maintains a gentle grade and provides easy walking through mature woods. This trail has signs at both ends and is blazed with yellow paint. At 0.6 mi. the Lost Farm Trail diverges right for the upper part of the Cliff Walk, and at 1.1 mi. the lower end of the Cliff Walk is on the right. The Parker Trail joins the Old Toll Road 0.6 mi. above NH 124 and 0.6 mi. below the Halfway House site.

Parker Trail (AMC Monadnock Map)
Distance from west side of reservoir outlet brook (1310')

   to Old Toll Road (1720'): 1.5 mi. (2.4 km.), 400 ft., 50 min.

Lost Farm Trail

This trail branches right from the Parker Trail 0.6 mi. from the state park and leads in 1.1 mi. to Emerson's Seat on the Cliff Walk. A fine circuit walk from the park headquarters combines this trail with the Cliff Walk, the Smith Connecting Link, and either the White Cross Trail or the White Dot Trail.

Lost Farm Trail (AMC Monadnock Map)

Distance from Parker Trail (1510')

   to Cliff Walk (2300'): 1.1 mi. (1.7 km.), 800 ft., 55 min.

METACOMET-MONADNOCK TRAIL

The Metacomet-Monadnock Trail, 160 mi. long, begins in the Hanging Hills of Meriden CT, and runs north along the traprock ridge that borders the Connecticut River. It traverses Mt. Tom and the Holyoke Range, and passes over the Northfield Hills and Mt. Grace. The New Hampshire section, 18.5 mi. long, includes Little Monadnock Mtn. and Gap Mtn. and terminates at Grand Monadnock. (Previous to this section, the trail parallels the state line for some distance and runs just inside New Hampshire for a short distance in one section; this part is not described below.) The trail is clearly marked by white rectangular paint blazes. Space constraints prevent its full and detailed coverage by this guide; what follows is a brief account of the entire trail and a more detailed account of two of its more important features, Little Monadnock Mtn. (1900 ft.) and Gap Mtn. (south peak, 1900 ft.; north peak, 1840 ft.). For a more detailed description of the entire Metacomet-Monadnock Trail, the *Metacomet-Monadnock Trail Guide*, published by the Berkshire Chapter of the AMC, is available from New England Cartographics, PO Box 369, Amherst, MA 01004.

    The best means of access to the south end of the New Hampshire section of the Metacomet-Monadnock Trail is from MA 32 0.5 mi. south of the Massachusetts–New Hampshire state line. The trail follows a woods road that passes south of the Newton Cemetery and descends moderately to cross Falls Brook at 0.7 mi. Here a spur path leads right about 100 yd. to the top of a waterfall. The main path swings left (north) and climbs, crossing the state line into New Hampshire at 1.1 mi. and continuing to Greenwood Rd. at 1.7 mi. It traverses to the north along a wooded ridge, then at 2.9 mi. turns right (east) onto an old road and bears left (northeast, then north) at a junction at 3.1 mi. At 4.7 mi. the trail reaches NH 119 and follows it to the left (west).

At 5.0 mi. the trail turns right onto an unmarked dirt road and ascends gradually, then at 5.4 mi. it turns left onto a woods road in a clearing. It runs along the east slope of Grassy Hill until it descends to cross Tully Brook at 6.8 mi., then climbs to Old Troy Rd. at 8.0 mi. It follows this road downhill to the right for 150 yd., then turns left through a stone wall and ascends to the wooded summit of Little Monadnock Mtn. at 9.2 mi., then descends to the junction at 9.5 mi. with the trail that ascends from Rhododendron State Park. The trail continues to descend past a fine north outlook, crosses a power line clearing at 10.0 mi., and turns right onto a dirt road at 10.8 mi. Continuing to descend, the road reaches homes and becomes improved gravel (Prospect St.) at 11.5 mi. At the bottom of the hill turn right onto Russell St., then left onto Depot St., and reach Troy village at 12.5 mi.

From Troy village the trail crosses the Ashuelot River and follows NH 12 south, then at 13.0 mi. turns left onto Quarry Rd. After crossing power lines, it continues straight on a woods road, then at 14.0 mi. leaves the road on the left. It then crosses Fern Hill in 100 yd. and descends across an area of old farmland with fields and stone walls. At 14.7 mi. it crosses a woods road near a gate and begins the serious ascent of Gap Mtn. At 15.1 mi. the unmarked side path to the south peak (the true summit) of Gap Mtn. leaves on the right, and the main trail continues to climb to the north peak of Gap Mtn., reaching the summit at 15.2 mi. Here, and along the ridge to the north, there are many excellent vistas featuring the impressive rocky crest of Mt. Monadnock, which rises about 1300 ft. higher only 6 mi. to the northeast. The trail descends across a succession of open ledges, passes a junction at 16.0 mi. where a former route of the trail, now blazed in blue, leaves on the left. The trail crosses Quarry Brook and ascends across Old County Rd. at 16.3 mi., then runs through the woods above a swampy area to NH 124 at 17.3 mi. It enters Monadnock State Park at 17.6 mi. as the Royce Trail, and ascends across the Cart Path to meet the White Arrow Trail in the small clearing of the former picnic grounds at 18.7 mi. It then follows the White Arrow Trail to the summit of Monadnock at 19.6 mi.

Gap Mountain

This small mountain in the town of Troy (south peak, 1900 ft.; north peak, 1840 ft.) is named for its double-humped summit, which is a prominent feature of the view south from Monadnock. It is crossed by the Metacomet-Monadnock Trail, which affords excellent views particularly from the ledges on the north side of the north peak. The higher south peak also offers views, but the side path to its summit has not been well maintained in the past and cannot be recommended to inexperienced hikers unless it is cleared, signed, and blazed. Refer to the USGS Monadnock Mtn. quadrangle. From the north, Gap Mtn. can be approached from the Old Toll Road parking area (fee charged) by following NH 124 west 0.4 mi. to the Metacomet-Monadnock Trail crossing. It is also possible to ascend from Old County Rd. (limited parking), which leaves NH 124 on the south 0.8 mi. west of the Old Toll Road parking area and crosses the Metacomet-Monadnock Trail in about 0.6 mi. From the south, one can ascend from one of several points on Quarry Rd., which leaves NH 12 0.5 mi. south of Troy village. A shorter route of ascent is available by leaving NH 12 just south of the Troy-Fitzwilliam town line, following Gap Mtn. Rd. for 0.8 mi., and turning left on Upper Gap Mtn. Rd. to a gate (parking available). Continue on the driveway past a house where the road becomes a woods road, passes a second gate, and meets the Metacomet-Monadnock Trail at the foot of Gap Mtn.

Gap Mountain (USGS Monadnock Mtn. quad)
Distance from Old Toll Road parking area (1490')

    to north peak of Gap Mtn. (1840'): 2.5 mi. (4.0 km.), 650 ft. (rev. 300 ft.), 1 hr. 35 min.

Distance from Upper Gap Mtn. Rd. (1380')

    to north peak of Gap Mtn. (1840'): 0.6 mi. (1.0 km.), 450 ft., 30 min.

Little Monadnock Mountain

This small mountain (1900 ft.) in the town of Fitzwilliam offers good views to the north from its northern ridge. It can be ascended by the Metacomet-Monadnock Trail from the north or the south, or by a path that ascends from Rhododendron State Park in Fitzwilliam, reached by following signs from NH 119 between Richmond and Fitzwilliam. A good loop hike can be made by ascending on the path from Rhododendron State Park, then following the Metacomet-Monadnock Trail south to Old Troy Rd., and returning to the starting point via Old Troy Rd. and Rhododendron Rd.

The trail from Rhododendron State Park begins by following the short Rhododendron Loop, then diverges and ascends to meet the Metacomet-Monadnock Trail 0.3 mi. north of the summit of Little Monadnock. For the summit, turn left here. The best viewpoint lies about 250 yd. downhill (to the right) from this junction.

Little Monadnock Mountain (USGS Monadnock Mtn. quad)
Distances from Rhododendron State Park (1200')

- *to* Little Monadnock Mtn. summit (1900'): 1.2 mi. (1.9 km.), 700 ft., 55 min.

- *to* starting point by complete loop via Metacomet-Monadnock Trail, Old Troy Rd., and Rhododendron Rd.: 4.1 mi. (6.5 km.), 800 ft., 2 hr. 25 min.

WANTASTIQUET MOUNTAIN

Wantastiquet Mtn. (1368 ft.) is a bluff that rises over 1100 ft. in 0.6 mi. from the Connecticut River directly across from Brattleboro VT. Refer to the USGS Brattleboro quadrangle. Excellent views across the Connecticut Valley are available from the flat summit of this mountain, which stands on the Chesterfield-Hinsdale town line about 3 mi. west of Pisgah State Park. Local legend states that the mountain is the lair of many rattlesnakes; this was probably true at one time, but no reliable sightings of venomous reptiles have been made for many years and they are now officially considered to have been extirpated from the area. The summit and northeast slopes are part of the Madame Sherri Forest, named for the theatrical costume designer who once owned this land and built a castle (now in ruins) on it.

For most of its length the trail is a gravel road that was cut to serve the quarries on the mountain. The trail begins on a side road that leaves NH 119 just east of the bridge over the Connecticut River leading to Vermont; this is about 7 mi. west of the junction of NH 119 with NH 63 in Hinsdale. There is parking about 0.2 mi. from NH 119. The trail passes between a pair of granite posts and ascends; avoid a lower road to the left that has a green gate. Almost immediately the trail passes through an orange gate, with a waterfall on a small stream on the right—avoid multiple side paths (except to view the waterfall or explore). The trail ascends past two switchbacks to another orange gate followed by a view to the west, then climbs by seven more switchbacks to a four-way intersection, where it turns right and climbs the last 50 yd. to the summit, marked by a monument to Walter H. Child. It is possible to scramble eastward across open ledges and small sections of brush to nearby Mine Ledge (1365 ft.) for additional views.

Wantastiquet Mountain Trail (USGS Brattleboro quad)

Distance from parking area (280')

> *to* summit of Wantastiquet Mtn. (1368'): 2.0 mi. (3.2 km.), 1100 ft., 1 hr. 35 min.

PISGAH STATE PARK

Pisgah State Park, located in the southwest corner of New Hampshire in the towns of Chesterfield, Winchester, and Hinsdale, is the largest state park in New Hampshire, covering an area of about 13,000 acres. It is largely undeveloped, but has a network of about 60 miles of multi-use trails. The park in general receives very light use, and is consequently a wilder place than might be expected—but also more satisfying for those looking for adventure and solitude. The terrain is mostly rolling terrain with fine woodlands and many attractive ponds but few open summits with views. Significant hills reached by trails include Hubbard Hill (1381 ft.), which has excellent views to the west, and the wooded Mt. Pisgah (1329 ft.).

Old Horseshoe Road

This historic dirt road heads southeast out of Chesterfield, loops around almost 180° like a horseshoe, and connects with the Old Winchester Road running northwest back into Chesterfield. The Horseshoe Rd. trailhead provides the major northern access to Pisgah State Park and the Old Chesterfield Road. Located at the birthplace of Harlan Fiske Stone (1872-1946), former attorney general and chief justice of the United States, the trailhead is situated on a scenic bluff overlooking the valleys and ridges of Pisgah State Park to the south. There is ample parking and an information board with maps available. It is reached by taking Holman Hill Rd. 0.3 mi. east from NH 63 in Chesterfield, then making a right onto Horseshoe Rd. (sign) and following it 1.4 mi. southeast to the parking area. A memorial for Harlan Fiske Stone is on the right.

The old road, lined with stone walls, descends past an orange gate. At 0.3 mi., the Old Horseshoe Road Connector follows the main road as it curves right and reaches the Old Winchester Road in an additional 0.3 mi., while the Old Horseshoe Road turns left onto an old grassy road signed "Habitat Trail." It enters a semi-open area filled with sumac trees, and soon the northwest fork of the South Woods Trail leaves on the left. The trail re-enters the woods and passes a small beaver bog and dam to the right. At 0.5 mi., it reaches a junction with the Old Chesterfield Road (left) and also the Old Winchester Road, which enters descending from the right through an area flooded by recent beaver activity. Waterproof footwear may be advisable here, depending on the water level.

Old Horseshoe Road (AMC Pisgah State Park Map)
Distance from Horseshoe Rd. trailhead (1060')

> *to* Old Chesterfield Road/Old Winchester Road (910'): 0.5 mi.
> (0.8 km.), 0 ft. (rev. 150 ft.), 15 min.

Legend

——— Park Access (Seasonal)

- - - - Multi-use trail

——— Hiking trail

— Gate

Ⓟ Parking

Key to Trails in Pisgah State Park

1 Davis Hill Tr
2 Hubbard Hill Tr
3 Resevoir Tr
4 Old Chesterfield Rd
5 South Woods Tr
6 Nash Tr
7 Fullam Pond Tr
8 Beals Road
9 Knob Tr
10 Winchester Road
11 Orchard Tr
12 Snow Brook Tr
13 South Link
14 Dogwood Swamp Tr
15 Chestnut Hill Tr
16 Parker Tr
17 North Ponds Tr
18 Lily Pond Tr
19 Pisgah Mtn Tr
20 Baker Tr
21 Kilburn Road
22 Kilburn Loop
23 Doolittle Tr
24 Hinsdale Tr

Key to Ponds

A Fullam Pond
B Lily Pond
C North Round Pond
D Baker Pond
E Kilburn Pond
F Pisgah Reservoir
G Tufts Pond

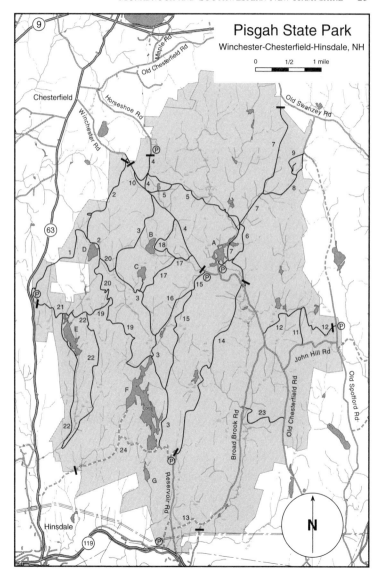

Pisgah State Park

Winchester-Chesterfield-Hinsdale, NH

0   1/2   1 mile

Chesterfield

Hinsdale

N

Old Winchester Road

This historic dirt road was once part of a main highway that connected Chesterfield with Winchester. It descends a broad ridge into the valley through which the Old Chesterfield Road runs, providing ample opportunities for various loops through the northwest section of the park. There is limited parking at this trailhead; for most longer trips, the Old Horseshoe Road trailhead with its large developed parking area should be used. To reach the Winchester Rd. trailhead, follow Winchester Rd. 1.3 mi. southeast of NH 63 in Chesterfield. Depending upon the road conditions and time of year, park as close to the locked gate as possible without obstructing the roadway or private drives.

The dirt road ascends straight ahead, enters Pisgah State Park (sign), and reaches the Hubbard Hill Trail (right) next to an information board and orange gate. It then descends, lined with stone walls. At 0.2 mi., the Old Horseshoe Road Connector follows the main road as it curves left and reaches the Old Horseshoe Road in an additional 0.3 mi., while the Old Winchester Road turns right onto an old woods road signed "Habitat Trail" and continues to descend. It skirts a semi-open area (left) filled with sumacs and enters a wet area created by recent beaver activity. Waterproof footwear may be advisable here, depending on the water level. The trail crosses stepping-stones through a particularly wet area next to a beaver dam (right) and meets the Old Chesterfield Road (straight ahead) and the Old Horseshoe Road (left) at a well-marked junction.

Old Winchester Road (AMC Pisgah State Park Map)
Distance from the Winchester Rd. trailhead (980')

> *to* Old Chesterfield Road and Old Horseshoe Road (910'): 0.6 mi. (1.0 km.), 0 ft. (rev. 50 ft.), 20 min.

Dogwood Swamp Trail

This interesting and scenic trail connects Reservoir Road with the Old Chesterfield Road near Fullam Pond. It passes over a complex subsidiary ridge with several old ponds at various stages in their succession into marshy bogs. The trail is marked with intermittent blue blazes and requires concentration and care to follow, as there are many unexpected turns which are poorly marked. Alert, experienced hikers should encounter few difficulties through this varied terrain; less experienced hikers may wish to take this trail with someone who has been over it before or may elect to take an alternative route. Difficult areas are highlighted in the description below. The trail begins on Reservoir Road, at a small parking area 1.5 mi. north of NH 119 via Reservoir Road itself or 1.4 mi. north of NH 119 via the Reservoir Trail and Reservoir Road, just before the gated road switchbacks up the small ridge to Pisgah Reservoir.

The Dogwood Swamp Trail ascends through hardwoods on an old woods road marked with sparse blue blazes up a prominent ridge, heading generally northeast. It enters a hemlock forest, swings right near a small frog pond (right), and at 0.8 mi. reaches the first of several heights-of-land, beginning a series of undulating descents and ascents along the complex ridge top. At 1.3 mi. it passes the first open marsh (left), crosses a snowmobile bridge over an outlet brook at the southwest end of another marsh with a small beaver dam (left), and descends gradually. After passing yet another marshy area with a small frog pond (left), the trail swings sharp right and then sharp left in a hemlock forest. At this left turn do not descend straight on an old logging road, which leads 0.9 mi. downstream to Broad Brook Rd. near the western terminus of the Doolittle Trail. Watch for small arrows and blazes to guide the way through this section.

Almost immediately the trail crosses a snowmobile bridge over an outlet brook and swings left near a large marshy area (left). It follows the southern border of this open area along an undulating ridge and reaches the final height-of-land at 2.1 mi., where it begins the long descent to Fullam Pond. It passes through a wet area and crosses several minor streams. After crossing a stream on a snowmobile bridge, the grade eases and the trail passes through an area with numerous blow-downs where the route should be followed with care. It passes through several wet areas past several large moss-covered boulders (left), joins a road coming from the left at a fork, and shortly thereafter reaches the Old Chesterfield Road at a point 1.1 mi. north of Broad Brook Rd. and 0.8 mi. south of the Chestnut Hill Trail and parking area.

Dogwood Swamp Trail (AMC Pisgah State Park Map)
Distances from Reservoir Road (620')

- *to* first height-of-land (920'): 0.8 mi., 300 ft., 35 min.
- *to* last height-of-land (1000'): 2.1 mi., 500 ft. (rev. 100 ft.), 1 hr. 35 min.
- *to* Old Chesterfield Road (680'): 3.3 mi. (5.3 km.), 500 ft. (rev. 300 ft.), 2 hr. 10 min.

Reservoir Trail

This old woods road connects Reservoir Road from the south to Old Chesterfield Road to the north, forming one of the major arteries through the center of the park. It intersects with many trails entering from the east and west, allowing for innumerable loops and circuits. It is scenic, with many fine viewpoints, and is easy to follow. It begins on Reservoir Road 0.5 mi. north of the Dogwood Swamp Trail parking area at the southeast corner of Pisgah Reservoir.

The trail follows the eastern shore of Pisgah Reservoir with many unmarked paths leading left to the attractive shoreline. It swings right at an intersection (sign), passes through several wet areas, and at 0.9 mi. reaches the Chestnut Hill Trail (right) at Snowmobile Sign #16. It continues to parallel the eastern shore but at a greater distance, and at 1.5 mi. it reaches the northeast corner of the reservoir, where the Pisgah Mountain Trail leaves left across a small bridge. The Reservoir Trail swings right (arrow), crosses a snowmobile bridge over an inlet brook, and passes a small beaver pond (left). After crossing a dry stream bed on another snowmobile bridge, it swings right, then left, and at 1.9 mi. reaches the Parker Trail (right). The trail swings left (arrows), crosses a small brook on a snowmobile bridge, and begins a gradual ascent, crossing several small bridges. After reaching a small rocky ridge it swings right, and at 2.6 mi. the North Ponds Trail leaves right at Snowmobile Sign #17.

The Reservoir Trail swings left and descends, and in less than 0.1 mi. an unblazed spur leaves right and runs 0.2 mi. to the southwest shore of North Round Pond (small sign), a beautiful and seldom-visited body of water, far from the most popular attractions of the park. The main trail continues to descend by sweeping switchbacks, crosses two snowmobile bridges, and at 3.3 mi. reaches the Baker Trail (left) at Snowmobile Sign #8. The Reservoir Trail now begins a persistent ascent through a hemlock forest along a small stream, crossing it several times. It reaches the height-of-land on a small ridge and begins a long gradual descent, passing through a clearing with a magnificent view northeast toward Mt. Monadnock and its surrounding hills. The trail descends past a group of small ledges and crosses several small streams, then swings right, then left, back into a hemlock forest. At 4.8 mi. it reaches the Old Chesterfield Road just past an orange gate. From here it is 0.1 mi. north on the Old Chesterfield Road to the junction with the Old Winchester Road and Old Horseshoe Road.

Reservoir Trail (AMC Pisgah State Park Map)
Distances from Reservoir Road (890')

> *to* Chestnut Hill Trail (940'): 0.9 mi., 50 ft., 30 min.

> *to* Pisgah Mountain Trail (910'): 1.5 mi., 50 ft., 45 min.

> *to* Parker Trail (940'): 1.9 mi., 100 ft. (rev. 50 ft.), 1 hr.

> *to* North Ponds Trail (990'): 2.6 mi., 150 ft., 1 hr. 20 min.

> *to* spur to North Round Pond (990'): 2.7 mi., 150 ft., 1 hr. 25 min.

> *to* Baker Trail (1090'): 3.3 mi., 250 ft., 1 hr. 45 min.

> *to* Old Chesterfield Road (910'): 4.8 mi. (7.7 km.), 450 ft. (rev. 350 ft.), 2 hr. 40 min.

Lily Pond Trail

This trail provides a side trip from the Old Chesterfield Road to Lily Pond, a beautiful body of water, heavily used by beavers and waterfowl, located only 0.5 mi. from the Old Chesterfield Road. Unfortunately the trail is scantily marked with orange ribbons for most of its length and is difficult to follow. Alert and experienced hikers should be able to follow the trail from ribbon to ribbon; others will need extra time and care, backtracking carefully to the path if no traces of markings or footway are seen. Persistent walkers will be rewarded by an extremely scenic trail with two interesting small beaver ponds along the way. The trail leaves the Old Chesterfield Road 0.9 mi. north of the Fullam Pond gate and parking area and 0.7 mi. south of the junction with the Old Winchester Road and the Old Horseshoe Road.

Leaving the Old Chesterfield Road, the Lily Pond Trail follows an old woods road through hemlocks to a small beaver pond (left) with a fine beaver lodge. From here, take extra care to find the way. The route skirts to the right of the pond and bears right uphill on an old woods road, crossing a small stream and ascending up a moderate slope to a flat area, where the trail swings left at the northeast corner of Lily Pond. From here it follows the eastern shore in a southerly direction. The pond is beautifully framed by larger hills to the west. With patience, beaver activity can be observed at the southern end of the pond near the large lodge. The trail swings left away from the pond at its southeast corner and descends with undulating grades. It passes by a wet area (left) before arriving at a small beaver pond (right) with a dam in progress. At the southeast corner of the pond, the trail ends at the green-blazed North Ponds Trail (no sign), 0.3 mi. from the Old Chesterfield Road (left).

Lily Pond Trail (AMC Pisgah State Park Map)
Distances from Old Chesterfield Road (820')

- *to* Lily Pond (960'): 0.5 mi., 150 ft., 20 min.
- *to* North Ponds Trail at small beaver pond (690'): 1.1 mi. (1.8 km.), 150 ft. (rev. 250 ft.), 40 min.

to starting point (820') via North Ponds Trail and Old Chesterfield Road: 2.0 mi. (3.2 km.), 300 ft., 1 hr. 10 min.

Parker Trail

This trail connects the Chestnut Hill Trail with the Reservoir Trail and
provides a shortcut to points on the northern part of the Reservoir Trail
from the Fullam Pond gate and parking area on the Old Chesterfield
Road. It ascends a large complex subsidiary ridge that runs south to
north through the center of the park, and meets the Reservoir Trail
south of its height-of-land on this ridge. Although it is a narrow path
for most of its length, it is well marked with yellow blazes and is fairly easy to follow as long as care is taken.

The trail makes a right turn onto an old woods road off the Chestnut Hill Trail 0.4 mi. south of the Old Chesterfield Road, and ascends
gradually through mixed hemlocks for 0.2 mi., where the route narrows to a small footpath after crossing a small stream on a log bridge.
Soon the path angles right into a shallow gully surrounded by hemlocks, which it ascends, crossing a seasonal stream and passing a
small marsh (left) in a beautiful hemlock and birch forest. At 0.9 mi.,
the trail reaches the height-of-land and descends gradually to the
Reservoir Trail, at a point 0.4 mi. north of the Mt. Pisgah Trail and 0.8
mi. south of the North Ponds Trail.

Parker Trail (AMC Pisgah State Park Map)
Distance from Chestnut Hill Trail (750')

to Reservoir Trail (920'): 1.0 mi. (1.6 km.), 150 ft., 35 min.

Chestnut Hill Trail

This trail connects the Old Chesterfield Road at the Fullam Pond gate
and parking area with the Reservoir Trail at a point 1.0 mi. north of
Reservoir Road. It crosses a large complex subsidiary ridge which
runs south to north through the middle of the park. It follows an old
woods road for its entire length, is marked with off-white blazes, and

with a few exceptions is easy to follow. The Fullam Pond gate and parking area is located 3.1 mi. north of the south gate on Old Chesterfield Road and 1.6 mi. south of the junction with the Old Winchester Road and Old Horseshoe Road. This trailhead, the most northern point that vehicles are permitted to drive to on the Old Chesterfield Road, may be reached by motorized vehicles from the south during the dry season (late spring through autumn; inquire locally).

The trail ascends gradually on an old woods road in a generally south-southwest direction past an orange gate into a mixed hemlock forest. After several small stream crossings, the Parker Trail (pale yellow blazes) leaves right at 0.4 mi. for the Reservoir Trail. The Chestnut Hill Trail swings left and ascends gradually into a hemlock grove on a small ridge where several wet areas are crossed. The trail zigzags and ascends through a hardwood forest, descends briefly to a snowmobile bridge over a small stream, then ascends again to the height-of-land where there are interesting views during the colder months. The path then descends to the Reservoir Trail (Snowmobile Sign #16) at a point 1.0 mi. north of Reservoir Road and 0.5 mi. south of the Mt. Pisgah Trail.

Chestnut Hill Trail (AMC Pisgah State Park Map)
Distance from Old Chesterfield Road at the Fullam Pond gate and parking area (690')

> *to* Reservoir Trail (950'): 2.2 mi. (3.5 km.), 450 ft. (rev. 200 ft.), 1 hr. 20 min.

North Ponds Trail

This trail connects the Old Chesterfield Road with the Reservoir Trail near its height-of-land on a long, complex subsidiary ridge. It provides access to Lily Pond by the Lily Pond Trail and to North Round Pond by the Reservoir Trail and a short spur path. Both of these splendid ponds merit time to explore, as they are probably the least visited of the major bodies of water in the park. The trail follows an old woods road marked with pale green blazes for its entire length, and is easy to

follow. It leaves the Old Chesterfield Road, 0.3 mi. north of the Fullam Pond gate and parking area and 1.3 mi. south of the junction with
the Old Winchester Road and Old Horseshoe Road.

The trail ascends gradually, passing a boggy area (left) and a
boundary marker (left) that marks the Chesterfield-Winchester town
line. The trail crosses a small stream and at 0.3 mi. reaches a double
green blaze, just before a snowmobile bridge over an outlet brook that
issues from a small beaver pond on the right. This is the southern terminus of the scantily marked Lily Pond Trail, which leaves to the
right, marked only by several orange ribbons. Although Lily Pond (0.5
mi. north from here) is well worth visiting, this trail should be
attempted only by experienced hikers who do not mind occasional
improvisational walking.

Continuing straight across the bridge, the North Ponds Trail
swings left, then right, and ascends the broad complex ridge, first
through hemlocks, then through mixed forest. It crosses a small
stream, reaches the height-of-land, and descends gradually to the
Reservoir Trail (Snowmobile Sign #17). From here it is 0.3 mi. to
North Round Pond by the Reservoir Trail and spur path, 2.6 mi. south
to Reservoir Road, and 0.8 mi. north to Baker Pond by the Reservoir
Trail and Baker Trail.

North Ponds Trail (AMC Pisgah State Park Map)
Distance from Old Chesterfield Road (690')

   to Reservoir Trail (990'): 1.1 mi. (1.8 km.), 300 ft., 40 min.

Baker Trail

Running south to north from Pisgah Reservoir to Baker Pond is a
chain of small, craggy, wooded hills that form the backbone of Pisgah
State Park. Some of these hills provide outstanding views east toward
Mt. Monadnock and west toward the Green Mtns. of Vermont. The
Baker Trail continues north from the Pisgah Mountain Trail, passes
over the northern half of this small range, swings east just south of

Baker Pond, and descends to the Reservoir Trail. It is marked with orange blazes and is easy to follow.

The trail begins in a small hemlock-lined gully where the Pisgah Mountain Trail swings west, 0.5 mi. east of the Kilburn Loop and 2.0 mi. north of Pisgah Reservoir. This junction is easy to miss due to the less-than-obvious small trail sign and orange blaze. The trail ascends gradually north on a small ridge then descends gradually with switchbacks into a shaded hemlock grove surrounded by boulder caves to the right and ledges to the left. It then ascends with switchbacks onto a ridge with an eastern lookout on semi-open ledges, swings left past a cellar hole (right), and at 0.6 mi. emerges onto an open ledge with a magnificent view of Mt. Monadnock and the nearby hills to the east. The path descends through mixed softwoods scattered with mountain laurels, then ascends gradually to a small clearing where the Hubbard Hill Trail leaves left toward Baker Pond and points north. The Baker Trail turns sharp right (east) onto an old woods road and descends gradually to the Reservoir Trail (Snowmobile Sign #8) at a point 0.7 mi. north of the North Ponds Trail and 1.5 mi. south of the Old Chesterfield Road.

Baker Trail (AMC Pisgah State Park Map)
Distances from Pisgah Mountain Trail (1230')

  to Hubbard Hill Trail (1130'): 1.1 mi., 0 ft. (rev. 100 ft.), 35 min.

  to Reservoir Trail (1090'): 1.5 mi. (2.4 km.), 0 ft. (rev. 50 ft.), 45 min.

Hubbard Hill Trail

This historic road ascends from the Winchester Rd. trailhead along a ridge to the summit of Hubbard Hill, then descends to Baker Pond and the Baker Trail. The view from the summit toward the Green Mtns. of Vermont is the finest in the park, and Baker Pond is an unspoiled, tranquil spot to observe waterfowl and beavers. The trail is marked with white blazes and is easy to follow.

The trailhead on Winchester Rd. is located 1.3 mi. southeast of NH

63 in Chesterfield, just before the road enters Pisgah State Park at the gate. There is limited parking. In a small clearing where the Old Winchester Road descends straight ahead, the Hubbard Hill Trail turns right onto an old woods road at an information board and ascends gradually past a chain-link gate, swings left (south) past an old cellar hole (left), and enters a partly cleared area at the site of an old farm. The road ascends sharply past two stone walls, then more gradually along a wooded ridge. After passing a spring (left), the road makes one long switchback (right, then left) up to the crest of the ridge at 1.2 mi. Here the north leg of a short loop path leads right 0.1 mi. to the summit of Hubbard Hill (1381 ft.), where there is a magnificent panorama of the southern Green Mtns. Stratton Mtn., Mt. Snow, and Bromley Mtn. are clearly visible over numerous farms and pastures along the Connecticut River valley in the foreground. Once the view has been savored, hikers may either backtrack on the north leg of the loop or continue ahead 0.1 mi. on the south leg back to the main trail at a point about 70 yd. south of the beginning of the north leg.

From the loop junction the old road descends gradually, making one long switchback (right, then left), and at 1.6 mi. the Davis Hill Trail enters on the right. The trail merges with a road coming from the left, then swings sharp left along the north shore of Baker Pond, where an unmarked path leads left to a scenic outlook across the length of the pond. The trail crosses snowmobile bridges over a spring and then an inlet brook, and swings right (south) along the eastern shore of Baker Pond through a hemlock forest. Another unmarked path (right) leads to a scenic outlook across the pond toward Davis Hill. At 2.0 mi., the Baker Trail is reached in a small clearing at a point 0.4 mi. from the Reservoir Trail and 1.1 mi. north of the Pisgah Mountain Trail.

Hubbard Hill Trail (AMC Pisgah State Park Map)
Distances from Winchester Rd. trailhead (980')

    to Hubbard Hill summit loop path (1350'): 1.2 mi., 350 ft., 45 min.

    to Davis Hill Trail (1150'): 1.6 mi., 350 ft. (rev. 200 ft.), 1 hr.

    to Baker Trail (1130'): 2.0 mi. (3.2 km.), 350 ft., 1 hr. 10 min.

Davis Hill Trail

This trail connects NH 63 at the Kilburn Road trailhead with the Hubbard Hill Trail at a point just north of Baker Pond, making possible a number of attractive loop hikes. The Kilburn Road trailhead is located on NH 63, 3.4 mi. south of Chesterfield and 3.9 mi. north of Hinsdale. There is an alternative snowmobile entrance on NH 63 0.3 mi. north of this trailhead.

The trail (sign) follows an old woods road in a northerly direction from a point near the trailhead. At 0.2 mi. it turns right onto another old road in a hemlock forest. The snowmobile entrance on NH 63 is 0.1 mi. to the left down this road. The trail ascends by several switchbacks, descends to cross a stream on a snowmobile bridge, then ascends again, passing the blue-blazed boundary markers at 0.9 mi. that signal the passage from Pisgah State Park into the Winchester Town Forest. At 1.0 mi. the height-of-land on Davis Hill is reached and the road descends through a hardwood forest and passes orange boundary markers (left) at 1.3 mi. as the trail re-enters Pisgah State Park in Chesterfield. The trail descends into a hemlock forest, swings to the right past an old stone wall, and crosses a small stream on a snowmobile bridge in an attractive glen. At 1.9 mi. the trail ends at the Hubbard Hill Trail (white blazes) at a point just north of Baker Pond and 0.5 mi. south of the fine western outlook on Hubbard Hill. From here, various circuits may be completed by taking either the Baker Trail, Reservoir Trail, or Pisgah Mountain Trail and returning to the Kilburn Road trailhead via the Kilburn Loop.

Davis Hill Trail (AMC Pisgah State Park Map)

Distances from Kilburn Road trailhead (1080')

- *to* height-of-land on Davis Hill (1410'): 1.0 mi., 350 ft., 40 min.
- *to* Hubbard Hill Trail (1150'): 1.9 mi. (3.1 km.), 350 ft. (rev. 150 ft.), 1 hr. 10 min.

Pisgah Mountain Trail

A ridge of small craggy, wooded peaks forms the backbone of Pisgah State Park, running south to north from Pisgah Reservoir to Baker Pond. Many of these hills offer excellent views of Mt. Monadnock to the east and the southern Green Mtns. to the west. The Pisgah Mountain Trail runs from the northern shore of Pisgah Reservoir over the southern half of this chain, connecting with the Baker Trail (which completes the ridge line traverse), then descends to the Kilburn Loop, which leads to Kilburn Pond and NH 63. Despite the low elevation of the summits, the trail is rugged, with several sharp ascents and descents, and takes longer than other trails in the park of comparable length. The hiker is rewarded, however, with several spectacular views and memorable moments that more than compensate for the effort involved. The trail is marked with pale yellow blazes and, with the exception of one short section, is easy to follow.

The trail leaves the Reservoir Trail at the northeast corner of Pisgah Reservoir, 1.5 mi. north of Reservoir Road. It crosses a bridge over an inlet brook with a beaver dam and skirts the northern shore of the reservoir through a hemlock forest. At 0.3 mi. the route swings to the right away from the reservoir and ascends a boulder-strewn slope alongside a beautiful stream lined with moss. It swings away from the stream, then swings left heading north onto the backbone of the ridge, passing a small clearing (right) with a view toward Mt. Monadnock and a striking view (right) back toward the northern shore of the reservoir. Soon thereafter the trail descends into a shallow gully, then ascends toward Mt. Pisgah. This section is poorly blazed and should be followed with care. At 1.2 mi. the high point of Mt. Pisgah (1329 ft.), a wooded knob, is reached.

The trail descends to a small stream, then ascends scattered ledges, emerging onto an open crag with pines at 1.7 mi., where there is a magnificent view of Mt. Monadnock. This spot is known locally as Parker's Perch. The path descends again into a hemlock glen, then swings left and ascends left into a small gully at 2.0 mi., where the Baker Trail leaves right to continue a traverse of the ridge north toward Baker Pond. This junction is easy to miss due to the small size of the Baker Trail sign and orange blaze.

The trail continues straight and descends past a small marsh (right) and moss-covered ledges (left), and crosses several small streams on snowmobile bridges. After passing a beaver bog and dam (left), the blue-blazed Kilburn Loop is reached. From here, turn left to complete the entire loop or turn right to reach Kilburn Road (0.4 mi.) and NH 63 (1.2 mi.) via the Kilburn Loop.

Pisgah Mountain Trail (AMC Pisgah State Park Map)
Distances from Reservoir Trail (910')

- *to* Mt. Pisgah (1329'): 1.2 mi., 400 ft., 50 min.

- *to* Baker Trail (1230'): 2.0 mi., 400 ft. (rev. 100 ft.), 1 hr. 10 min.

- *to* Kilburn Loop (1080'): 2.5 mi. (4.0 km.), 400 ft. (rev. 150 ft.), 1 hr. 25 min.

Kilburn Loop

One of the most popular hiking and snowmobile routes in the park, the Kilburn Loop provides an attractive overview of Pisgah State Park from an easily accessible trailhead. In a relatively short distance, the trail passes Kilburn Pond and its outlet brook, several marshy areas with small bogs, and attractive hemlock forests. The route is well blazed with blue diamond markers, well signed, and easy to follow. It is also a comfortable length to complete in half a day, making it an ideal family hike. The trailhead, which is shared with the Davis Hill Trail, is located on NH 63, 3.4 mi. south of Chesterfield and 3.9 mi. north of Hinsdale. There is ample parking.

The trail begins by following Kilburn Road, an old gravel road that heads east directly out of the parking area through two gateposts and past a mailbox to the right. It ascends gradually, swings right, begins a gentle descent, and enters the Kilburn Loop on the right at 0.6 mi. The loop is described here in a counter-clockwise direction. It follows an old woods road marked by blue diamond blazes and runs generally south. Almost immediately it passes within sight of Kilburn Pond, an attractive body of water lined with rocky outcroppings and hemlocks. The trail follows the western shore, passing numerous unmarked paths (left) leading to fine viewpoints overlooking the pond. Several of these spots by themselves justify a walk along this route and merit additional time. At 1.4 mi. the trail reaches the southwestern corner of the pond, where an old woods road leaves left. The trail bears right here, avoiding an old woods road (right), and descends parallel to a large outlet brook (left), crossing several small streams. At 1.9 mi. there are views to the left through the trees to a smaller pond (not shown on the park map). The trail passes this pond, then descends in earnest, crossing the outlet brook and a tributary stream on snowmobile bridges. The road makes a hard left where an old woods road leaves right to exit the park, then at 2.7 mi. begins the northward climb to complete the loop. The trail passes a smaller pond (left) that is seen through the trees, and shortly reaches red boundary blazes which indicate the Hinsdale-Winchester town line. After passing a small spring (right) and swinging left onto a snowmobile bridge that crosses an outlet brook emerging from a small marsh (right), the Kilburn Loop leaves the old road and becomes a footpath in a hemlock forest.

The trail passes another pond that is seen through the trees to the left, crosses a small wet area, then ambles through a rock-strewn hardwood forest, ascending gradually into another hemlock forest. At 4.4 mi. the trail reaches its high point on a small ridge, then descends gradually by several switchbacks and reaches the Pisgah Mountain Trail (right) at 5.2 mi., where the loop merges with an old woods road coming from the left. The trail descends by one sweeping switchback, crosses a large inlet brook on a snowmobile bridge, then turns left (west) onto Kilburn Road at 5.5 mi. It passes an old woods road (left) and a small marshy area (right), and swings around the north shore of Kilburn Pond (left). It then ascends gradually, and at 5.7 mi. reaches the starting point of the Kilburn Loop (left), 0.6 mi. east of the trailhead.

Kilburn Loop (AMC Pisgah State Park Map)
Distances from the Kilburn Road trailhead (1080')

> *to* western end of Kilburn Loop (1130'): 0.6 mi., 50 ft., 20 min.

> *to* southern end of Kilburn Loop (980'): 2.7 mi., 100 ft. (rev. 150 ft.), 1 hr. 25 min.

> *to* Pisgah Mountain Trail (1080'): 5.2 mi., 200 ft., 2 hr. 40 min.

> *to* eastern end of Kilburn Loop (1050'): 5.5 mi., 200 ft. (rev. 50 ft.), 2 hr. 50 min.

> *to* Kilburn Road trailhead (1080') via complete loop: 6.3 mi. (10.1 km.), 250 ft., 3 hr. 20 min.

South Woods Trail

The trail connects the Old Horseshoe Road and Old Chesterfield Road with the Fullam Pond Trail. The central section is extremely difficult to follow due to a lack of blazes and an indistinct footway. It should be attempted only by experienced hikers who are willing to spend extra time locating the trail. Both ends of the trail split off into north and south forks with separate entrances. The western forks coincide with part of the Habitat Trail, a self-guiding nature path with numbered posts keyed to an informational brochure that may be obtained from the park office. The southwest fork passes a beaver pond where water may flood the trail, so waterproof footwear may be desirable.

The northwest fork (the least wet approach) leaves the Old Horseshoe Road in an overgrown clearing filled with sumacs, 0.3 mi. south of the Horseshoe Rd. trailhead and 0.2 mi. north of the junction of the Old Chesterfield Road and Old Winchester Road. It enters the woods, passes a stone wall, and descends on an old woods road lined with stone walls to the point where the southwest fork comes in on the right at 0.5 mi.

The southwest fork leaves the Old Chesterfield Road just south of the convergence of the Old Horseshoe Road and Old Winchester

Road. It descends gradually on an old woods road that coincides with the Habitat Trail, crosses two culverted brooks, and at 0.1 mi. makes a left onto an old grassy road signed "Wildlife Trail." The trail follows this road to the eastern shore of a large beaver pond in a beautiful open marsh, crosses the beaver dam (use caution) to the northeast corner of the pond, and heads into the woods bearing right onto another old woods road. This section of trail is extremely wet. The trail descends gradually past a stone wall and meets the northwest fork (left) at 0.4 mi. From here, the Habitat Trail turns left onto the northwest fork and ends at the Old Horseshoe Road.

The South Woods Trail turns right at this junction (or continues straight if you are coming in on the northwest fork), crosses a stream on a snowmobile bridge past a large marshy area (left), crosses a brook on a log bridge, then crosses a small stream on a regular bridge. From here the route narrows to a trail and is extremely difficult to follow in places; it may require backtracking if the footway is lost. The route bypasses a small bog (left), crosses several small streams, then turns right onto an old woods road (no signs, arrows, or blazes). It skirts to the right of an open wetland area, re-enters the woods, and climbs over a small hill into a hemlock forest, where a large brook is crossed on a bridge. The old road follows the north bank of this brook downstream, recrosses the brook on a bridge, and at 1.6 mi. reaches a junction where the trail forks again.

The northeast fork (easier to follow) bears left and ascends gradually to Fullam Pond Trail at a point just south of its junction with the Nash Trail.

The southeast fork continues along the large brook, crosses a fairly significant tributary brook without a bridge, and meets the Fullam Pond Trail at a point 0.1 mi. south of the Nash Trail and 0.5 mi. north of Fullam Pond Dam. There are plans to abandon this trail segment in the near future.

South Woods Trail (AMC Pisgah State Park Map)
Distances from the junction of the Old Chesterfield Road and Old Horseshoe Road (910')

- *to* convergence of northwest and southwest forks (840'): 0.5 mi., 0 ft. (rev. 50 ft.), 15 min.

- *to* divergence of northeast and southeast forks (690'): 1.6 mi., 0 ft. (rev. 150 ft.), 50 min.

- *to* Fullam Pond Trail (690'): 1.9 mi. (3.1 km.), 0 ft., 55 min.

Old Chesterfield Road

Once the highway between Winchester and Chesterfield, this historic road is now the southeast-to-northwest artery through Pisgah State Park. The southern 3.3-mi. section may be used by motorized vehicles during the dry season (late spring through autumn; inquire locally for details) but is gated the remainder of the year. There are many historical exhibits and sites along the first 1.5 mi. as the road passes through the remains of an early-nineteenth-century farming and industrial community. An interesting 3.5-mi. loop, which includes many of the historical exhibits in the park, may be made by combining the Doolittle Trail with the northern section of the Broad Brook Road and the southern section of the Old Chesterfield Road. Accompanying literature may be obtained by contacting the state park office.

There is a small area for parking at the southern trailhead, 2.8 mi. northwest of Winchester. The road heads north, and in 0.2 mi. it passes an orange gate (locked during winter and early spring) and descends gradually on a well-graded gravel roadway. It passes the cider mill site (left, sign #1) shortly before reaching the Doolittle Trail (left) next to an old barn site (sign #2) at 0.4 mi. The road continues past the Benjamin Doolittle Homestead (right, sign #3), then a small pond (right), and ascends gradually past the Jediah Eaton Homestead (left, sign #4), the Ebenezer Hutchinson Homestead (left, sign #5), and a small parking area for the historic sites (right, signs #6 and #7). At 1.1 mi., the road reaches an orange gate that is locked during winter and early spring and at night during the rest of the year. Here John Hill Road leaves right and runs to Old Spofford Road.

The Old Chesterfield Road descends gradually to several culverted streams, passes the Nathan Field Homestead (right, sign #8), crosses a culverted brook, and ascends gradually. It passes Cheese Rock (right), a white pine stand (left, sign #10), and reaches the northern end of Broad Brook Road (left) at 1.5 mi. Heading generally northwest, the road passes an old woods road (left), and at 1.7 mi. the Snow Brook Trail comes in on the right at an orange gatepost next to an old woods road. The road descends gradually past a small clearing (left) into an open marshy area through which Broad Brook flows.

At 2.5 mi. the Old Chesterfield Road reaches the Nash Trail (right) at a small parking area, then swings left (west), crosses Broad Brook on a bridge and shortly reaches the Dogwood Swamp Trail (left) in a small clearing. The road curves several times through an open bog and at 3.1 mi. reaches the road to the Fullam Pond parking area (right), opposite Snowmobile Sign #13 (left). The Old Chesterfield Road continues straight ahead, passes through a small flooded area, and at 3.3 mi. reaches the Chestnut Hill Trail (left) at a small parking area. This is the northern limit of motorized travel permitted on this road.

The road now becomes a graded woods road and ascends gradually past a locked orange gate, passes the Winchester-Chesterfield boundary markers (right), and at 3.6 mi. reaches the North Ponds Trail (left) at Snowmobile Sign #14. The road descends gradually past a small beaver bog with lodge and dam (right), and at 4.2 mi. reaches the northern terminus of the Lily Pond Trail (left). The road continues through a wet area (left), crosses a culverted stream, and ascends gradually. At 4.4 mi. the road passes an unmarked woods road (right) that connects to the South Woods Trail near a beaver pond in 0.3 mi. The main road crosses several culverted streams, then descends gradually to the Reservoir Trail, which comes in on the left at an orange gate at 4.7 mi. The road then crosses a culverted stream and at 4.8 mi. reaches the southwest terminus of the South Woods Trail (right), which is a link to the Habitat Trail. The Old Chesterfield Road ends just beyond at an area of recent beaver activity, where the Old Winchester Road and Habitat Trail lead straight uphill 0.6 mi. to the Winchester Rd. trailhead and the Old Horseshoe Road leaves right uphill 0.5 mi. to the Horseshoe Rd. trailhead and parking area.

Old Chesterfield Road (AMC Pisgah State Park Map)
Distances from southern trailhead (880')

> *to* Broad Brook Road (710'): 1.5 mi., 50 ft. (rev. 200 ft.), 45 min.

> *to* Nash Trail (660'): 2.5 mi., 150 ft. (rev. 150 ft.), 1 hr. 20 min.

> *to* Chestnut Hill Trail and locked gate (680'): 3.3 mi., 150 ft., 1 hr. 45 min.

> *to* Old Winchester Road and Old Horseshoe Road (910'): 4.8 miles (7.8 km.), 400 ft., 2 hr. 35 min.

Doolittle Trail

This short trail connects the Old Chesterfield Road with the Broad Brook Road. It descends into the Broad Brook valley through the remains of an early New Hampshire farming and industrial community with several numbered exhibits and sites scattered along the bank of the brook (accompanying literature may be obtained from the state park office). An interesting loop may be made by hiking the Doolittle Trail from east to west, heading north on the Broad Brook Road, then going south on the Old Chesterfield Road back to the starting point. The Doolittle Trail is generally easy to follow with the exception of a short segment near the eastern terminus where care must be taken.

The trail leaves the Old Chesterfield Road on an old grassy road, 0.2 mi. north of the southern gate and 0.7 mi. south of John Hill Road. It passes through an old orchard and overgrown field past several stone walls, then bears right off the old road into the forest (no sign). The trail turns left onto a footpath (sign) and ascends a small hill. This section should be followed with care as the footway is faint with few blazes or markings. The route swings right and then left, descends gradually, then turns left onto an old woods road (sign). From here on, the trail is easier to follow.

The trail passes over a small hill, descends through a hemlock forest to the Old Broad Brook Meadow (left, sign #23) at 0.7 mi., then swings right (north) and ascends through mixed pines. The trail crosses a stream on a snowmobile bridge and follows Broad Brook upstream, passes the Water Mill Dam Site (left, sign #22) at 0.9 mi., then swings left (west) and crosses Broad Brook and a tributary stream on two snowmobile bridges. Soon it meets the Broad Brook Road, 1.0 mi. south of Old Chesterfield Road and 2.0 mi. north of the south gate and South Link Trail.

Doolittle Trail (AMC Pisgah State Park Map)
Distances from Old Chesterfield Road (910')

- *to* Broad Brook Road (590'): 1.1 mi. (1.8 km.), 0 ft. (rev. 350 ft.), 35 min.

- *to* starting point by complete loop via Doolittle Trail, Broad Brook Road, and Old Chesterfield Road: 3.3 mi. (5.3 km.), 400 ft. (rev. 50 ft.), 1 hr. 50 min.

Broad Brook Road

This is an extremely scenic and historic walk through the valley of Broad Brook, which was once the location of a thriving nineteenth-century farming and industrial community. The southern section of the road is open to hikers and snowmobiles only; it passes through attractive open marshes and flood plains. The northern mile passes through the remains of an early New Hampshire industrial settlement with foundations of mills, homesteads, schools, and water canals used to harness the streams to provide energy for the early mills. Motorized vehicles are allowed through this section from late spring through autumn (inquire locally). There are numbered exhibits and sites; accompanying literature may be obtained from the state park office.

There are several ways of access to Broad Brook Road. From late spring through autumn, hikers in vehicles may enter from the north by the Old Chesterfield Road, or from the south from the new Reservoir Road trailhead by way of the new South Link. Hikers on foot may also enter the road directly from NH 119 from the Broad Brook Road junction (little parking available here). By any of these routes, this trail presents an interesting perspective on a former way of life that flourished well before the settlement of much of the rest of the United States.

From the new Reservoir Road trailhead (on NH 119, 2.2 mi. east of Hinsdale), the access trail follows a woods road that leads uphill past an orange gate and crosses a power line clearing. At 0.2 mi. the route turns right and follows the Connector Trail, a snowmobile trail that passes through an attractive pine grove and reaches Reservoir Road at 0.4 mi. A short distance downhill to the right from here, at 0.5 mi., the South Link leaves on the left and ascends on an old woods road through mixed hemlocks, then descends through mixed forest to reach the Broad Brook Road at 1.1 mi. from the parking area on NH 119. This point is 0.6 mi. north of NH 119 (at a point 3.2 mi. east of Hinsdale) and 0.1 mi. north of the locked south gate where Broad Brook Road enters Pisgah State Park (parking very limited here).

From the junction with the South Link, the Broad Brook Road leads gradually uphill past an open marsh and flood plains (right) and moss-covered ledges (left), and finally runs alongside Broad Brook itself (right). At 2.9 mi. it reaches the Historic Sites parking area and turn-around (left) which is the southern limit for motorized vehicle travel during the summer season. From here the road parallels Broad Brook through the remains of an early New Hampshire settlement with over a dozen historical exhibits on either side of the road. Included are the sites of steam mills, dams, barns, homesteads, water mills, a boarding-house, and a school. At 3.0 mi. the road reaches the western terminus of the Doolittle Trail (right), which provides access to several other historical sites. In another half-mile the road crosses Broad Brook next to the site of the William King Water Mill and ascends gradually away from the brook, passing several historical sites, and reaches the Old Chesterfield Road 0.5 mi. north of John Hill Road and 1.6 mi. south of the Fullam Pond parking area.

Broad Brook Road (AMC Pisgah State Park Map)
Distances from new Reservoir Road trailhead on NH 119 (390')

- *to* Broad Brook Road via connector trail and South Link (560'): 1.1 mi., 200 ft., 40 min.

- *to* Historic Sites parking area (590'): 2.9 mi., 200 ft., 1 hr. 30 min.

- *to* Doolittle Trail (590'): 3.0 mi., 200 ft., 1 hr. 35 min.

- *to* Old Chesterfield Road (710'): 4.0 mi. (6.4 km.), 350 ft., 2 hr. 10 min.

Snow Brook Trail

This scenic trail meanders in a westerly direction from the Old Spofford Road to the Old Chesterfield Road. It follows an old woods road for its entire length through attractive evergreen forests, along the bank of Snow Brook, and beside open marshlands. Although the route is longer and more serpentine than the park map indicates, it is easy to follow.

The eastern trailhead may be found by driving north on the Old Spofford Road, 4.8 mi. from Winchester, 3.5 mi. north of the road to Westport (see map), and 0.2 mi. north of John Hill Road. It has ample parking. The trail follows an old woods road through an orange gate into a mixed hemlock forest, swings right past a small marshy area (left), passes a stone wall, and begins a gradual descent, swinging left and then right into a beautiful mossy glen. After several more turns, it crosses Snow Brook on a snowmobile bridge, then continues to follow its course downstream. The road passes a small beaver bog (left), then swings left and re-crosses Snow Brook on another bridge. At 0.9 mi. the Orchard Trail leaves right (Snowmobile Sign #21) for Old Spofford Road. A short distance beyond, the Orchard Trail leaves left (Snowmobile Sign #21) for John Hill Road.

From here the trail swings right, crosses Snow Brook on a snowmobile bridge, ascends an embankment away from the brook, and skirts the south side of a large open marsh. It enters a pine forest and ascends to the Old Chesterfield Road, 0.2 mi. north of the Broad Brook Road and 1.3 mi. south of the Fullam Pond parking area.

Snow Brook Trail (AMC Pisgah State Park Map)
Distances from Old Spofford Road trailhead (920')

- *to* Orchard Trail (850'): 0.9 mi., 0 ft. (rev. 50 ft.), 25 min.
- *to* Old Chesterfield Road (720'): 1.8 mi. (2.9 km.), 0 ft. (rev. 150 ft.), 55 min.

John Hill Road

This partly paved, partly gravel road connects the Old Spofford Road with the Old Chesterfield Road. It is suitable for hikers in all seasons, and is also used by all-terrain vehicles and snowmobiles. It is gated on both ends. To find out when the road is open to vehicles, consult the state park office. The road leaves the Old Spofford Road 0.2 mi. south of the trailhead for the Snow Brook Trail and 4.6 mi. north of Winchester. Hikers are encouraged to park at the trailhead for the Snow Brook Trail, where there is ample space.

The road descends through a wire gate with orange posts past a beaver pond (left), then ascends to a height-of-land at 0.4 mi. Here the road swings right and descends past a wet area. At 0.6 mi. an unmarked woods road (the Orchard Trail) leaves right (north) and runs to a turnaround in a small clearing. After passing another old road (right) and a small clearing with utility lines (right), the road swings left and descends to the Old Chesterfield Road at an orange gate, 0.5 mi. south of Broad Brook Road and 0.9 mi. north of the south gate.

John Hill Road (AMC Pisgah State Park Map)
Distances from Old Spofford Road (920')

- *to* Orchard Trail (900'): 0.6 mi., 0 ft., 20 min.
- *to* Old Chesterfield Road (750'): 1.2 mi. (1.9 km.), 0 ft. (rev. 150 ft.), 40 min.

Orchard Trail

This somewhat ill-defined trail travels north from John Hill Road, crosses the Snow Brook Trail, then swings east to the Old Spofford Road. Its trailheads are not obvious, and a small section north of the Snow Brook Trail is minimally marked with ribbons and is extremely difficult to follow. The landowner has forbidden the use of the north end of this trail for the time being.

The southern trailhead leaves John Hill Road on an unmarked dirt road, which begins at a point 0.6 mi. west of Old Spofford Road and 0.5 mi. east of Old Chesterfield Road. Almost immediately the road reaches a turnaround where the trail bears right onto an old woods road (sign) and enters the woods. It passes two stone walls, descends gradually to a beaver bog, passes another stone wall, crosses a small stream, and at 0.6 mi. reaches a woods road marked only with Snow-mobile Sign #21. This is the Snow Brook Trail. The Orchard Trail turns right on this woods road, ascends gradually along the bank of Snow Brook, soon reaches another Snowmobile Sign #21, and turns left onto a trail (sign). From here to the northern trailhead, the trail is closed at present, but a description is included in case it is opened to public use in the future.

The trail crosses Snow Brook on a snowmobile bridge and ascends a small embankment. From here the trail is extremely difficult to follow, with a faint footway marked only by occasional ribbons. In 0.1 mi. the trail crosses a collapsed bridge over a small stream, then turns right onto an unmarked old woods road. From here the trail is easier to follow. It crosses two culverted streams, leaves Pisgah State Park (signs), passes two stone walls, and emerges onto the Old Spofford Road in a small clearing, 0.7 mi. north of the trailhead for the Snow Brook Trail (parking) and 2.1 mi. south of Beal's Road trailhead. At the landowner's request there are no signs or blazes here.

Orchard Trail (AMC Pisgah State Park Map)
Distances from John Hill Road (900')

   to Snow Brook Trail (850'): 0.6 mi., 0 ft. (rev. 50 ft.), 20 min.

   to Old Spofford Road (980'): 1.3 mi. (2.1 km.), 150 ft., 45 min.

Reservoir Road

This attractive trail from NH 119 to the south shore of Pisgah Reservoir uses a well-graded gravel road for most of its length. The trip may be extended to an 8-mi. loop by continuing on the Hinsdale Snowmobile Trail to NH 63 and walking south on NH 63 0.6 mi. to Hinsdale, then east on NH 119 for 2.2 mi. back to the trailhead. Some of the views from the shore of the reservoir are excellent.

There are now two approaches to Reservoir Road: one follows the access trail from the new trailhead and parking area, 2.2 mi. east of Hinsdale on NH 119, and meets Reservoir Road, while the other follows the first part of Reservoir Road (no parking here), which begins 0.3 mi. east of the new trailhead. Both are described below.

From the new trailhead, a woods road (marked by blue diamonds) ascends past an orange gate and through a power line clearing. At 0.2 mi. the Connector Trail, a snowmobile trail, leaves right uphill and runs 0.2 mi. through an attractive pine grove to Reservoir Road. The main trail continues straight uphill on an old woods road, then quickly fades to a trail through mixed hemlocks and reaches Reservoir Road at 0.5 mi. Turn left here for Pisgah Reservoir (no sign).

From the base of Reservoir Road at NH 119 (no parking), the gravel road ascends past an orange gate and immediately enters Pisgah State Park (signs). There is a view of the paper mill on the Ashuelot River to the left. The road crosses a power line clearing and at 0.4 mi. reaches the South Link (right), which leads 0.6 mi. to Broad Brook Road at a point 0.1 mi. north of its southern gate. The main road leads straight 0.1 mi. to the Connector Trail, a snowmobile link that descends on the left 0.2 mi. back down to the access trail from the new trailhead at a point 0.2 mi. north of the new trailhead. The road then continues another 0.2 mi. to reach the access trail, which enters on the left (sign).

The Reservoir Road crosses a brook, passes two beaver ponds (right) in a marshy area, and at 1.4 mi. reaches the Dogwood Swamp Trail (right) across from a small parking area. The road now swings left, passes another orange gate with a mailbox (left), and begins a series of switchbacks up the side of a ridge. After a 0.5-mi. climb, the grade eases and the trail descends gradually to the Reservoir Trail (right), which serves as one of the major north-south arteries in the park. The road swings left around the south end of Pisgah Reservoir, passing several unmarked paths (right) which lead to the shore. At 2.2 mi., the road reaches a spillway at the southern end of the reservoir, where there are magnificent views north over the water toward Mt. Pisgah. On the other side of the spillway, the road continues as the Hinsdale Snowmobile Trail, which leads 2.8 mi. down to NH 63. Use caution if you cross the spillway; if the spillway cannot be crossed due to high water or winds, an unmarked bypass road to the left avoids the spillway and dam area.

Reservoir Road (AMC Pisgah State Park Map)

Distances from the new Reservoir Road trailhead (400')

- *to* Reservoir Road (560'): 0.5 mi., 200 ft., 20 min.

- *to* Dogwood Swamp Trail (620'): 1.4 mi., 250 ft., 50 min.

- *to* Reservoir Trail (940'): 2.0 mi., 600 ft., 1 hr. 20 min.

- *to* spillway at southern end of Pisgah Reservoir (890'): 2.2 mi. (3.5 km.), 600 ft., 1 hr. 25 min.

Hinsdale Snowmobile Trail

This woods road is actively used in winter as part of one of the major snowmobile corridors through Pisgah State Park. An attractive loop can be made by combining this trail with the Reservoir Trail, a 0.6-mi. walk along NH 63 to Hinsdale, and a 2.2-mi. walk along NH 119 to the Reservoir Road trailhead. Hikers should be aware that there are few trail markings such as signs and blazes along this route, with the exception of a small number of snowmobile signs at major intersections. Take care to follow the route closely so that inadvertent wrong turns can be quickly corrected; a topographical map and compass would be particularly useful. Several viewpoints along the shore of Pisgah Reservoir are extremely memorable. Hikers wishing to attempt the complete loop should park their vehicles either in Hinsdale or at the Reservoir Road trailhead, since parking is not permitted at the start of this trail. From Hinsdale, follow NH 63 north on foot for 0.6 mi. to a small woods road over a small bridge on the right.

The trail ascends on this woods road, crossing the small snowmobile bridge, then swings hard left into the woods, bears left where an old woods road leaves right, and swings right. At 0.4 mi. the trail turns left at a three-way intersection, enters a power line clearing, bears left again, and ascends across the clearing back into the woods. There are several old woods roads on either side of the main road that should be avoided. The main road enters a mixed hemlock forest, and at 1.3 mi. reaches an old camp on the left just before crossing a snowmobile bridge over a small beaver pond. The road passes through orange gateposts and enters Pisgah State Park (signs). The road makes the first of several crossings over a small brook as it follows the course of this stream uphill. It swings right through a semi-open area with evidence of old beaver activity and crosses the stream three times before entering a small open marsh on the left. The trail crosses the stream three more times in a fine hemlock forest, then leaves the stream behind as it climbs to higher ground.

At 2.1 mi. the trail reaches Snowmobile Sign #20 at a three-way intersection. To reach a beautiful cove on the western shore of Pisgah Reservoir, follow the unmarked road straight ahead. It leads 0.4 mi. over a small rocky ridge and then down to the shore of the reservoir.

The main route turns right at this intersection and continues on the unmarked road, heading generally southeast. It crosses a small stream on a snowmobile bridge, then passes over some corduroy in a wet area and swings right. At the height-of-land the road passes a stone wall, then descends gradually on a relatively flat ridge, swinging left to cross a long corduroy snowmobile bridge over a wet area, then another snowmobile bridge over a stagnant stream. The trail swings right and reaches Snowmobile Sign #19, where it swings left. After passing over yet another bridge, the trail emerges onto the southwest corner of Pisgah Reservoir at 2.8 mi. To reach the Reservoir Trail, cross a concrete barrier to a spillway on the southern shore of the reservoir. From here, there are good views north over the open water toward Mt. Pisgah. On the other side of the spillway, the road continues as the Reservoir Trail, which leads 2.1 mi. down to the Reservoir Road trailhead on NH 119, 2.2 mi. east of Hinsdale. Use caution if you cross the spillway; if the spillway cannot be crossed due to high water or winds, an unmarked bypass road to the right avoids the spillway and dam area.

Hinsdale Snowmobile Trail (AMC Pisgah State Park Map)
Distances from NH 63 (330')

- *to* three-way intersection at power line clearing (590'): 0.4 mi., 250 ft., 20 min.
- *to* Pisgah State Park boundary (770'): 1.3 mi., 450 ft., 55 min.
- *to* spur trail to western cove of Pisgah Reservoir (890'): 2.1 mi., 550 ft., 1 hr. 20 min.
- *to* western cove of Pisgah Reservoir via spur trail (890'): 2.5 mi., 550 ft., 1 hr. 30 min.
- *to* Pisgah Reservoir spillway and Reservoir Road (890'): 2.8 mi. (4.5 km.), 550 ft., 1 hr. 40 min.
- *to* starting point (from any point) by complete loop via Reservoir Trail, Hinsdale Snowmobile Trail, NH 63, and NH 119: 7.8 mi. (12.6 km.), 900 ft., 4 hr. 20 min.

Old Spofford Road

This woods road runs south from the Beal's Road trailhead to the trailhead for the Snow Brook Trail. The southern half may be driven during the dry season from late spring through late autumn; however, parking is limited, and hikers are encouraged to use the designated trailhead parking areas. The northern half of this trail is extremely wet (particularly in spring) and may be flooded under a foot of water, making rubber boots or waders desirable. During the winter, the road is used by snowmobiles and may be well packed at times. The route is fairly obvious throughout its length despite the lack of signs or blazes. The Beal's Road trailhead can be reached by following Old

Swanzey Rd. 1.8 mi. southeast from Tuttle Rd. Turn right onto a dirt road (sign) and follow it 0.6 mi. south to a small clearing with trail signs and limited parking.

The trail follows the unsigned dirt road south, passing a beaver pond to the right almost immediately. The woods road on the right at 0.1 mi. bypasses the wet areas that lie ahead, running on higher terrain, but is unblazed, unsigned, and difficult to follow. Shortly thereafter the main road passes through a boggy area which may be flooded with a great deal of water. There is a stone wall to the right which may be used as a bypass if necessary. Several unmarked woods roads on either side should not be followed. At 0.5 mi. the trail passes through another extremely wet area with an old beaver lodge to the left. The road then enters a mixed hemlock forest and becomes temporarily drier. A small brook is crossed at 0.8 mi. and, after a short descent, another significant wet, marshy area is crossed at 1.1 mi. Shortly, a small brook is forded and the Old Spofford Road ascends gradually to higher and drier ground.

A small parking area to the left marks the northern limit for motorized travel during the dry season. An attractive white pine grove on the right is followed by a small beaver pond with lodge and dam. At 1.9 mi., red-blazed boundary markers are passed as the road leaves Chesterfield and enters Winchester. Within a short distance, a small parking area appears on the left marked by a yellow ribbon, with an unmarked woods road to the right. (This is the northern end of the Orchard Trail. Due to negotiations between the landowner and the state park, there are no signs or blazes and hikers are currently forbidden to use the northern part of the trail that crosses private land; hikers are encouraged to use the section of the Orchard Trail from John Hill Road to the Snow Brook Trail only.) From here, it is 0.7 mi. south past several private homes to the trailhead for the Snow Brook Trail with its ample parking, and 0.2 mi. beyond to John Hill Road.

Old Spofford Road (AMC Pisgah State Park Map)
Distances from Beal's Road trailhead (980')

- *to* northern limit of motorized travel (890'): 1.2 mi., 0 ft. (rev. 50 ft.), 35 min.

- *to* Chesterfield-Winchester town line (950'): 1.9 mi., 100 ft., 1 hr.

- *to* Orchard Trail (980'): 2.1 mi., 150 ft., 1 hr. 5 min.

- *to* Snow Brook Trail trailhead (920'): 2.7 mi. (4.3 km.), 150 ft. (rev. 50 ft.), 1 hr. 25 min.

- *to* John Hill Road (920'): 2.9 mi. (4.7 km.), 150 ft., 1 hr. 30 min.

Nash Trail

This trail connects the Old Chesterfield Road with the Fullam Pond Trail. It parallels the eastern shore of Fullam Pond with a connecting spur leading down to the Fullam Pond Dam and the southern terminus of the Fullam Pond Trail. It is not blazed but is well signed and easy to follow throughout its length.

Leaving the Old Chesterfield Road at a small parking area just south of the bridge over Broad Brook, the trail follows an old grassy road in a northerly direction past two wooden gateposts. After a short distance, Broad Brook, which drains Fullam Pond and runs south to the Ashuelot River, may be seen on the left in a small clearing. At 0.4 mi. a red boundary marker is reached as the trail passes from Winchester into Chesterfield and swings right. Shortly thereafter, a connecting spur leaves left downhill on an old grassy road. In 0.1 mi. the spur reaches the southern terminus of the Fullam Pond Trail, crosses Fullam Pond Dam on a grated walkway, and ends 0.1 mi. beyond at the eastern shore of Fullam Pond.

The main trail swings right and then left, passes a stone wall, crosses a small stream on a snowmobile bridge, swings left again, and ends at the Fullam Pond Trail just north of the South Woods Trail. From here it is 0.6 mi. south to the Fullam Pond Dam by the Fullam Pond Trail, 0.6 mi. north to Beal's Road by the Fullam Pond Trail, and

2.0 mi. northwest to the Horseshoe Rd. trailhead by the South Woods Trail and the Old Horseshoe Road.

Nash Trail (AMC Pisgah State Park Map)
Distances from Old Chesterfield Road (660')

> *to* spur to Fullam Pond Dam (690'): 0.5 mi., 50 ft., 15 min.
>
> *to* Fullam Pond Dam and Fullam Pond Trail via spur (680'): 0.6 mi., 50 ft., 20 min.
>
> *to* Fullam Pond Trail and South Woods Trail, northeast branch (690'): 1.2 mi. (1.9 km.), 50 ft., 40 min.

Fullam Pond Trail

This old road runs south from Old Swanzey Rd. to Fullam Pond, 50 yd. east of the Fullam Pond Dam at the Nash Trail Spur. Although the road is wide and easy to follow, the northern end has virtually no signs or blazes, so the trail is easier to follow from south to north. It crosses the small northeast arm of Fullam Pond on a small causeway—the park map makes it appear that the trail does not cross the pond—then leads directly to the short spur that runs from the Nash Trail to the Fullam Pond Dam at its southeast corner. The trail (no signs or blazes) leaves Old Swanzey Rd. 1.2 mi. southeast of Tuttle Rd. between a large white house (right) and a log cabin home (left) on an unmarked woods road with a chain-link gate. Permission should be requested from the owners of the white house before leaving cars here.

The trail follows the old road generally south into Pisgah State Park (signs) at 0.2 mi. Swing left, then right at an unmarked intersection where care should be made not to turn left onto one of several old roads. The route ascends gradually to a height-of-land at 0.8 mi. and shortly thereafter passes a beaver pond (left) in a wet marshy area. The road then descends gradually, following an enlarging stream (which eventually becomes an inlet brook for Fullam Pond), crossing it several times. Shortly after a snowmobile bridge over this stream, Beal's

Road is reached (left) at 1.6 mi., marked only by Snowmobile Sign #1 in a hemlock forest.

The trail continues to descend, making several crossings of the same stream, which has now enlarged to a small brook. The Nash Trail (left) and the northeast fork of the South Woods Trail (right) are reached at 2.2 mi. Shortly after crossing another snowmobile bridge, the southeast fork of the South Woods Trail (right) is reached. The trail now follows a large inlet brook south as it enters the northern cove of Fullam Pond. At 2.5 mi. the road crosses the northeast corner of Fullam Pond on a causeway with a small spillway in the center. The trail re-enters the woods, with numerous unmarked paths (right) leading to the eastern shore of Fullam Pond. The trail ends at the unmarked Nash Trail Spur, 0.1 mi. west of the Nash Trail and 50 yd. east of the Fullam Pond Dam and the pond's eastern shore.

Fullam Pond Trail (AMC Pisgah State Park Map)
Distances from Old Swanzey Road (1030')

- *to* Pisgah State Park boundary (1030'): 0.2 mi., 0 ft., 5 min.
- *to* beaver pond at height-of-land (1050'): 0.9 mi., 50 ft., 30 min.
- *to* Beal's Road at Snowmobile Sign #1 (790'): 1.6 mi., 50 ft. (rev. 250 ft.), 50 min.
- *to* Nash Trail and South Woods Trail, northeast fork (690'): 2.2 mi., 50 ft. (rev. 100 ft.), 1 hr. 10 min.
- *to* spillway at northeast corner of Fullam Pond (680'): 2.5 mi., 50 ft., 1 hr. 15 min.
- *to* Nash Trail spur, just east of Fullam Pond Dam (680'): 2.8 mi. (4.5 km.), 50 ft., 1 hr. 35 min.

Beal's Road

This historic road ascends from the Beal's Road trailhead along the southern side of Beal's Knob and descends past a historic eighteenth-century graveyard on its way to the Fullam Pond Trail. It is well signed at its trailhead and easy to follow; however, it is designated only by Snowmobile Sign #1 at its junction with the Fullam Pond Trail. Beal's Road trailhead may be reached by following Old Swanzey Rd. 1.8 mi. southeast from Tuttle Rd. Turn right onto a signed dirt road and follow it 0.6 mi. south to a small clearing with trail signs and limited parking.

From the trailhead, the route passes an orange gate and follows an old grassy road, almost immediately reaching the lower junction of the Beal's Knob Trail (right). Both trails are marked with blue diamond blazes as part of the Beal's Knob Cross-Country Ski Loop over the summit. The road passes the northern shore of a significant beaver pond with its lodge (left) and ascends 0.4 mi. to a height-of-land and the upper junction of the Beal's Knob Trail (right), which leads in 0.4 mi. to the summit of Beal's Knob with its fine view of Mt. Monadnock.

No longer marked by blue blazes, Beal's Road descends into the forest and passes the Latham Beal Cemetery (1790) with its weathered stone markers. The road swings right, enters a mixed softwood forest, and descends gradually to the Fullam Pond Trail (Snowmobile Sign #1), 1.6 mi. south of Old Swanzey Rd. and 1.1 mi. north of the Fullam Pond Dam.

Beal's Road (AMC Pisgah State Park Map)
Distances from Beal's Road trailhead (990')

- *to* Beal's Knob Trail, upper junction (1080'): 0.4 mi., 100 ft., 15 min.

- *to* Latham Beal Cemetery (840'): 0.7 mi., 100 ft. (rev. 250 ft.), 25 min.

- *to* Fullam Pond Trail at Snowmobile Sign #1 (790'): 1.1 mi. (1.8 km.), 100 ft. (rev. 100 ft.), 35 min.

Beal's Knob Trail

This trail, marked with blue diamond cross-country ski blazes, ascends Beal's Knob, an attractive lookout with fine views east toward

Mt. Monadnock. It leaves the Beal's Road just beyond the orange gate at the Beal's Road trailhead and ascends a grassy road around the north side of the Beal's Knob. At 0.3 mi. the trail swings left (south) through a mixed hemlock forest and reaches a three-way junction, where a spur trail leaves left 0.2 mi. to the summit of Beal's Knob with its fine view. The main trail bears right, passes a stone wall, swings left onto an old road, passes two more stone walls, and ascends gradually to the Beal's Road at its height-of-land. From here it is 0.7 mi. right (west) to the Fullam Pond Trail and 0.4 mi. left (east) back downhill to the Beal's Road trailhead.

Beal's Knob Trail (AMC Pisgah State Park Map)
Distances from Beal's Road trailhead (990')

- *to* spur path to Beal's Knob summit (1100'): 0.4 mi., 100 ft., 15 min.
- *to* Beal's Knob summit via spur path (1180'): 0.6 mi., 200 ft., 25 min.
- *to* Beal's Road at height-of-land (1080'): 0.6 mi. (1.0 km.), 100 ft. (rev. 100 ft.), 20 min.
- *to* starting point by complete loop to Beal's Knob summit via Beal's Knob Trail, spur path, and Beal's Road: 1.4 mi. (2.2 km.), 200 ft., 50 min.

HYLAND HILL

Hyland Hill (1509 ft.) is located in Westmoreland, west of Keene and about 10 mi. north-northeast of Pisgah State Park. A high fire tower on its summit provides an excellent view, dominated by Mt. Monadnock, of southwestern New Hampshire, southeastern Vermont, and the adjoining section of Massachusetts. Refer to the USGS Keene quadrangle. From NH 12 west of Keene, in the village of East Westmoreland, take South Village Rd. south toward Westmoreland for 0.5 mi., then turn left on Hurricane Rd. and follow it for about 1.5 mi. to a dirt road on the right just past the height-of-land, marked only by a sign depicting a fire tower. The trail, a jeep road, ascends northwest for 0.5 mi., then turns left (southwest) and continues to climb. At 0.8 mi. it turns left again at a fork and continues south with easier grades to the summit and fire tower.

Hyland Hill Trail (USGS Keene quad)
Distance from Hurricane Rd. (1010')

   to summit of Hyland Hill (1509'): 1.2 mi. (1.9 km.), 400 ft., 50 min.

WAPACK TRAIL

This trail follows the ridge of the Wapack Range, running mostly along the skyline for over 21 mi. from Watatic Mtn. in Ashburnham MA over Barrett and Temple mountains and across the Pack Monadnocks in New Hampshire. There are many open ledges with fine views, and the spruce forest found in several places is similar to that of a more northern region. Refer to the USGS Ashburnham, Peterborough South, Peterborough North, and Greenfield quadrangles. The trail is blazed with yellow triangles and marked by cairns on open ledges. An organization named Friends of the Wapack (PO Box 115, West Peterborough, NH 03468) has been established to protect and maintain the trail; this group publishes a detailed guidebook and map to the Wapack Trail.

Section I. Watatic Mountain

The southern end of the Wapack Trail begins in a small parking area off MA 119, about 1.5 mi. west of its junction with MA 101 northeast of Ashburnham and 1.5 mi. east of the Massachusetts–New Hampshire border. The first part of the trail coincides with the Mid-State Trail. It passes a small pond and ascends to a junction where it turns right; here the State Line Trail continues straight for 1.0 mi. and rejoins the Wapack Trail at the state line. The Wapack Trail climbs past two viewpoints to a shelter (Camp Gardner) in poor condition, then swings left and reaches the site of the former fire tower at the summit of Mt. Watatic (1836 ft.) at 1.2 mi., where there is a sweeping view. Here the old route of the Wapack Trail leaves on the right and makes a steep 0.6-mi. descent on a heavily used and badly eroded path along the power and telephone lines to MA 119, 0.7 mi. west of its junction with MA 101 northeast of Ashburnham (0.8 mi. east of the current trailhead of the Wapack). The Wapack Trail turns left and descends northwest across old ski trails and through spruce woods that are a state bird sanctuary, then crosses overgrown pastures on Nutting Hill, passing the summit, a ledgy area in a clearing, at 2.0 mi. Here the Mid-State Trail turns left and joins the State Line Trail in a short distance. The Wapack Trail then descends to a junction near cellar holes (obscured by bushes) that mark the Nutting Place, settled by James Spaulding just before the American Revolution and continued by his son-in-law, Jonas Nutting, until about 1840.

From the Nutting Place junction the trail continues north on a long-abandoned road into beech woods, and at 2.4 mi. it crosses a wall that runs east-west on the Massachusetts–New Hampshire border, where the Mid-State Trail and State Line Trail end on the left. A few yards west of the trail, close to the wall, are two stone survey monuments, one erected in 1834. The trail continues north past the old woods roads and cellar holes of long-deserted farms, and reaches Binney Hill Rd. at 3.5 mi. This part of Binney Hill Rd. is no longer maintained, and it is possible to drive in from NH 119 for only about 0.3 mi. to an area where parking is limited because of private residences. The trail turns left (west) on this road and follows it for 0.2 mi. to the point where the Barrett Mtn. section of the Wapack Trail turns to the right off the road.

Section II. Barrett Mountain

The Barrett Mtn. section of the Wapack Trail runs from Binney Hill Rd. to Wapack Lodge on NH 123/124. Shortly after leaving Binney Hill Rd. at 3.7 mi. (sign, "Pond Trail"), the trail crosses a small brook, then skirts the Binney Ponds near their west shores. (Flooding from beaver dams may require a detour here.) The trail traverses the ridge of Barrett Mtn., nearly 3 mi. long and partly wooded, with four summits (the highest is 1885 ft.) and numerous outlooks. Two private trails intersect the Wapack Trail along this ridge, so hikers should be especially careful to identify the Wapack Trail at any junctions. In the saddle between the third and fourth summits, the trail crosses the location of one of the oldest roads from Massachusetts to the hill towns, the Boston Road, built in 1753. After descending from the northern end of Barrett Mtn., the trail enters an area where it encounters several ski trails, ascends an outlying knoll, then descends to Wapack Lodge, now a private residence (no longer identified by a sign) located on NH 123/124 on the site of a house built in 1776 by Deacon John Brown of Concord MA.

Section III. Kidder Mountain

The Wapack Trail next crosses the lower western slopes of Kidder Mtn. (1805 ft.). From Wapack Lodge it crosses the highway at 9.1 mi. and enters a dirt road opposite the lodge driveway, and soon enters the woods. At 9.7 mi. the trail turns left on an old grassy road with bordering stone walls and crosses under a power line 150 yd. beyond. (A blue-blazed side trail leads right from here along the power lines, then left into the woods through a recently logged area to the summit of Kidder Mtn. at 0.9 mi., where there are good views) The Wapack Trail descends to a junction with a gravel road from the left at a pond on the right. Here it turns right onto a woods road, crosses the pond outlet, and ascends gradually to the Wildcat Hill–Conant Hill saddle, where there is an old homestead site to the right. The trail descends gradually, still on the old roadway, and crosses the outlet of a beaver pond on the right. It then bears left onto Todd Rd. at 11.0 mi. and continues to Nashua Rd. (the road from Temple to Jaffrey) at 11.4 mi.

Section IV. Temple Mountain

The trail crosses Nashua Rd. and continues straight ahead along Sharon Rd. for 0.4 mi., bears right at a fork, then turns right 30 yd. beyond to follow a dirt road for a short distance before entering the woods. (From Sharon Rd. north, the trail passes through private land known as Avelinda Forest. Please observe the No Fires—No Smoking rules posted in the forest.) The trail then ascends the south end of Temple Mtn., which has several bare summits, though the highest summit, Holt Peak (2045 ft.), is broad, wooded, and viewless, while the southern summit, Burton Peak (2010 ft.), has limited views in several directions. At 13.2 mi., a short distance south of Burton Peak, the Berry Pasture Trail leaves left and descends 0.9 mi. through an abandoned pasture and down an old woods road to end at Mountain Rd., at a point 0.6 mi. northeast of the Sharon Arts Center on NH 123.

A short distance south of Holt Peak, the trail crosses a stone wall, then turns sharp left and parallels the wall a short distance before climbing to the summit at 14.3 mi. (An alternate route, used mostly as a ski bypass and marked by old red blazes, continues straight ahead beyond the wall, swings to the east of the summit, and rejoins the main trail 0.3 mi. north of the summit.) The trail follows the ridge, which has wide views, especially toward Grand Monadnock. Stone monuments mark the Sharon-Temple town line, which also follows this ridge. From the north summit the trail descends through the Temple Mountain Ski Area to NH 101 in Peterborough Gap at 16.2 mi., a few yards east of the road up South Pack Monadnock, which leaves NH 101 at the height-of-land.

Section V. Pack Monadnock

This extended ridge culminates in two open peaks, Pack Monadnock (2290 ft.), usually called South Pack Monadnock, and North Pack Monadnock (2276 ft.); *pack* is an Indian word meaning "little." The mountain stands between the towns of Peterborough and Temple and is a well-known landmark in southern New Hampshire and eastern Massachusetts. On the summit of South Pack is a small state reservation, General James Miller Park. (To reach the park, drive up the road that starts at the parking lot located just off NH 101, about 100 yd. west of the Temple Mtn. parking lot.)

The Wapack Trail crosses NH 101 just east of the state park sign, enters the woods, and reaches a trail junction 25 yd. east of the parking area (sign, "Foot Trails," at the east end of the parking area). The blue-blazed trail on the right is the former route of the Wapack Trail, now the Marion Davis Trail. (This trail angles up the east side of the mountain, then climbs moderately, passing near two radio towers, and reaches the automobile road at the summit just to the right of a small shed.) The official Wapack Trail is somewhat more difficult than the former route, particularly for descent. It continues north from the trail junction near the parking area, crosses the automobile road, and immediately scrambles up a steep ledge. Turning northwest, it skirts the crest of ledges with views southwest and passes two crevice caves. The trail turns east through woods and over ledges, crosses a hollow, then runs north, angling upward parallel to the automobile road through a beautiful hemlock forest to the Summit Loop Trail, which enters on the right and continues straight ahead, making a loop around the summit 0.5 mi. long. The Wapack Trail then turns sharp right and ascends following the Summit Loop Trail to the fire tower on the summit of South Pack at 17.6 mi. Here the Summit Loop Trail diverges and descends into the woods to the left of the shed where the Marion Davis Trail also leaves the summit area. The Wapack Trail continues north from the north end of the summit road to the left of a stone lean-to (sign, Wapack) and descends gradually over ledges, crossing the Summit Loop Trail. A short distance to the left on the Summit Loop Trail is the upper end of the Raymond Trail, which descends 1.6 mi. to East Mountain Rd. at a point 1.2 mi. northwest of the Miller State Park lower parking area via East Mountain Rd., Old Mountain Rd., and NH 101.

The Wapack Trail leads down the wooded north slope past a spring, ascends over the knoll sometimes called the Middle Peak, and reaches the junction with the Cliff Trail on the right at 19.3 mi. (The Cliff Trail is a longer and rougher but more scenic alternative route from here to the summit of North Pack. It descends sharply downhill for 0.3 mi., then swings north and ascends several rocky knolls with excellent views toward the southern Wapack Range and Grand Monadnock. At 0.7 mi. the grade eases and the trail follows an undulating ridge, rejoining the Wapack Trail at the summit of North Pack at 1.2 mi.) The main Wapack Trail ascends directly to the summit of North

Pack at 20.0 mi. This ledgy peak provides fine views of central New Hampshire, the Contoocook River valley, and, on a clear day, Mt. Washington and other White Mtn. peaks. The trail descends north, northwest, then north again through overgrown pastures (take care to distinguish the trail from other paths), and ends at Old Mountain Rd., 2.6 mi. west of NH 31 (via Old Mtn. Rd. to Russell Station Rd.).

Wapack Trail (USGS Ashburnham, Peterborough South, Peterborough North, and Greenfield quads)

Distances from MA 119 (1250')

- *to* Watatic Mtn. summit (1836'): 1.2 mi., 600 ft., 55 min.
- *to* Binney Hill Rd. near Binney Ponds (1360'): 3.7 mi., 800 ft. (rev. 700 ft.), 2 hr. 15 min.
- *to* Barrett Mtn., south summit (1826'): 5.1 mi., 1500 ft. (rev. 200 ft.), 3 hr. 20 min.
- *to* Barrett Mtn., north summit (1850'): 7.5 mi., 1950 ft. (rev. 450 ft.), 4 hr. 45 min.
- *to* NH 123/124 (1450'): 9.1 mi., 2050 ft. (rev. 500 ft.), 5 hr. 35 min.
- *to* Nashua Rd. (1240'): 11.4 mi., 2250 ft. (rev. 400 ft.), 6 hr. 50 min.
- *to* Temple Mtn., main summit (Holt Peak, 2045'): 14.3 mi., 3250 ft. (rev. 200 ft.), 8 hr. 45 min.
- *to* NH 101 (1480'): 16.2 mi., 3350 ft. (rev. 700 ft.), 9 hr. 45 min.
- *to* South Pack Monadnock summit (2290'): 17.6 mi., 4200 ft., 10 hr. 55 min.
- *to* North Pack Monadnock summit (2276'): 20.0 mi., 4850 ft. (rev. 650 ft.), 12 hr. 25 min.
- *to* Old Mountain Rd. (1310'): 21.6 mi. (34.8 km.), 4850 ft. (rev. 950 ft.), 13 hr. 15 min.

CROTCHED MOUNTAIN

Crotched Mtn. (2066 ft.) is in Francestown and Bennington, with a south spur in Greenfield. There are excellent views from scattered ledges around the summit. Refer to the USGS Greenfield, Peterborough North, Hillsboro, and Deering quadrangles.

Greenfield Trail

From NH 31 0.9 mi. north of Greenfield, follow a road with the sign "Crotched Mountain Rehabilitation Center." Pass Gilbert Verney Drive on the right 1.4 mi. from NH 31 and park 0.1 mi. farther where there is a gated road on the left. (No Trespassing signs do not apply to hikers.) There is no trail sign, and the trail is not marked except for some carefully placed cairns. Pass through a gate and by a sandpit. The trail bears left, passing a private camp on the right. Bear right onto an older road at 0.3 mi, traveling through overgrown blueberry barrens. Bear right again at a fork (0.5 mi). Take the left fork (cairn) where the trail enters mature woods. The trail continues to Lookout Rock, which has an excellent view west and south and an impressive view of Mt. Monadnock. The Bennington Trail soon enters left at a stone wall, and the two trails coincide to the summit.

Greenfield Trail (USGS Greenfield and Peterborough North quads)

Distances from Crotched Mtn. Rehabilitation Center (1300′)

- *to* Bennington Trail (1750′): 1.4 mi., 450 ft., 55 min.
- *to* Crotched Mtn. summit (2066′): 1.8 mi. (2.9 km.), 750 ft., 1 hr. 15 min.

Bennington Trail

From NH 31, 1.6 mi. south of Bennington, take the road with signs reading "Summus Mons Campground" and "Mountain Rd." for 0.5 mi. to the campground entrance. The trail follows a dirt road right (sign), which may be passable for cars for 0.2 mi. The trail turns sharp right here (sign) and follows an old logging road to a double cairn and sign, where it turns left. Follow it with care. It passes a spring, then begins to climb more steeply to a junction with the Greenfield Trail. The two trails then coincide to the summit.

Bennington Trail (USGS Greenfield and Peterborough North quads)

Distances from campground entrance (960')

- *to* Greenfield Trail (1750'): 1.2 mi., 800 ft., 1 hr.
- *to* Crotched Mtn. summit (2066'): 1.6 mi. (2.5 km.), 1100 ft., 1 hr. 20 min.

FOX STATE FOREST

This 1,455-acres preserve in the town of Hillsborough features a network of about 20 mi. of nature trails and multi-use trails. The environmental center, where an informational brochure with a map of the trail system can usually be obtained, is located about 2 mi. from the center of Hillsborough on Hillsborough Center Rd. (which leaves US 202/NH 9 in Hillsborough village roughly opposite NH 149). Refer to the USGS Hillsboro Upper Village and Hillsboro quadrangles. There are few distant views, except for the cleared view south to Monadnock from the observation tower on the side of Monroe Hill, but there are almost unlimited possibilities for short, medium, and even long woods walks by stringing together trail sections according to the desires of the visitor. The Ridge Trail, 10 mi. long, is the central artery through the park, circling through Fox State Forest and connecting with most of the other trails. Short nature walks are available on the popular Tree I.D. Trail and Mushroom Trail, while Mud Pond and Black Gum Swamp offer somewhat longer walks. Black Gum Swamp, which supports a stand of black gum (also known as tupelo) trees—quite rare in New Hampshire—is of particular interest to students of the New Hampshire woodlands.

SKATUTAKEE AND THUMB MOUNTAINS

Skatutakee Mtn. (1998 ft.) and Thumb Mtn. (1978 ft.), located in the town of Hancock, offer interesting views particularly to the south from their open ledges. Refer to the USGS Marlborough quadrangle. The trails on these mountains, as well as a number of other trails nearby, are maintained by the Harris Center for Conservation Education, which is the focal point of a 7000-acre tract of land that is maintained primarily as wildlife habitat by the cooperative effort of the Harris Center, the New Hampshire Audubon Society, the Society for the Protection of New Hampshire Forests, the New Hampshire Fish and Game Department, the town of Hancock, and a number of private landowners. To reach the Harris Center follow NH 123 west from its junction with NH 137 for 2.2 mi.; turn left at a small Harris Center sign and follow Hunt Pond Rd. for 0.4 mi.; then turn left on King's Highway and follow it another 0.5 mi. to the Harris Center's parking lot. From here the Harriskat Trail leads to the summit of Skatutakee Mtn., which has the best views; on the return a loop hike may be made by taking the Thumbs Up Trail from Skatutakee Mtn. to Thumb Mtn., then descending to the parking lot via the Thumbs Down Trail. The Bee Line Trail ascends Skatutakee Mtn. from the south.

Harriskat Trail

This white-blazed trail begins on King's Highway (sign) opposite the main building of the Harris Center, just northwest of a sign for the Briggs Preserve. At 0.2 mi. it turns sharp right onto an older route of the trail (descending, turn sharp left off the old route). It crosses a wet area with several large boulders and at 0.6 mi. reaches the junction with the Thumbs Down Trail to Thumb Mtn. The Harriskat Trail bears left uphill, then soon swings left onto a broad ridge and climbs across a stone wall, ascending with alternating moderate climbs and nearly level sections on the contour. At 0.9 mi. the trail runs level across a small boulder field, and at 1.2 mi. an unmarked, unsigned side trail enters on the left at a sharp right turn where the main trail is signed

"Harris Center" for the descent. The trail now runs mostly through stands of conifers, and high up it passes a narrow outlook left through trees to Crotched Mtn. It climbs on ledges, then runs level across more ledges and reaches the summit, which is the highest of several jumbled ledges in an extensive open area. Here there are good views of Crotched Mtn., the Wapack Range, and Monadnock. The Bee Line Trail enters here; the Thumbs Up Trail to Thumb Mtn. leaves the Bee Line Trail on the right about 40 yd. from the summit.

Harriskat Trail (USGS Marlborough quad)
Distances from King's Highway (1290')

> *to* Thumbs Down Trail (1400'): 0.6 mi., 100 ft., 20 min.

> *to* summit of Skatutakee Mtn. (1998'): 1.6 mi. (2.5 km.), 700 ft., 1 hr. 10 min.

> *to* starting point by complete loop via Harriskat Trail, Thumbs Up Trail, and Thumbs Down Trail: 4.9 mi. (7.9 km.), 900 ft., 2 hr. 55 min.

Thumbs Up Trail

This trail connects the summits of Skatutakee Mtn. and Thumb Mtn. From the summit of Skatutakee; descend on the Bee Line Trail for about 40 yd., then turn right (sign, "Thumb," which is not obvious). The trail is well marked with white plastic triangles, though the footway is not always well beaten. The trail descends through a dark coniferous forest and, at the foot of the descent from Skatutakee Mtn. at 0.3 mi., makes a very sharp left turn, then soon leaves the dark coniferous forest and winds about a great deal on a fairly level ridge. At 1.0 mi. the trail reaches the junction where the Thumbs Down Trail (marked by yellow blazes) enters on the right. The Thumbs Up Trail now ascends steeply to the summit of the first knob of Thumb Mtn., where it levels, descends slightly, crosses a stone wall, and resumes a moderate ascent to the summit of Thumb Mtn. at 1.3 mi. The trail continues 50 yd. to a ledge with views to Monadnock and the Wapack Range.

Thumbs Up Trail (USGS Marlborough quad)
Distances from summit of Skatutakee Mtn. (1998')

   to junction with Thumbs Down Trail (1820'): 1.0 mi., 50 ft. (rev. 250 ft.), 30 min.

   to summit of Thumb Mtn. (1978'): 1.3 mi. (2.0 km.), 200 ft., 45 min.

Thumbs Down Trail

This trail descends from the Thumbs Up Trail at a junction 0.3 mi. east of the summit of Thumb Mtn., completing the Skatutakee-Thumb loop. Since this loop is described in this guide for the clockwise direction, the Thumbs Down Trail is described here for the descent. Marked by yellow blazes, it descends from the junction at the foot of Thumb Mtn. across several stone walls and reaches the north shore of Jacks Pond at 0.6 mi., at a point where a side path descends to the right 20 yd. to the edge of the pond. In another 100 yd. the trail makes a right-angle turn to the left and follows a woods road downhill, crossing the outlet brook from Jacks Pond. At 1.0 mi. the trail bears to the right off the road, crosses a good-sized brook, and runs to the junction with the Harriskat Trail 0.6 mi. from the Harris Center. If you are ascending by the Thumbs Down Trail, bear right (slightly downhill) at this junction.

Thumbs Down Trail (USGS Marlborough quad)
Distance from junction with Thumbs Up Trail (1820')

   to junction with Harriskat Trail (1400'): 1.1 mi. (1.8 km.), 0 ft. (rev. 400 ft.), 35 min.

Bee Line Trail

This trail ascends Skatutakee Mtn. from the south. The trailhead is located on Old Dublin Rd. 1.1 mi. southwest of its junction with King's Highway (this junction is 0.7 mi. southeast of the Harris Center). Loop hikes can be made in combination with the direct trails from the Harris Center by means of the 1.8-mi. walk along King's Highway and Old Dublin Rd., both country gravel roads with little traffic.

The white-blazed trail ascends moderately on an old woods road lined with stone walls and furnished with rock culverts. At 0.3 mi. the trail levels and then climbs at gentle to easy grades. At 0.9 mi. it turns to the right off the road in an overgrown pasture and (now marked with light-green blazes) descends slightly to cross the bed of a small brook. It then begins a fairly steep ascent and crosses a stone wall. The grade becomes moderate, and the trail passes boulders with a limited outlook. The terrain becomes ledgy, and at a ledge—where there is a 5-ft.-high conical boulder about 10 yd. ahead in a level section—there is a fine view in the downhill direction of Monadnock framed by trees. At 1.4 mi. the trail crosses a stone wall on a ledge, and the grade become easy as the trail wanders around the summit ledges. The Thumbs Up Trail to Thumb Mtn. diverges left (sign, "Thumb," which is hard to see in ascending direction) about 40 yd. before the trail reaches the summit of Skatutakee Mtn., where there are good views of Crotched Mtn., the Wapack Range, and Monadnock.

Bee Line Trail (USGS Marlborough quad)
Distance from Old Dublin Rd. (1160')

  to summit of Skatutakee Mtn. (1998'): 1.5 mi. (2.5 km.), 850 ft., 1 hr. 10 min.

Harris Center Trails

The Harris Center maintains several other trails that provide interesting walks, mostly over fairly easy terrain. The *Dandelyon Trail* (yellow blazes) runs from the Harris Center, crosses the Boulder Train Trail twice, and ends at a collection of erratic boulders at 0.5 mi. The *Boulder Train Trail* (blue blazes) is a loop 1.1 mi. long, with numbered stops keyed to an informational booklet available at the Harris Center. It involves more ascent and descent relative to its length than the other trails. It crosses the Dandelyon Trail twice, making possible an easy 0.2-mi. side trip to the boulders reached by that trail. The *Channing Trail* (red blazes) leaves the northeast corner of the Boulder Train Trail and makes a big 1.9-mi. loop back to King's Highway 0.7 mi. northwest of the Harris Center. The *Babbitt Trail* (red blazes) makes a 1.4-mi. loop in the woods northeast of NH 137. There is a connector trail, 0.2 mi. long, that runs between the trailhead of the Babbitt Trail on NH 137 and the Channing Trail at a point 1.4 mi. from the Harris Center via the Dandelyon Trail and Boulder Train Trail.

PIERCE RESERVATION

Pierce Reservation comprises almost 3500 acres owned by the Society for the Protection of New Hampshire Forests.

Trout-n-Bacon Trail

The Trout-n-Bacon Trail provides access to secluded Trout Pond and views from Bacon Ledge. Follow NH 123 north for 1.7 mi. from its junction with NH 9 to Mill Village. One trailhead is reached by following Shedd Hill Rd. (paved) north for 0.8 mi. to the trailhead, marked by an SPNHF sign (limited parking; do not block the woods road). The other is reached by following Old Antrim Rd. (gravel, also called Barrett Pond Rd.) 0.9 mi. east from Mill Village to a small parking area. Hiking the complete loop requires walking these two segments of road.

The trail leaves Old Antrim Rd. and follows a woods road. At 0.7 mi. a cross-country ski trail continues on the road, bypassing Bacon Ledge and Round Mtn., while the Trout-n-Bacon Trail leaves the road on the right and continues uphill, finally scrambling to the top of Bacon Ledge (1959 ft.) at 1.1 mi., where there are excellent views in all directions. (A short side path can be used to bypass the scramble up the ledge in adverse conditions.) Past Bacon Ledge the trail winds around on the ridge of Round Mtn. (1959 ft.), then descends, passing the junction at 1.9 mi. where the cross-country ski trail rejoins from the left. The trail continues to descend to a clearing near a camp at 2.6 mi. The trail follows the right edge of the clearing uphill past the camp. In a short distance the continuation of the main trail turns left on another woods road, while a spur path continues down to beautiful Trout Pond on the original road. From the junction below the camp, the main trail soon reaches another woods road junction, where it turns left and runs to Shedd Hill Rd. at 4.3 mi.

Trout-n-Bacon Trail (USGS Stoddard quad)

Distances from Old Antrim Rd. (1340')

- *to* Bacon Ledge (1959'): 1.1 mi., 600 ft., 50 min.
- *to* Trout Pond (1598'): 2.7 mi., 750 ft. (rev. 500 ft.), 1 hr. 45 min.
- *to* Shedd Hill Rd. (1540'): 4.3 mi. (6.9 km.), 1000 ft. (rev. 300 ft.), 2 hr. 40 min.
- *to* starting point by complete loop via Trout-n-Bacon Trail, Shedd Hill Rd., and Old Antrim Rd.: 6.0 mi. (9.6 km.), 1050 ft., 3 hr. 30 min.

DEPIERREFEU–WILLARD POND WILDLIFE SANCTUARY

This New Hampshire Audubon Society reservation in the town of Antrim contains most of Willard Pond, as well as Bald Mtn. (2037 ft.) and Goodhue Hill (1621 ft.). Several trails provide access to these features. Refer to the USGS Stoddard quadrangle. The trailhead is reached by following NH 123 west from Hancock village for 3.7 mi., then turning right and following Willard Pond Rd. for 1.6 mi.

In addition to the trails that make a loop over Bald Mtn., there are several shorter trails. The *Mill Pond Trail* makes an 0.4-mi. loop around Hatch Mill Pond. The *Goodhue Hill Trail* follows the south leg of the Mill Pond Trail for 0.1 mi., then climbs another 0.9 mi. and 450 ft. (45 min.) to an outlook ledge on Goodhue Hill with a view to the south-southwest. The *Tudor Trail* follows the west shore of Willard Pond for 0.2 mi. until it reaches the junction with the Bald Mountain

Trail. It then turns left and climbs past mossy boulders and ledges and returns to the starting point at 0.5 mi. The *Pine Point Trail,* reached in 0.7 mi. by following the Tudor Trail and Bald Mountain Trail along the west shore of Willard Pond, continues another 0.4 mi. along the shore of the pond to Pine Point, a majestic promontory with large white pines on the north shore of the pond.

Bald Mountain Trails

The Bald Mountain Trail and the Tamposi Trail provide the opportunity for a loop hike over Bald Mtn., whose summit affords a fine view. The Bald Mountain Trail follows the Tudor Trail for 0.2 mi., then continues along the west shore of Willard Pond, passing through a small boulder field. At 0.7 mi. the Pine Point Trail continues along the shore, while the Bald Mountain Trail swings left and ascends, gradually at first, passing a number of interesting boulders. At 1.2 mi. it crosses a yellow-blazed path and swings right, reaching the ledgy outlook with the best view on the trail at 1.4 mi., providing a magnificent panorama to the south. It reaches the small clearing at the summit at 1.5 mi. Here it meets the Tamposi Trail, which descends directly to the parking area in 1.1 mi.

Bald Mountain (USGS Stoddard quad)

Distances from parking area (1160')

> *to* summit of Bald Mtn. (2037') via Bald Mountain Trail: 1.5 mi. (2.4 km.), 900 ft., 1 hr. 10 min.

> *to* starting point by complete loop via Bald Mountain Trail and Tamposi Trail: 2.6 mi. (4.2 km.), 900 ft., 1 hr. 45 min.

MONADNOCK-SUNAPEE GREENWAY

The Monadnock-Sunapee Greenway, 49 mi. long, continues north from Mt. Monadnock to Sunapee Mtn. The SPNHF and AMC cooperatively built and continue to manage this trail, which runs mostly over hills and along ridges between these two major peaks in southwest New Hampshire. Volunteer maintenance and other support of this trail is coordinated by the Monadnock-Sunapee Greenway Trail Club, PO Box 164, Marlow, NH 03456. Because a large part of this trail is located on private property, users should be particularly aware of their status as guests and avoid thoughtless behavior that could jeopardize this privilege. Camping is permitted at designated sites only. Space constraints prevent its full and detailed coverage by this guide; what follows is a brief account of the entire trail and a more detailed account of two of its more important features (in addition to Mt. Monadnock and Sunapee Mtn.), Pitcher Mt. (2162 ft.) and Lovewell Mtn. (2470 ft.). The *Monadnock-Sunapee Greenway Guide,* which also includes additional details on several side trails in the Mt. Sunapee area, is available from the SPNHF, 54 Portsmouth St., Concord, NH 03301 (603-224-9945).

(1) *Monadnock to NH 101.* From the summit of Mt. Monadnock, the Greenway descends on the Dublin Trail for 2.2 mi., then turns left (west) on Old Troy Rd. At 2.7 mi. the trail turns to the right off Old Troy Rd., following a woods road at first. It descends across a valley and climbs to Old Marlborough Rd. at 3.7 mi. It follows this road to the right (east), then at 4.0 mi. it turns left, passes around a swamp, and ascends to the top of a low ridge. Here it meets a well-used woods road and follows it to the right, swinging to the north and descending to meet NH 101 at 5.6 mi. just after passing a beaver pond (left).

(2) *NH 101 to NH 9.* The Greenway continues straight across NH 101 and ascends a woods road (sign, "Monadnock Wilderness Girl Scout Campsite"). At 6.0 mi. it passes the primitive Leighton State Forest Campsite, then ascends on woods roads across a power line clearing. It crosses a low, flat ridge and descends to Howe Reservoir, crossing the outlet brook at Eliza Adams Gorge at the foot of the dam on a bridge at 6.9 mi. The Greenway continues to Brown Rd., follows it left for 100 yd., then at 7.3 mi. turns to the right onto a gravel road and continues past a private picnic area (left) and a millpond (right). It joins Seaver Rd. and follows it across Chesham Rd. at 7.9 mi., then continues northwest on Seaver Rd. past Chesham Pond almost to the

foot of Silver Lake at 8.8 mi. Here, just after crossing the outlet brook from Silver Lake, it bears right at a fork, then turns right onto a gravel driveway, and finally diverges left into the woods on a woods road. This woods road runs past Childs Bog Dam at 9.4 mi. and continues to Nelson Rd. at 10.1 mi. The trail crosses this road and runs through the woods to Cabot Rd. at 11.2 mi., which it follows to the left. From here to Nelson village the trail follows well-maintained roads. At 12.2 mi. Cabot Rd. joins Tolman Pond Rd. (in the opposite direction, take the right fork), which continues to Harrisville Rd. at 12.6 mi. This road is followed to Nelson village. At 13.0 mi., just before reaching the Nelson Congregational Church, the trail makes a right turn onto Log Cabin Rd., which it follows past several houses, keeping straight ahead as it becomes a woods road that climbs across a height-of-land and descends to the outlet of a beaver pond, which it crosses on a bridge at 14.0 mi. The woods road climbs again over the sag between Felt Hill and Tolman Hill and descends to NH 9 at 15.4 mi.

(3) *NH 9 to NH 123.* After following NH 9 about 100 yd. to the right (east), the Greenway turns left onto High St. At 15.7 mi. it bears right onto an old woods road, then turns left onto another woods road at 15.9 mi. and follows it uphill across a power line clearing to the height-of-land at 16.9 mi. The woods road then descends, passing a trail on the right at 17.4 mi. that connects the Greenway to Daniel Upton Forest. The Greenway continues to descend as the road improves and becomes Center Pond Rd., passing along the east shore of Center Pond. It then climbs away from the pond, and at 19.1 mi. the Greenway turns left onto a gated woods road and follows a succession of old roads and foot trails past the spur path (right) to Parker Hill Campsite at 20.0 mi. The trail continues through the woods, crossing a private gravel road at 20.5 mi., and at 22.0 mi. it reaches a gravel road and follows it to the right, passing a gate just before reaching NH 123 at 22.1 mi. The trail follows NH 123 to the right (south) to the parking area for Pitcher Mtn. at 22.3 mi.

(4) *NH 123 to NH 31.* About 70 yd. from NH 123, the Greenway bears right at a fork where the blue-blazed steeper, more direct route

to the summit of Pitcher Mtn. bears left. The Greenway climbs to the summit of Pitcher Mtn. at 22.7 mi., then descends on an old grassy road through blueberry barrens, and the direct blue-blazed summit trail enters on the left in about 70 yd. The Greenway now follows a succession of blazed paths and woods roads (follow with care) through woods and areas that have not yet fully recovered from a 1941 forest fire. It crosses the open summit of Hubbard Hill (1896 ft.) at 25.3 mi. and descends past the side path (right) to Fox Brook Campsite at 25.8 mi. After crossing Fox Brook, it ascends to the summit of Jackson Hill (2057 ft.) at 26.6 mi., then descends north, then east, then north again, then east again. It crosses Barney Brook south of Ashuelot Pond on a snowmobile bridge at 28.6 mi., and at 29.0 mi. reaches Old King's Highway and follows it downhill to the left (north). At 29.6 mi. the Greenway passes an old church and graveyard in a rather desolate spot along this old deserted road with no houses nearby; this is regarded as the first church of the Seventh-Day Adventist denomination. At 30.0 mi. the Greenway bears right onto the paved Faxon Hill Rd., and at 30.3 mi. the trail leaves the paved road to follow a paved driveway on the right. The trail now climbs to the summit of Oak Hill (1959 ft.) at 31.1 mi., then descends past General Washington Lean-to at 32.5 mi. The trail soon reaches Symonds Lane and turns left, then turns right onto Faxon Hill Rd. and follows it to NH 31 at 32.8 mi.

(5) *NH 31 to Washington-Bradford Road.* The Greenway crosses NH 31 and bears right (east) through the public buildings of Washington village. At 33.4 mi. it takes a sharp left onto the Washington-Bradford road, passes Halfmoon Pond, then turns right at 34.7 mi. and ascends a rough old woods road to the height-of-land at 35.5 mi. Here it turns left and becomes a footpath, ascending Lovewell Mtn. (2470 ft.), passing viewpoints, and reaching the ledgy summit at 37.0 mi. The Greenway descends the long north ridge into a ravine at 38.3 mi., then makes a short climb over a lesser northern ridge and continues to the old Washington-Bradford road at 39.3 mi. This road is not pass-

able for most cars at most times for the first half-mile or so south from this trail crossing.

(6) *Washington-Bradford Road to Sunapee Mountain.* **Note:** This is the wildest section of the trail; except at the ends, there are only a few side approach routes, and they are fairly long. Therefore this trail section demands a degree of preparation and commitment far greater than the rest of the trail requires.

The Greenway continues across the road, crosses Bog Brook, and ascends into Pillsbury State Park, reaching the summit of Kittredge Hill (2116 ft.) at 40.6 mi. It descends into a deep col, then crosses a flat hump and descends into a lesser col where the Bear Pond Trail enters on the left. (This trail runs 1.8 mi. to the picnic area in the main visitor area of Pillsbury State Park, off NH 31.) The trail winds around two significant humps on the south ridge of Sunapee Mtn., then reaches the junction where the Five Summers Trail enters on the left at 44.8 mi. (This trail runs 3.9 mi. to the picnic area in the main visitor area of Pillsbury State Park, off NH 31, sharing the last 0.5 mi. with the Bear Pond Trail.) The Greenway climbs to Lucia's Lookout, a fine viewpoint toward Monadnock over the land crossed by the Greenway, at 45.0 mi. The Greenway now runs along the ledgy, lumpy ridge until it descends on the east side to reach the south end of Lake Solitude at 47.8 mi. It follows the west shore to the north end of the lake, where it meets the Andrew Brook Trail, which ascends from the east, at 48.1 mi. Here it also meets the Lake Solitude Trail from the summit of Sunapee Mtn., with which it coincides for the remainder of its length—and now becomes heavily used, in contrast to the light use received by many miles of the trail south of this point. At 48.2 mi. the Newbury Trail and a trail from the top of the Mt. Sunapee State Park gondola lift enter on the right. The trail climbs sharply, and at 48.3 mi. a side path leads left onto White Ledge, where there are fine views down to the lake and out to the east. At 48.9 mi. the trail comes out on the ski slopes, and in 30 yd. more the Goshen Trail enters on the left. The Greenway follows ski trails the rest of the way to the summit lodge at 49.1 mi.

Pitcher Mountain Trails

This small mountain (2162 ft.) in the town of Stoddard has a summit fire tower that offers an excellent view for little effort. Refer to the USGS Stoddard quadrangle. The parking lot is located on the northeast side of NH 123, 4.5 mi. north of its junction with NH 9 and 3.1 mi. south of its junction with NH 10. About 70 yd. above the parking area the trails divide; the left-hand path (with blue blazes) is the shorter, steeper trail, while the right-hand path (with white blazes) is the less steep Monadnock-Sunapee Greenway. The two trails rejoin about 70 yd. from the summit after the Greenway has already passed over it.

Pitcher Mountain Trails (USGS Stoddard quad)

Distances from NH 123 (1870')

- *to* summit (2162') by either path: 0.4 mi. (0.7 km.), 300 ft., 20 min.
- *to* starting point via complete loop: 0.8 mi. (1.4 km.), 300 ft., 35 min.

Lovewell Mountain

This mountain (2470 ft.), located in the town of Washington and crossed by the Monadnock-Sunapee Greenway, offers interesting views from a number of scattered ledges. Refer to the USGS Lovewell Mtn. quadrangle. From Washington village on NH 31, follow the gravel road that leads east from the village church and school for 0.5 mi., then turn sharp left and follow the old Washington-Bradford road past Halfmoon Pond; the best parking may be at the Halfmoon Pond boat launch at 1.4 mi. from NH 31. At 1.9 mi. turn right onto a rough jeep road (limited parking). As this road is not passable for the vast majority of vehicles, the trail description begins here.

The road (part of the Monadnock-Sunapee Greenway) climbs to a level area at 0.9 mi., where ledges run down to the road past the stone wall that parallels it. Here the foot trail turns left and ascends through old pastures, and at 1.8 mi. enters a level section. At the end of this section, the trail turns left and ascends a steep, rough section, then continues on a fairly steep, rough, and ledgy pathway through mostly dark, mature coniferous woods. At 2.1 mi. a side path leads left 100 yd. to a piped spring, and in a short distance another side path leads right 60 yd. to a southeast outlook. The trail reaches the summit cairn at 2.3 mi., then descends north along a broad ridge, crosses a shallow sag and a minor hump. It then swings around to the west and descends into a ravine, where it crosses a small brook at 3.6 mi. and climbs to the crest of a lesser ridge. From there it descends, crossing several stone walls and passing the remains of old farms—a number of old cellar holes and foundations, and the remnants of an apple orchard. The trail continues to descend across several more stone walls and at 5.5 mi. reaches the old Bradford-Washington road at a point 1.9 mi. north of the junction with the jeep road where the description of this trail begins. This road is passable by cars only to a point about a half-mile south of this trail crossing.

Monadnock-Sunapee Greenway (USGS Lovewell Mtn. quad)
Distances from junction of old Washington-Bradford road and jeep road (1540')

- *to* summit of Lovewell Mtn. (2470'): 2.3 mi. (3.7 km.), 950 ft., 1 hr. 40 min.

- *to* crossing of old Washington-Bradford road (1610'): 5.5 mi., 1200 ft. (rev. 1100 ft.), 3 hr. 20 min.

- *to* starting point via old Washington-Bradford road: 7.4 mi. (11.9 km.), 1300 ft. (rev. 100 ft.), 4 hr. 20 min.

SUNAPEE MOUNTAIN

Sunapee Mtn. (2726 ft.), the northern terminus of the Monadnock-Sunapee Greenway, is an irregular, massive, heavily wooded mountain located in the town of Newbury at the south end of Lake Sunapee. Lake Solitude near its summit is unique for its high elevation, remoteness, and beauty of setting. Nearby are cliffs that rise 300 ft. to White Ledge, where there is a fine view southeast over the wild country of the Merrimack-Connecticut watershed. Refer to the USGS Newport quadrangle. Mt. Sunapee State Park is on NH 103, 7 mi. east of Newport. There is a state-owned but now privately managed ski area on the north slope of the mountain. In addition to the trails described below, the mountain is easily climbed via the ski slopes (direct routes are about 1.5 mi. long); there is also a trail that leads from the top of the gondola lift in about a mile to Lake Solitude, which can be used to make a loop trip to the summit and Lake Solitude from the ski area. A hikers' trail map is usually available at the ski area.

Lake Solitude Trail

This very popular trail, which connects the summit of Sunapee Mtn. with beautiful Lake Solitude and the ledges that overlook it—ledges that are only slightly lower than the summit itself—is also the northern end of the Monadnock-Sunapee Greenway. From the summit of Sunapee Mtn., the trail descends along the far right edge of the ski slopes, with excellent views to the north. At 0.2 mi. the trail leaves the ski trails and enters the woods; just 30 yd. before this point the Goshen Trail, here a woods road, enters on the right. The Lake Solitude Trail follows a bumpy ridge through fine woods, and at 0.8 mi. a side path on the right leads across White Ledge to a fine viewpoint down to the lake and out to the east. The main trail descends sharply, passing a junction on the left at 0.9 mi. with the Newbury Trail and the trail from the top of the gondola lift, and ends at its junction with the Andrew Brook Trail at the north end of Lake Solitude.

Lake Solitude Trail (USGS Newport quad)

Distance from summit of Sunapee Mtn. (2726')

>   *to* Lake Solitude (2510'): 1.0 mi. (1.6 km.), 250 ft. (rev. 450 ft.), 40 min.

Andrew Brook Trail

This trail ascends to beautiful Lake Solitude from the east and offers access to the summit of Sunapee Mtn. via the Lake Solitude Trail. Leave NH 103 0.8 mi. east of its junction with NH 103A in Newbury, and follow Mountain Rd. 1.2 mi. to a woods road on the right just before Mountain Rd. crosses a bridge. There is limited parking here; do not block the woods road.

The trail follows the woods road for 0.5 mi., then bears right across Andrew Brook and follows it upstream. It recrosses the brook at 1.0 mi. and 1.4 mi., finally reaching Lake Solitude at a point where severe damage from illegal camping is evident. It follows the north shore of the pond and meets the Monadnock-Sunapee Greenway, which enters on the left (south) and follows the Lake Solitude Trail uphill toward the summit of Sunapee Mtn. Even if you do not intend to visit the summit, you should not miss the views from White Ledge, which is reached by following the Lake Solitude Trail uphill for 0.2 mi., then turning left across the ledges on a spur path to the outlook.

Andrew Brook Trail (USGS Newport quad)

Distances from Mountain Rd. (1330')

- *to* Lake Solitude at the Lake Solitude Trail junction (2510'): 2.0 mi. (3.2 km.), 1200 ft., 1 hr. 35 min.

- *to* summit of Sunapee Mtn. (2726') via Lake Solitude Trail: 3.0 mi. (4.8 km.), 1650 ft. (rev. 250 ft.), 2 hr. 20 min.

Newbury Trail

This trail ascends from Newbury village at the southern tip of Lake Sunapee to the Lake Solitude Trail at a point just above Lake Solitude. It is probably best to park in Newbury village, but there is limited parking on the road just below the trailhead. Follow the road that leaves NH 103 directly opposite the information booth, then take the second right, which leads in a short distance to the path, which is marked by an orange blaze on a telephone pole on the right side of the road.

The trail climbs steadily, passing the red-blazed path that leads to the right 0.2 mi. to Eagle's Nest, a ledgy outlook with a fine view across Lake Sunapee. The main trail continues to climb, becoming steep as it approaches another excellent outlook at 1.0 mi. It soon passes a path from the ski area that enters on the right, then follows a ridge to the South Peak of Sunapee Mtn. (2608') and continues along a bumpy ridgecrest with little change of elevation. At 2.0 mi. it meets the Lake Solitude Trail a short distance above the lake; the trail from the top of the gondola lift also enters here.

Newbury Trail (USGS Newport quad)
Distances from side road off NH 103 near Newbury village (1150')

  to Lake Solitude Trail (2510'): 2.0 mi. (3.2 km.), 1400 ft., 1 hr. 40 min.

  to summit of Sunapee Mtn. (2726') via Lake Solitude Trail: 2.9 mi. (4.6 km.), 1850 ft. (rev. 250 ft.), 2 hr. 25 min.

Goshen Trail

This trail, which follows an old woods road that was used to transport the materials to construct the summit lodge, provides an easy if unexciting rote to the summit of Sunapee Mtn. from the west. It begins in the town of Goshen, which is notable as the birthplace of John Gunnison, an early explorer of the west whose name was given to a town, a river, and a national forest in Colorado. Follow NH 103 about a mile west from the complicated traffic circle at the ski area entrance, then take Brook Rd. (sign) south for 2.5 mi. to the point where the road makes a 90° turn to the west. There is some parking available here but very little beyond.

Follow the gravel road across a bridge; just after it starts to climb, the trail turns left onto a gated gravel road with signs forbidding the use of motorized vehicles. At 0.7 mi. the road enters a clearing and bears left, soon crossing a brook on a bridge and beginning to climb more seriously. At 1.4 mi. it passes to the right of a small gravel pit, and the old road becomes much rougher, climbing to reach the ski trail used by the Lake Solitude Trail at 2.4 mi., just after passing a large boulder. For the summit, turn left and follow the left edge of the ski trails; for Lake Solitude, turn right and enter the woods in 30 yd. On the descent, the entrance to the Goshen Trail is somewhat camouflaged, but once identified—it passes a beech tree with a light-blue blaze and a large boulder after 40 yd.—the trail is unmistakable.

Goshen Trail (USGS Newport quad)

Distance from Brook Rd. (1350')

>   *to*   summit of Sunapee Mtn. (2726'): 2.6 mi. (4.1 km.), 1400 ft., 2 hr.

SAINT-GAUDENS NATIONAL HISTORICAL SITE

The estate where the noted sculptor Augustus Saint-Gaudens lived and worked from 1892 until his death in 1907 is now maintained by the National Park Service as a National Historical Site. It is located in the town of Cornish on NH 12A almost exactly halfway between Claremont and West Lebanon. In addition to the grounds of the estate itself, where there is an attractive 0.9-mi. loop walk that includes a path along the beautiful wooded ravine of Blow-Me-Up Brook, there is a forested area of about 80 acres called the Blow-Me-Down Natural Area. In this area an interesting loop walk of 2.3 mi. can be made. The route starts at the parking lot, runs 0.3 mi. across the estate grounds to the point where the Blow-Me-Down Trail enters the woods, then descends to a trail junction where it follows the Sycamore Trail 0.1 mi. to the bank of Blow-Me-Down Brook opposite a stand of sycamore trees. Returning to the main trail, the route runs past Blow-Me-Down Pond to NH 12A at the Cornish Colony Historic Marker (another possible entrance point for the loop). The route then follows the trail back past the pond to the Return Trail, which it follows back to the main grounds of the estate.

Section 2
Cardigan and Kearsarge

This section covers the northern part of the hill country of western New Hampshire, south of the White Mountains, where the main backbone of the mountains continues as a jumble of medium-sized mountains that generally do not group naturally into ranges. This area includes the highest and most impressive of these mountains, Mt. Cardigan, which with its subsidiary peaks supports the most extensive and interesting trail system in the region. Also included is Mt. Kearsarge, only about 200 ft. lower than Cardigan and equally impressive due to its comparative isolation from other mountains and its relatively great rise from base to summit. Plymouth Mtn., Cardigan's neighbor on the other side of Newfound Lake, also has trails that are described here.

In the past few years the Sunapee-Ragged-Kearsarge Greenway, a loop trail about 80 mi. long that connects these three major mountains in western Merrimack County, has been under development. A route has been established but improvements are still being made—mostly reroutings off roads and onto woods trails. This trail uses existing trails on Mt. Kearsarge and Sunapee Mtn. and a partly new route on Ragged Mtn. (2286 ft.), which has had a number of trails in the past that have usually lacked sufficient maintenance to make them attractive to the average hiker. In addition to the trails described in this book for Sunapee Mtn. (see Section 1) and Mt. Kearsarge that are parts of the Sunapee-Ragged-Kearsarge Greenway, the western part of the trail on Bog Mtn. is described in this section. Information on this trail and volunteer maintenance activities can be obtained from the Sunapee-Ragged-Kearsarge Greenway Coalition, PO Box 1684, New London, NH 03257-1684.

Mount Cardigan

Plymouth Mountain

Bog Mountain   *106*

Mount Kearsarge

MOUNT CARDIGAN

The outstanding peak of west central New Hampshire, Mt. Cardigan (3155 ft.) is located in Orange (near Canaan) and Alexandria (near Bristol). Excellent views are available from the steep-sided rock dome of "Old Baldy" itself, as well as from the South Peak (2864 ft.)—also noted for its blueberries in season—and from Firescrew (3064 ft.), the north peak, named for a spiral of fire and smoke that rose from it during the conflagration in 1855 that denuded the upper slopes of the mountain. Though relatively low, Cardigan provides a great variety of terrain, from low hardwood forests to the wind-swept summit. Its trails vary from gentle woods walks, to the West Ridge Trail (a traditional first "big mountain climb" for children), to the Holt Trail, with upper ledges that constitute one of the more difficult scrambles among the regular hiking trails in New England. From the east, you can make a fine circuit by ascending Cardigan by the Holt, Cathedral Forest, and Clark trails—or by taking the much more challenging Holt Trail all the way—and returning over Firescrew via the Mowglis and Manning trails.

In addition to Cardigan itself, there are excellent views from several of the smaller mountains on the two long ridges that run easterly toward Newfound Lake. On the northeast ridge, traversed by the Elwell Trail all the way from the edge of the lake to the north shoulder of Cardigan, Little Sugarloaf (1002 ft.), Sugarloaf (1370 ft.), and Bear Mtn. (1847 ft.) are easily accessible and offer excellent views. On the southeast ridge, traversed by the Skyland Trail, Church Mtn. (2270 ft.), Grafton Knob (2201 ft.), Crane Mtn. (2423 ft.), and Orange Mtn. (2684 ft., also sometimes called Gilman Mtn.) offer interesting outlooks.

Most of the mountain is contained in a state forest of more than 5000 acres. Adjacent to the park is the AMC's 1000-acre Cardigan Reservation, which occupies much of Shem Valley and portions of the east slopes of the mountain. The AMC Cardigan Lodge complex (which includes a main lodge, a cottage, a campground, and a small lodge called Hi-Cabin high on the upper east slope of the mountain) provides meals and lodging to the public during the summer season. A trail map showing hiking and ski trails is available at the lodge. Nearby Newfound Lake, with a major public beach at Wellington State Park, offers swimming, boating, and fishing. For reservations at the lodge contact the Manager, AMC Cardigan Lodge, RFD, Bristol, NH 03222 (603-744-8011). The usual approach is from Bristol, easily accessible from I-93. Turn left (west) from NH 3A at the stone church at the foot of Newfound Lake, continue straight ahead through the crossroads at 1.9 mi., bear right at 3.1 mi., and turn left at 6.3 mi. At 7.4 mi. from the church, turn right on a gravel road, then bear right at 7.5 mi. at the red schoolhouse and continue to the lodge at 8.9 mi. This road is plowed in winter, but must be driven with great care.

While many of the trails on Mt. Cardigan are heavily used and well beaten, others, noted in the individual descriptions, are lightly used, sparsely marked, and receive little maintenance. Such trails may be difficult to follow if not recently maintained, in the early part of the season when a footway is not clearly established, or in the fall when covered by leaves. Although these trails are not recommended for the inexperienced, they may be followed fairly readily by experienced hikers, although you should carry map and compass, keep track of your location on the map, and carefully follow whatever markings do exist. Mt. Cardigan is covered by the AMC Cardigan Map; the mountain itself and most of the trails are shown on the USGS Mt. Cardigan quadrangle, with lesser amounts of outlying areas on the Newfound Lake, Grafton, and Danbury quadrangles.

Volunteer maintenance efforts at Cardigan are led by the Cardigan Highlanders, whose address is PO Box 104, Enfield Center, NH 03749-0104. The AMC Cardigan Lodge Committee (c/o AMC, 5 Joy St., Boston, MA 02108) also sponsors several volunteer work weekends each year. The Cardigan region was hit hard by the January 1998 ice storm, and some disruption in trails, with possible changes and relocations, may be expected for another year or two. Hikers should be alert and be prepared at least to return to their starting point if a trail is impassable. It would be wise to check with Cardigan Lodge before attempting the less popular trails.

West Ridge Trail

This is the main trail to Mt. Cardigan from the west, as well as the shortest and easiest route to the summit. From NH 118, 0.5 mi. north of Canaan, turn right at a large Cardigan State Park sign. Bear right 2.7 mi. from NH 118, shortly after crossing Orange Brook. At 3.4 mi. bear left to a parking area at 4.1 mi., where there are picnic tables and restrooms.

The well-beaten trail, blazed in orange, starts at a sign in the parking area. At 0.4 mi. it turns left onto a woods road, and at 0.5 mi. the South Ridge Trail diverges right at a sharp turn. The West Ridge Trail soon turns left off the woods road, crosses a small brook on a bridge, and climbs to a junction with the Skyland Trail right. It then crosses Cliff's Bridge and reaches the site of the Hermitage (a shelter removed in 1991) at 1.1 mi. Shortly beyond the Hermitage site, an unsigned branch of the South Ridge Trail (marked by a cairn) leads to the right to the warden's cabin. The West Ridge Trail—marked by cairns, paint on the rocks, and blaze boards—ascends the broad, open summit ledges and joins the Clark Trail just below the summit. Descending hikers should take note that this trail, and no other, is marked by cairns and blaze boards.

West Ridge Trail (AMC Cardigan Map)
Distance from Cardigan State Park parking area (1930')

> *to* Mt. Cardigan summit (3155'): 1.5 mi. (2.5 km.), 1250 ft., 1 hr. 20 min.

South Ridge Trail

This trail provides access to Mt. Cardigan, South Peak, and Rimrock, and also makes possible a scenic loop in combination with the West Ridge Trail. It is blazed in orange below Rimrock and white above. It diverges right from the West Ridge Trail 0.5 mi. from the state park parking area, crosses a brook and climbs, rather steeply at times, to Rimrock, where it crosses the Skyland Trail at 0.7 mi. (Descending, follow the left of two lines of cairns on the ledge below Rimrock.) The trail continues across marked ledges and passes the summit of South Peak at 1.0 mi., where a poorly marked spur descends on the right to the Hurricane Gap Trail. The South Ridge Trail turns left and descends to the junction with the Hurricane Gap Trail on the right (the former portion of the Hurricane Gap Trail west of the South Ridge Trail has been closed). It then turns sharp right at a junction (left is the branch trail that leads 0.2 mi. to the West Ridge Trail near the Hermitage site) and continues to the warden's cabin, where it ends at the Clark Trail.

South Ridge Trail (AMC Cardigan Map)
Distance from West Ridge Trail (2250')

> *to* Clark Trail (2900'): 1.3 mi. (2.1 km.), 700 ft., 1 hr.

Distance from Cardigan State Park parking area (1930')

> *to* starting point by complete loop via West Ridge, Clark, and South Ridge trails: 3.6 mi. (5.8 km.), 1300 ft., 2 hr. 25 min.

Orange Cove Trail

This trail, which is really a dirt road (the old Groton-Orange highway) used as an access trail, provides a direct approach from the west to Mowglis Trail, Cilley's Cave, Hanging Rocks, and Crag Shelter. Follow access directions above for the West Ridge Trail, but bear left 2.7 mi. from NH 118 immediately after crossing Orange Brook. Follow this road 1.2 mi. to the end of the pavement. The trail has no sign but is easy to follow. It passes the state park boundary, bears left at a fork, and climbs easily past a large beaver pond at 1.0 mi. to end at the Mowglis Trail in the col between Cilley's Cave and Cataloochee Mtn. The Mowglis Trail continues straight ahead on the old road to Groton, or turns sharp right on a foot path to Cilley's Cave and Mt. Cardigan.

Orange Cove Trail (AMC Cardigan Map)
Distance from end of paved road (1850')

> *to* Mowglis Trail (2310'): 1.6 mi. (2.5 km.), 450 ft., 1 hr.

Mowglis Trail

This trail provides access to Cardigan and Firescrew from the north. From Hebron village on the north end of the lake, follow signs to Sculptured Rocks State Geological Site on the Cockermouth River, an interesting glacial gorge with potholes that is a popular picnic spot with a good swimming hole. Continue 1.0 mi. farther on Sculptured Rocks Rd. to a point just beyond the green bridge over Atwell Brook. The trail (no sign) follows the old Groton-Orange road, which forks left and follows Atwell Brook, ascending at a moderate grade. It may be possible to drive 1.4 mi. to a logging road fork, where the trail keeps right on the old road. The trail ascends past the state park boundary at 2.4 mi. to a junction with the Orange Cove Trail at 3.5 mi. in the col between Cilley's Cave and Cataloochee Mtn. Here the Orange Cove Trail continues ahead on the old road, while the white-blazed Mowglis Trail turns left and climbs briefly to a junction with the Elwell Trail at 3.7 mi. Soon after this junction a spur trail (sign) leads left 80 yd. to Cilley's Cave, a lonely, rocky retreat where it is said a hermit once lived, and about 0.3 mi. farther another spur leads left to Hanging Rocks.

Hanging Rocks is an interesting glacial formation that forms a natural shelter. About 100 yd. from the Mowglis Trail the spur forks. The right fork leads 0.1 mi. across the top of the ledge, with a fine view east, and the left fork descends 0.1 mi. among the rocks at the foot of the ledge. There is a steep connecting link at the far end of these two paths.

The Mowglis Trail then ascends more steeply, and at 4.6 mi. passes Crag Shelter (an open shelter accommodating fifteen with no reliable water source) and continues to a north outlook, where the trail turns sharp right and climbs to the summit of Firescrew at 5.1 mi., where it meets the Manning Trail. It descends across wide ledges deeply marked by glacial action and passes a side trail left, marked by a sign painted on the rocks, that descends 0.2 mi. and 200 ft. to Grotto Cave and a smaller boulder cave. The main trail then ascends steeply to the summit of Mt. Cardigan.

Mowglis Trail (AMC Cardigan Map)

Distances from Sculptured Rocks Rd. (800')

> *to* Elwell Trail (2450'): 3.7 mi., 1650 ft., 2 hr. 40 min.
>
> *to* Firescrew summit (3064'): 5.1 mi., 2300 ft., 3 hr. 40 min.
>
> *to* Mt. Cardigan summit (3155'): 5.7 mi. (9.2 km.), 2500 ft., 4 hr.

Elwell Trail

The Elwell Trail extends over 10 mi. from Newfound Lake to the Mowglis Trail 2.0 mi. north of Mt. Cardigan. It is named in honor of Col. Alcott Farrar Elwell, who directed Camp Mowglis for fifty years and helped develop many of the trails in this region. Recent logging has caused disruption and required some relocations, and the January 1998 ice storm added its severe destruction to the situation. The upper (western) part of the trail should be attempted with caution and an alternate backup plan.

The trail begins on West Shore Rd. about 100 yd. north of the entrance to Wellington State Park. At 0.5 mi. it passes a spur trail that leads left 0.2 mi. to Goose Pond, crosses the open summit of Little Sugarloaf at 0.8 mi., continues along the ridge, and finally climbs steeply to the summit of Sugarloaf at 1.7 mi. About 100 yd. past this summit the trail turns sharp left, descends steeply, then runs fairly level across the old Alexandria-Hebron turnpike.

It then climbs by steep switchbacks with rough footing, passing the junction on the right with the Bear Mountain Trail. It reaches the summit ridge of Bear Mtn. at 3.3 mi., where there are several fine outlooks across Newfound Lake. The Elwell Trail continues along the ridge, crosses under power lines, enters recent logging, and passes a junction on the right with the northern part of the Welton Falls Trail at 4.6 mi. At 5.3 mi. the southern part of the Welton Falls Trail descends to the left, and the Elwell Trail ascends gradually with occasional steep pitches past several scenic outlooks to a fork, where the right branch leads in a short distance to the summit of Oregon Mtn. (2239 ft.). At the top of a gravel log landing the trail turns sharp right (north) onto the Old Dicey Road and travels through a clear-cut marked by blazed two-by-fours until it resumes its old route at the junction with the Carter Gibbs Trail (right) at 7.7 mi. It then crosses a brook and climbs gradually to the summit of Mowglis Mtn. (2370 ft.) at 8.7 mi., where a tablet on the right honors Camp Mowglis. It descends again to the next col at 9.8 mi., where the Back 80 Trail diverges left for Cardigan Lodge, then climbs fairly steeply to a spur trail leading left 130 yd. to Cilley's Cave (sign) and descends slightly to end at the Mowglis Trail.

Elwell Trail (AMC Cardigan Map)

Distances from West Shore Rd. (600')

   to Sugarloaf summit (1370'): 1.7 mi., 900 ft. (rev. 150 ft.), 1 hr. 20 min.

   to Bear Mtn. summit (1847'): 3.3 mi., 1750 ft. (rev. 350 ft.), 2 hr. 30 min.

   to Mowglis Mtn. summit (2370'): 8.7 mi., 3100 ft. (rev. 850 ft.), 5 hr. 55 min.

   to Mowglis Trail junction (2450'): 10.4 mi. (16.7 km.), 3550 ft. (rev. 350 ft.), 7 hr.

Bear Mountain Trail

This trail provides an alternative route up the steep eastern side of Bear Mtn. from the old Alexandria-Hebron turnpike to the Elwell Trail 0.5 mi. south of the summit of Bear Mtn. To reach the trailhead, follow Bear Mtn. Rd., which leaves West Shore Rd. 2.0 mi. south of Hebron and 2.5 mi. north of Wellington State Park. After 0.3 mi., follow the gravel road to the left as the paved road swings right toward a housing development. Depending upon driving conditions, it may be advisable to park here and walk the remainder of the way. Follow the gravel road (the old Alexandria-Hebron turnpike) 0.7 mi. uphill to the trail, which is on the right 0.2 mi. below the junction of the road with the Elwell Trail in the saddle between Sugarloaf Mtn. and Bear Mtn. There is a small parking area just above the trailhead.

. The trail ascends to a small stream, swings right, and immediately attacks the steep, rocky eastern slope of Bear Mtn. by longer, then shorter switchbacks. It reaches the Elwell Trail 0.5 mi. above its junction with the old Alexandria-Hebron turnpike and 0.5 mi. below the main summit of Bear Mtn.

Bear Mountain Trail (AMC Cardigan Map)

Distance from old Alexandria-Hebron turnpike (800')

   to Elwell Trail (1600'): 0.5 mi. (0.7 km.), 800 ft., 40 min.

Carter Gibbs Trail

This trail leaves Sculptured Rocks Rd. at a small gravel turnout on the south side, 0.2 mi. east of the Sculptured Rocks parking area. Due to logging activity it is currently very difficult to follow and cannot be recommended except to experienced route-finders, but it is being retained in this guide in the hope that it will be restored. It may be possible to drive the first 1.2 mi. Leaving Sculptured Rocks Rd., it follows a gravel road for about 0.5 mi., then turns left where a right fork crosses Dane Brook on a snowmobile bridge. In another 0.3 mi. it bears right at a fork and follows an old logging road that gradually peters out. The trail then climbs more steeply to the height-of-land between Oregon Mtn. and Mowglis Mtn., where a side path (sign) leads right 0.2 mi. to an outlook on Carter's Knob. The main trail then descends sharply 0.3 mi. to the Elwell Trail opposite the upper terminus of the Old Dicey Road.

Carter Gibbs Trail (AMC Cardigan Map)

Distance from Sculptured Rocks Rd. (750')

   to Elwell Trail (1850'): 3.0 mi. (4.8 km.), 1400 ft. (rev. 300 ft.), 2 hr. 10 min.

Welton Falls Trail

This trail provides a route from Hebron to the Elwell Trail. The section continuing south of the ridgecrest to Welton Falls Rd., which has been almost impossible to follow for many years, has been reopened, though storm damage may make it obscure and impractical to follow in the near future. This section is important since it makes possible a number of attractive loop trips involving sections of the Elwell Trail. The trail diverges left from Hobart Hill Rd. 0.8 mi. from the village square in Hebron. The only sign at the trailhead is a small Mowglis trail marker. The trail starts up a gravel driveway, then follows an old road across a brook through a ruined farm. It makes a sharp right turn in a log yard, then angles up the hillside to another old road. It turns left and ascends this road, passing under power lines, and reaches the Elwell Trail at the top of the ridge at 1.5 mi. Here it turns right and coincides with the Elwell Trail for 0.7 mi., then diverges left in a spruce grove just before the Elwell Trail descends a steep pitch.

The Welton Falls Trail passes a white quartz boulder and descends steeply, then moderately, through patches of mature woods and brushy clear-cuts. It turns left onto a grassy logging road that descends to a grassy log yard. As the road begins to climb slightly, the trail turns right onto a footpath through a field, descends and crosses Templeton Brook, then follows old woods roads past a logged area (left) and bears left through a wet log landing area to a gravel driveway. Turn right and follow this driveway to Welton Falls Rd. just north of the bridge over Fowler River (Clark Brook on the USGS map).

Welton Falls Trail (AMC Cardigan Map)

Distances from Hobart Hill Rd. (650')

- *to* Elwell Trail, east junction (1650'): 1.5 mi., 1000 ft., 1 hr. 15 min.
- *to* Elwell Trail, west junction (1800 ft.): 2.2 mi., 1200 ft., 1 hr. 40 min.
- *to* Welton Falls Rd. (900'): 4.0 mi. (6.4 km.), 1200 ft. (rev. 1200 ft.), 2 hr. 35 min.

Old Dicey Road

Follow the route described above for Cardigan Lodge but bear right 6.3 mi. from the stone church and follow Welton Falls Rd. for another 1.2 mi. Where the good road turns sharp right uphill, continue straight ahead to a bridge over the stream coming from Welton Falls. Park along the road, being careful not to block side roads. Follow the road, which is the Old Dicey Road, across the bridge. At 0.2 mi. from the bridge, the Manning Trail diverges left on a cart track, while the Old Dicey Road continues to a clearing at 1.1 mi. Here the Back 80 Loop continues straight ahead. Beyond this point the Old Dicey Road has been severely disrupted by damage from the January 1998 ice storm. It turns right and climbs up a gravel logging road to a landing at the top. Here the Elwell Trail enters on the right, and the trails turn left and run together through a clear-cut marked by blazed two-by-fours to the junction with the Carter-Gibbs Trail.

Old Dicey Road (AMC Cardigan Map)
Distance from the bridge on Welton Falls Rd. (1000')

>   *to* Carter-Gibbs Trail (1850'): 2.0 mi. (3.3 km.), 850 ft., 1 hr. 25 min.

Back 80 Loop

This short trail connects the Old Dicey Road with the Back 80 Trail and makes possible a circuit to Welton Falls from Cardigan Lodge. It follows an old road straight ahead from the clearing where the Old Dicey Road turns right, then bears left to cross two brooks within a short distance, and ascends across another brook and the 93Z Ski Trail to meet the Back 80 Trail at a cellar hole.

Back 80 Loop (AMC Cardigan Map)
Distance from Old Dicey Road (1400')

>   *to* Back 80 Trail (1750'): 0.8 mi. (1.2 km.), 350 ft., 35 min.

Back 80 Trail

This trail diverges right from the Holt Trail about 100 yd. west of Cardigan Lodge and follows an old logging road. At 0.3 mi. the Short Circuit Ski Trail diverges right, and at 0.4 mi. the Whitney Way Ski Trail diverges left. At 0.8 mi., where the Alleeway Ski Trail turns left, the Back 80 Trail turns sharp right and reaches a cellar hole. The trail to the right here is the Back 80 Loop to Welton Falls; the Back 80 Trail turns left (follow the trail with care from here on). It crosses the 93Z Ski Trail, then a brook at a scenic little waterfall. It turns sharp left at 1.2 mi. at the east corner of Back 80 Lot and runs along the northern border of the lot. The trail goes around a flowage from a beaver dam, which may force a detour through the woods at 1.8 mi. It passes a junction with the Duke's Link Ski Trail, then turns sharp right, crosses a brook, turns left, and follows the brook and the edge of another beaver pond to the back corner post (marked Draper-NHFS-AMC). The trail then ascends gradually across a brook to end at the Elwell Trail in the col between Mowglis Mtn. and Cilley's Cave. For the summit of Mt. Cardigan, turn left on the Elwell Trail and ascend to the junction with the Mowglis Trail on a section of trail that is usually relatively easy to follow.

Back 80 Trail (AMC Cardigan Map)

Distance from Holt Trail (1400')

   to Elwell Trail (2000'): 2.4 mi. (3.9 km.), 600 ft., 1 hr. 30 min.

Manning Trail

This trail was constructed by the AMC as a memorial to the three Manning brothers—Robert, Charles, and Francis—who were killed by a train during a blizzard in 1924 while hiking on a section of railroad near Glencliff that was once often used as a shortcut between Dartmouth Outing Club trails. The trail diverges left from the Old Dicey Road 0.2 mi. from the bridge on Welton Falls Rd., follows a cart path to the Fowler River, crosses on stones, and enters the Welton Falls Reservation (NHDP). It continues up the river to a deep, mossy ravine and the main falls. There are many attractive falls and rapids, as well as spectacular potholes, above and below the main falls. From Welton Falls the trail climbs and descends many small ridges, usually in sight of the river. Then at 1.1 mi. it turns right, crosses the river without a bridge (difficult at high water), and ascends to a plateau, where it passes through a grove of spruces. It crosses the 93Z Ski Trail, then descends through a picnic area to Cardigan Lodge. (To reach the Manning Trail to Welton Falls from the lodge, ascend through a picnic area to the road at the right of the fireplace.)

The Manning Trail continues past the lodge, coincides with the Holt Trail for 0.3 mi., then diverges right and passes the old Holt cellar hole. The Duke's Ski Trail leaves to the right, then the Manning Trail turns right at an arrow, crosses back over the Duke's Ski Trail, and climbs through the woods to the first ledges. It passes a small brook, then climbs again to a great open ledge with fine views. At the top of this ledge it turns left through scrubby woods, ascending steeply at times, then follows cairns and paint markings across flat ledges to the cairn where it ends at the Mowglis Trail, just below the summit of Firescrew. The summit of Mt. Cardigan is reached by turning left on the Mowglis Trail.

Manning Trail (AMC Cardigan Map)

Distances from Old Dicey Road (1050')

   to   Cardigan Lodge (1392'): 1.6 mi., 400 ft., 1 hr.

   to   Mowglis Trail near Firescrew summit (3060'): 4.0 mi. (6.4 km.), 2050 ft., 3 hr.

Distance from Cardigan Lodge (1392')

   to   Mt. Cardigan summit (3155') via Manning Trail and Mowglis Trail: 3.0 mi. (4.8 km.), 1950 ft. (rev. 200 ft.), 2 hr. 30 min.

Holt Trail

This is the shortest but far from the easiest route from Cardigan Lodge to the summit of Mt. Cardigan. The upper ledges are very steep, and the scramble up these ledges is much more difficult than on any other trail in this section and one of the most difficult in New England; it may be dangerous in wet or icy conditions. Allow extra time for this challenging and strenuous climb. The trail is named for the founder of Camp Mowglis, Elizabeth Ford Holt.

From Cardigan Lodge the Holt Trail follows a gravel road to a junction with the Manning Trail, then a woods road almost to the Bailey Brook bridge. It crosses the bridge and continues to Grand Junction, where the Cathedral Forest Trail diverges left, providing an easier ascent of Mt. Cardigan via Cathedral Forest and the Clark Trail. The Alexandria Ski Trail also diverges left here, and shortly beyond the Alleeway Ski Trail diverges right. The Holt Trail continues along Bailey Brook to a point directly under the summit, climbs steeply on a rocky path through woods, then emerges on open ledges and makes a rapid, very steep ascent over marked ledges to the summit.

Holt Trail (AMC Cardigan Map)

Distances from Cardigan Lodge (1392')

  to Grand Junction (1700'): 1.1 mi., 300 ft., 40 min.

  to Mt. Cardigan summit (3155'): 2.2 mi. (3.6 km.), 1750 ft., 2 hr.

Cathedral Forest Trail

This trail diverges left from the Holt Trail at Grand Junction and ascends to the Clark Trail in the Cathedral Forest, providing the easiest route to the summit of Cardigan from the east. About 100 yd. above the junction the Vistamont Trail branches left to Orange Mtn. Ascending in graded switchbacks past the huge but rapidly decaying dead trunk of the Giant of the Forest, the trail joins the Clark Trail at a large cairn.

Cathedral Forest Trail (AMC Cardigan Map)
Distance from Holt Trail at Grand Junction (1700')

   to Clark Trail (2250'): 0.6 mi. (1.0 km.), 550 ft., 35 min.

Distance from Cardigan Lodge (1392')

   to Mt. Cardigan summit (3155') via Holt, Cathedral Forest, and
   Clark trails: 2.6 mi. (4.2 km.), 1750 ft., 2 hr. 10 min.

Clark Trail

This trail begins on the Woodland Trail 1.2 mi. from Cardigan Lodge,
continuing straight ahead on an older road at a point where the Woodland Trail turns sharp left on the logging road it has been following. It
passes an old cellar hole, enters the state reservation at a level grade
in a beautiful forest, then climbs steeply to cross the Vistamont Trail
at 0.8 mi. The grade becomes easier, and the Clark Trail reaches the
Cathedral Forest, where the Cathedral Forest Trail enters from the
right at 1.1 mi. As the trail continues a moderate ascent, the Alexandria Ski Trail enters right near P. J. Ledge, and 30 yd. farther the Hurricane Gap Trail leaves left for Hi-Cabin and the Hermitage site. The
Clark Trail continues past a side trail left that leads to a spring and Hi-
Cabin, then climbs on ledges and through scrub to the warden's cabin
at 1.8 mi., where it meets the South Ridge Trail. Turning right, it follows marked ledges steeply to the summit.

Clark Trail (AMC Cardigan Map)
Distance from the Woodland Trail (1600')

   to Mt. Cardigan summit (3155'): 2.0 mi. (3.2 km.), 1550 ft., 1 hr.
   45 min.

Hurricane Gap Trail

This trail connects the east side of the mountain to the South Ridge
Trail in the col between Cardigan and South Peak. The former western half passed through a fragile area—a wet depression with luxuri-
ant mosses, easily damaged by footsteps—and has been closed to all

use. The trail leaves the Clark Trail just above P. J. Ledge, passes an unsigned spur right to a spring, then reaches the AMC Hi-Cabin, where another spur trail leads right 60 yd. to the spring and 40 yd. farther to the Clark Trail. It climbs past a spur that leads 0.1 mi. left to South Peak, then ends at the South Ridge Trail at 0.4 mi. at the height-of-land.

Hurricane Gap Trail (AMC Cardigan Map)
Distance from Clark Trail (2600')

  to South Ridge Trail (2800'): 0.4 mi. (0.7 km.), 200 ft., 20 min.

Vistamont Trail

The Vistamont Trail connects the Holt Trail with the Skyland Trail at Orange Mtn. (sometimes also called Gilman Mtn.). It leaves the Cathedral Forest Trail left about 100 yd. above Grand Junction and rises over a low ridge, where it crosses the Clark Trail at 0.6 mi. It drops to cross a branch of Clark Brook, then ascends by switchbacks up the east spur of Orange Mtn., climbing moderately on open ledges to the Skyland Trail 80 yd. southeast of the rocky summit, where there are fine views.

Vistamont Trail (AMC Cardigan Map)
Distance from Cathedral Forest Trail (1750')

  to Skyland Trail (2650'): 1.6 mi. (2.6 km.), 1000 ft., 1 hr. 20 min.

Woodland Trail

This trail runs from Cardigan Lodge to the Skyland Trail just northwest of the summit of Church Mtn., giving direct access from Cardigan Lodge to the interesting outlooks from the ledges along the Skyland Trail. It leaves the parking lot to the left of the pond, crosses the outlet brook on a bridge, and passes the east entrance of the Kimball Ski Trail. It continues through woods past the Brock Farm cellar hole and field, then turns right on a rough dirt logging road at 0.7 mi. At

1.2 mi., where the Clark Trail continues straight ahead on an older road, the Woodland Trail follows the more recent logging road as it turns sharp left and descends across a brook, then climbs to a large beaver pond at 2.1 mi. From here on the trail is harder to follow and great care must be used. It ascends along the inlet brook, crosses it, and doubles back along the edge of the pond, then climbs moderately past a corner post marked "Draper" in a boggy area near a large boulder. Finally it rises more steeply to end at the Skyland Trail on the northwest shoulder of Church Mtn.

Woodland Trail (AMC Cardigan Map)
Distance from Cardigan Lodge (1392')

   to Skyland Trail (2250'): 3.3 mi. (5.2 km.), 900 ft., 2 hr. 5 min.

Skyland Trail

This trail runs from Alexandria Four Corners to the West Ridge Trail just below the former site of the Hermitage shelter. It follows the western and southern boundaries of Shem Valley, and in 4.5 mi. crosses five of the six peaks that extend south and southeast from Cardigan summit. It is lightly marked for much of its distance and, particularly between Brown Mtn. and Orange Mtn., must be followed with great care. It is, however, a very scenic route.

The trail starts at Alexandria Four Corners, reached by following signs from the stone church at the foot of Newfound Lake to Alexandria village. Continue through the village on the main road, which turns sharp right, then left. Pass under the power lines and then, as the main road turns sharp left for Danbury, continue straight ahead for about 4.0 mi. to the crossroads (sign, "Rosie's Rd."). Best parking is here; do not block roads above.

The trail follows the road that runs right (north) from the corner and soon bears left at a fork. At 0.3 mi. it turns sharp left (arrow) on a short road to a clearing, and ascends moderately through woods to the edge of an open field and a dilapidated cabin in the woods. It climbs through woods again to an outlook near the wooded summit of Brown Mtn.

(2270 ft.), then turns left and crosses the col to the east knob of Church Mtn. at 1.1 mi., where there is another outlook. It continues over the flat, wooded summit of Church Mtn. and past a junction (right) at 1.3 mi. with the Woodland Trail coming up from Cardigan Lodge, then follows the ridge top over Grafton Knob to Crane Mtn. at 2.1 mi., with good views from several ledges near the summit. The Skyland Trail continues to Orange Mtn. at 3.3 mi., where the Vistamont Trail enters 80 yd. before the summit. There are excellent views from the summit ledges. The trail descends to a col, then climbs fairly steeply to Rimrock at 4.3 mi., where it crosses the South Ridge Trail. It descends along a ledge (follow the right of two lines of cairns), drops rather steeply, and soon enters the West Ridge Trail just below the Hermitage site.

Skyland Trail (AMC Cardigan Map)
Distances from Alexandria Four Corners (1800')

- *to* South Ridge Trail at Rimrock (2900'): 4.4 mi., 1850 ft. (rev. 750 ft.), 3 hr. 10 min.
- *to* West Ridge Trail (2650'): 4.6 mi. (7.3 km.), 1850 ft. (rev. 250 ft.), 3 hr. 15 min.
- *to* Mt. Cardigan summit (3155') via South Ridge Trail and Clark Trail: 5.4 mi. (8.7 km.), 2150 ft. (rev. 50 ft.), 3 hr. 45 min.

Distance from Cardigan Lodge (1392')

- *to* Mt. Cardigan summit (3155') via Woodland Trail, Skyland Trail, South Ridge Trail, and Clark Trail: 7.4 mi. (11.9 km.), 2350 ft. (rev. 600 ft.), 4 hr. 55 min.

Ski Trails at Cardigan Lodge

The AMC maintains a number of ski trails in the woods around Cardigan Lodge, in addition to the hiking trails, many of which are also skiable. A map available at the lodge shows most of these trails and their ratings, which range from novice cross-country to expert alpine terrain on the ledges of Cardigan and Firescrew. Some of these trails were cut as alpine trails in the days before modern tows became common. Ski trails are not maintained for summer use, and hikers are requested not to use them.

PLYMOUTH MOUNTAIN

Plymouth Mtn. (2193 ft.) lies in Plymouth, northeast of Newfound Lake. The true summit is wooded, but nearby open ledges afford excellent views. Refer to the USGS Ashland quadrangle.

Plymouth Mountain Trail

This trail, which has been in use for many years, is the easiest route to the summit of Plymouth Mtn. At the crossroads on NH 3A near the head of Newfound Lake, where the lakeshore road to Hebron village runs west, go east on Pike Hill Rd. and bear left at the first fork at 0.3 mi. The road becomes very rough immediately after the last house, and since no parking is allowed in that area, the best place to park may be at the fork at 0.3 mi., or at a point about 0.9 mi. from NH 3A where there are small open areas just off the sides of the road. At 1.4 mi. from NH 3A, after the second bridge over the brook and 0.2 mi. past a snowmobile trail that leaves on the right opposite the last house, the trail leaves to the right on an old logging road (sign). It is marked by stenciled Camp Mowglis signs. It crosses a brook (follow trail with care), follows another old road uphill, and turns sharp left where a branch trail enters right. (Descending, turn sharp right here where the branch trail, marked by a Mowglis sign, goes almost straight ahead.) The trail ascends to an outlook over Newfound Lake, becomes less steep, crosses a false summit, and climbs to the true summit, where it meets the Sutherland Trail from Plymouth. From here an open ledge 30 yd. straight ahead (east) on the Sutherland Trail (for which the only sign at the summit reads "Outlook") provides fine views of Franconia Notch and the White Mtns., while a line of cairns leads right (southwest) to an outlook over Newfound Lake to Mt. Cardigan. The impressive outlook from the East Cliff can be reached by following the Sutherland Trail for 0.2 mi. and then a side path (sign) for another 0.2 mi.

Plymouth Mountain Trail (USGS Ashland and Newfound Lake quads)
Distances from NH 3A (737')

   to start of foot trail (1320'): 1.4 mi., 600 ft., 1 hr.

   to Plymouth Mtn. summit (2193'): 2.9 mi. (4.6 km.), 1500 ft., 2 hr. 10 min.

Sutherland Trail

This recently opened trail from Plymouth on the north side of the mountain makes a longer but more satisfying ascent than the traditional route. The ledges near the summit have not yet lost their coating of lichens and are very slippery in wet conditions. From US 3/NH 25 at the south end of downtown Plymouth, take Warren St. for 0.2 mi. to a crossroads with four-way stop signs and "Dangerous Intersection" signs. Go through this intersection with a slight jog to the right onto Texas Hill Rd.; at 2.3 mi. pass the junction with Hebron Rd., where there is a boulder in the triangular island between the converging roads. At 2.6 mi. the trail begins on a gravel road on the right with a mailbox labeled "502"; parking is available on the shoulder opposite the gravel road.

Follow the gravel road as it makes a long switchback, then bears left and becomes a dirt logging road where a driveway leads right to a house. It swings around a rock outcrop on the left, and reaches the trailhead on the left at 0.6 mi. (small sign), just as the logging road starts to descend gradually. The trail climbs through old-growth conifers, then young hardwoods in a logged area. It passes a wet area, then runs through more old conifers and then young hardwoods again. It passes along the top of a steep slope in old conifers, then swings left uphill. At 1.1 mi. it turns sharp right where a side path leads left 40 yd. to an interesting rocky knob (no view). The trail climbs to a ridgecrest, drifts off to the right side, then comes back to the ridgecrest at a ferny spot. It crosses a small brook at 1.5 mi., then continues climbing until it encounters a low rocky knob and runs along its ledgy margin to a trail junction (signs) at 2.0 mi. The side path to the left here runs 100 yd. to an excellent north outlook from the knob, which is locally called "Pike's Peak." In another 100 yd. the main trail reaches the rough upper ledges of the mountain, which are slippery when wet. There are an unusual number of small rocky knobs in the area that is crossed by the trail between here and the summit, and in fact the summit area itself is composed of several of these knobs. At 2.2 mi. the trail reaches the junction (signs) with the path that leads 0.2 mi. to the left to the excellent viewpoint from the East Cliff, and continues over ledges to the summit and the Plymouth Mountain Trail at 2.4 mi. At the summit the start of the Sutherland Trail is marked only by a sign that reads "Outlook."

Sutherland Trail (USGS Ashland quad)
Distance from Texas Hill Rd. (830')

> *to* summit of Plymouth Mtn. (2193'): 2.4 mi. (3.8 km.), 1400 ft., 1 hr. 55 min.

BOG MOUNTAIN

This small mountain (1787 ft.) in the town of Wilmot, now reached by the Sunapee-Ragged-Kearsarge Greenway, provides excellent views from several ledges, particularly south to Kearsarge from a ledge part of the way up. Refer to the USGS New London quadrangle. Take NH 4A west from Wilmot village for about 2.0 mi., passing along the south edge of extensive boggy areas on Kimpton Brook, which give the mountain its name and afford views across to it. Turn right on Stearns Rd. and follow it 0.4 mi. to the bridge over Kimpton Brook, where parking space is available (take care not to block any road). Follow Stearns Rd. uphill for another 0.4 mi. until it becomes almost level at the top of the hill, where the Bog Mountain Trail begins on the right (sign) opposite the trailhead for the Kimpton Brook Trail (sign), the continuation of the Greenway to NH 4A. The trail climbs moderately through beautiful woods, reaching a fine outlook ledge to the south at 0.5 mi. from Stearns Rd. It continues to climb, winding around on or near the ridgecrest, until it reaches a broad open ledge with excellent views at 1.1 mi., which most people would consider the summit. The true summit is a ledge (no view) in the woods about 100 yd. to the east of the north end of this ledge, reached by a white-blazed path. The Sunapee-Ragged-Kearsarge Greenway continues down the southeast side of the mountain toward Wilmot village, but since the permanent location of the path from the village to the base of the mountain had not been formally established at press time, this part of the trail cannot be described here at the present time.

Bog Mountain Trail (USGS New London quad)
Distances from Stearns Rd. at the Kimpton Brook bridge (1030')

  to Bog Mountain Trail (1200'): 0.4 mi., 150 ft., 15 min.

  to summit of Bog Mtn. (1787'): 1.5 mi. (2.4 km.), 750 ft., 1 hr. 10 min.

MOUNT KEARSARGE

Mt. Kearsarge (2930 ft.) is a high, very prominent isolated mountain located in Warner, Wilmot, Andover, and Salisbury. It has a bare summit, topped by a fire tower, with magnificent views in all directions. Mt. Kearsarge probably was discovered shortly after the Pilgrims landed. On a seventeenth-century map (Gardner's) it appears as "Carasarga," but since Carrigain's map of 1816 "Kearsarge" has remained the accepted spelling. Refer to the USGS Andover quadrangle for the summit and most of the upper part of the mountain, and to the Warner, Bradford, and New London quadrangles for the lower slopes.

Wilmot (Northside) Trail

From NH 11 between Wilmot Flat and Elkins, take Kearsarge Valley Rd. south, then follow signs to Winslow State Park and the site of the old Winslow House (caretaker's cabin, picnic area, water, and parking; there is a substantial admission fee in season). The trail starts from the parking area to the left of a service garage, at the same point as the Barlow Trail. It is well beaten and marked with red paint. It crosses under power lines and climbs moderately to the foot of Halfway Rock, where it climbs more steeply. It then angles to the left, climbing moderately again past an outlook to the north, then turns south and ascends over increasingly bare ledges, marked with orange paint. It meets the new Barlow Trail about 100 yd. below the summit.

Wilmot Trail (USGS Andover quad)
Distance from parking area, Winslow State Park (1820')

    to Mt. Kearsarge summit (2930'): 1.1 mi. (1.8 km.), 1100 ft., 1 hr. 5 min.

Barlow Trail

This new trail was cut and opened in 1998 and named in memory of Peter Barlow. It is a very scenic trail that provides a gentler alternative to the steeper and rockier Wilmot Trail. It is particularly enjoyable for the descent of the mountain.

    The trail leaves the parking area at the same place as the Wilmot Trail, crosses under the power line, and descends slightly for the first 0.1 mi. It angles around toward the east side of the mountain, climbing at easy to moderate grades, and at 0.7 mi. it bears left at a rock outcrop where there is an arrow placed for the benefit of descending hikers. More ledges are encountered—but not views, yet. At 1.2 mi. a side path leads right 25 yd. to an excellent northern outlook ranging from Cardigan through the White Mtns. to the Ossipee Range. Soon there is the first restricted view from the trail itself, and more extensive views are reached at short intervals. The trail turns sharp right on an open ledge and climbs to its top, reaching the end of the mountain's east shoulder at 1.4 mi. (For the descending hiker approaching this point, it appears for a short distance that one is about to step off the edge of the mountain—an exciting prospect.) The Barlow Trail passes a small pond in a swampy area (right) and dips down on the south side of the ridge to pass around a sharp canyon-like formation on the ridgecrest, then wanders back across to the north side of the ridge to join the Wilmot Trail (sign) on the open ledges 100 yd. below the summit.

Barlow Trail (USGS Andover quad)

Distance from parking area, Winslow State Park (1820')

   to Mt. Kearsarge summit (2930'): 1.6 mi. (2.6 km.), 1150 ft., 1 hr. 25 min.

Warner (Southside) Trail

Leave NH 103 in Warner and follow signs to the gate at Rollins State Park. There is a substantial admission fee in season, and the gate is often closed on weekdays before Memorial Day and after Labor Day. There is a picnic area with tables, fireplaces, and water. The road then mainly follows the route of the old carriage road along the crest of Mission Ridge and ends at a parking area 3.7 mi. above the toll gate. There are toilets, picnic tables, and fireplaces here, but no water. From there the trail follows the old carriage road, now badly eroded, to a ledge with a fine view. The trail then swings left and rises to the foot of the summit ledges and, blazed in silver across the ledges, continues to the summit and fire tower.

Warner Trail (USGS Andover quad)

Distance from parking area, Rollins State Park (2600')

   to Mt. Kearsarge summit (2930'): 0.6 mi. (1.0 km.), 350 ft., 30 min.

Lincoln Trail

This interesting and varied trail runs from Kearsarge Valley Rd. along a meandering route up the western ridge of Black Mtn. to the summit of Mt. Kearsarge via the parking area at Rollins State Park. It is lightly used, particularly compared with the other shorter, more popular trails from Winslow and Rollins state parks, and passes Baker's Ledge with its attractive western outlook. It is well marked with white blazes. The trail begins on Kearsarge Valley Rd. at a turnout 0.4 mi. south of the golf course entrance and 0.4 mi. north of North Rd. It is signed initially as the "Link Trail," because the original route of the Lincoln Trail started at Kearsarge Regional High School off North Rd.—what was once a link to the main trail has become the official trail.

The trail leaves the parking area and ascends gradually through a mixed forest 0.5 mi. to a wide woods road, where it turns left uphill (signs) and coincides with a snowmobile trail. It follows the road straight through a large clearing (where there is a snowmobile trail map to the right), and at 1.5 mi. turns left onto an older woods road (trail sign) uphill in company with the snowmobile route. At 2.0 mi. a short spur leaves left to Baker's Ledge, which has a fine view west toward Sunapee Mtn. and Lovewell Mtn. The Lincoln Trail soon turns right onto a footpath where the snowmobile route continues straight toward Wilmot. The trail zigzags to a grassy knoll where there are views of Lovewell Mtn. to the west and Mt. Cardigan to the north, then continues on alternately ascending and level grades across the western shoulder of Black Mtn., a subsidiary peak on the southern flank of Mt. Kearsarge. After a moderate ascent through an attractive birch grove, the trail reaches the western end of the upper parking area in Rollins State Park and turns left uphill. From here, at a sign, the summit of Mt. Kearsarge may be reached in either 0.4 mi. via the steep and rocky Lincoln Trail (left) or in 0.5 mi. by the heavily used and more gradual Rollins Trail (right). On the descent, the Lincoln Trail leaves the Rollins Trail at a flat ledge 0.1 mi. below the summit. It is unsigned and unblazed at this point so as not to attract inexperienced hikers to the short steep, rocky section, which may be hazardous in wet or icy conditions.

Lincoln Trail (USGS Andover, Warner, and Bradford quads)

Distances from Kearsarge Valley Rd. (850')

- *to* Baker's Ledge (1650'): 2.0 mi., 800 ft., 1 hr. 25 min.
- *to* Rollins State Park parking area (2600'): 4.2 mi., 1750 ft., 3 hr.
- *to* Mt. Kearsarge summit (2930'): 4.6 mi. (6.4 km.), 2100 ft., 3 hr. 20 min.

Section 3

The Merrimack Valley

The Merrimack River divides the southern part of New Hampshire nearly in half. For more than two centuries it has been the central artery of the state, providing a route for transportation and travel and a supply of water power that helped establish the state's three largest cities: Manchester, Nashua, and Concord. The Merrimack was once said to "turn more spindles than any other river in the world"—a reference to the massive textile industry that spawned the mills in Manchester and Nashua as well as in the Massachusetts cities of Haverhill, Lawrence, and Lowell. Manchester, a sleepy village with less than a thousand residents in 1830, was the largest town in the state with a population of nearly 14,000 in 1850 and had grown to almost 57,000 by 1900. The extent of the river-powered industry is most noticeable to the casual visitor in the almost unbroken line of old brick mill buildings—now preserved as a historical landmark—that borders the river across from the Everett Turnpike in Manchester below Amoskeag Falls. The falls themselves (now the site of a fishways educational center), along with the rapids below them, remain an impressive sight despite having been dammed for well over a century.

Though there are no high mountains in the Merrimack Valley, there are a number of interesting hills and other features, as well as a myriad of historical sites along the river itself. The state of New Hampshire is engaged in a long-term project to construct a trail, called the New Hampshire Heritage Trail, along the Merrimack Valley from the Massachusetts border to—eventually—the Canadian line via Franconia Notch and the Connecticut River Valley. This is a tremendously complex and difficult project due to the large amount of development along the river corridor, but many sections of trail already exist and offer a variety of walks both in flood-plain and riverbank natural areas and in urban areas with a wealth of history. The major hiking area covered in this section is 9300-acre Bear Brook State Park several miles east of the river, roughly between Concord and Manchester. Trails are also described on the Uncanoonuc Mtns. in Goffstown, Hooksett Pinnacle in Hooksett, and Oak Hill in Loudon and Concord.

In addition, short walks with an emphasis on ecology and conservation are available at the state headquarters of the New Hampshire Audubon Society and the Society for the Protection of New Hampshire Forests, both located in Concord. The Audubon Society headquarters, located on Silk Farm Rd., is easily reached by following signs from I-89 at Exit 2; the principal trail is a loop that descends to the shore of Turkey Pond. The SPNHF headquarters is on Portsmouth St., reached from I-93 at Exit 16 either by following East Side Drive uphill to the right and then turning right on Portsmouth St. (sign, "Conservation Center") or by turning right onto Eastman St. then sharp left onto Portsmouth St. at a small park. The main building, which incorporates a number of advanced energy-conservation measures, is situated on top of a bluff overlooking the river, while the trails lie on the flood plain at the foot of the trail; loop hikes of 1.5 mi. or more are possible.

Uncanoonuc Mountains

Bear Brook State Park (cont.)

Oak Hill   *141*

UNCANOONUC MOUNTAINS

These two nearly symmetrical and almost perfectly paired rounded hills in the town of Goffstown are visible from many points in the Merrimack Valley. Refer to the USGS Pinardville quadrangle. The

North Mtn. (1324 ft.) is wooded but offers some views from the summit area, and can be reached fairly easily by an unofficial but well-beaten trail. The South Mtn. (1315 ft.) supports what is probably the finest forest of communications towers in New Hampshire (even though the former fire tower has been removed), giving it a distinctively bristly appearance even from a considerable distance. There is a paved road to the unattractively overdeveloped summit, and the actual high point is now within a fenced-off area. A hiker who nonetheless finds this mountain irresistibly attractive and wishes to ascend on foot would probably do best to seek out the grade of the former incline railway, which once carried fashionable tourists to the summit. From NH 114 0.6 mi. east of its junction with NH 13, take Wallace Rd., immediately passing Goffstown High School, then turn right onto Mountain Base Rd. at 1.5 mi. and follow it 1.0 mi. to its end at the small town beach on Uncanoonuc Lake. The old railroad grade can be found easily just behind the beach, climbing rather steeply to the summit in about 0.6 mi. and 650 ft.

North Mountain Trail

To reach the trail to the North Mtn., start from NH 114 in Goffstown, just east of the junction with NH 13, and follow Mountain Rd. south, bearing left at 0.9 mi. The trailhead is on the right at 1.4 mi., nearly opposite a small parking area that has been created by blocking a woods road with large rocks. The trail is marked with white blazes, circles, and painted can tops. It climbs the bank above the road and soon passes through a stone wall and in front of a small cave. It climbs steeply through a fine hemlock forest, then moderates, passes an outlook, and approaches the summit, passing a side path which leads down to a view of Manchester.

North Mountain Trail (USGS Pinardville quad)
Distance from Mountain Rd. (625')

> *to* summit of North Mtn. (1324'): 0.6 mi. (1.0 km.), 700 ft., 40 min.

HOOKSETT PINNACLE

This small but steep-sided hill (485 ft.) in the town of Hooksett rises abruptly from the edge of the Merrimack River. It also overlooks picturesque Pinnacle Pond on its west side, a pond that borders on I-93, making the hill and pond a familiar and attractive landmark from the interstate just north of the Hooksett tollbooth. The interesting summit monolith is composed of a tough, erosion-resistant quartzite that has enabled it to survive the leveling current of the Merrimack River; the land on both sides of it, now essentially a terrace about 100 ft. above the river level, was once evidently part of the river's flood plain. The summit offers some interesting views of the river and nearby hills, and (unfortunately) intimate views of the interstate. Thoreau, in *A Week on the Concord and Merrimack Rivers*, praises the view of the river that this little peak provided at a time when the river itself was the interstate, and the sounds made by the main means of transportation in the valley could not compete with the roar of nearby Hooksett Falls. He comments that the Pinnacle affords "a scene of rare beauty and completeness, which the traveler should take pains to behold." An imaginative modern visitor might be able to reconstruct the bucolic scene that Thoreau enjoyed from its ledges. Refer to the USGS Manchester North quadrangle.

To climb the hill, go west on Pine St. from NH 3A a short distance north of the traffic lights at the junction where the main bridge crosses the Merrimack, connecting the two sides of Hooksett village. After 0.1 mi. on Pine St., turn left on Ardon Drive and continue 0.2 mi. to a paved turnaround at the end of the road. (Since this is a residential area, visitors should be scrupulous about not disturbing the residents; cars can be carefully parked in the turnaround without interfering with traffic or privacy.) Several beaten paths climb a few yards up the bank above the turnaround to a woods road. Follow the woods road to the right as it climbs up the west flank of the hill to the south ridge, where it swings north to the summit.

Hooksett Pinnacle (USGS Manchester North quad)
Distance from Ardon Drive turnaround (310')

> *to* summit of Hooksett Pinnacle (485'): 0.3 mi. (0.5 km.), 200 ft.,
> 15 min.

BEAR BROOK STATE PARK

This 9300-acre park lies mostly in Allenstown, with smaller portions
in the towns of Deerfield, Hooksett, and Candia. In this area of generally rolling terrain there are only a few significant hills—including
Hall Mtn. (941 ft.), Bear Hill (835 ft.), and Catamount Hill (721 ft.)—
but there are many interesting streams, ponds, and wetlands, and
extensive and varied stands of fine forest. There is a wide-ranging system of multi-use trails, most of which are woods walks with few summits or long-distance views. These trails are shown on the AMC Bear
Brook State Park Map, included with this book, and the park's trail
maps, which are available at the park's tollbooth and information
offices. The park is also covered by four USGS quadrangles that meet
almost in the center of the park, a short distance to the northwest of
Bear Hill: Suncook (northwest), Gossville (northeast), Manchester
North (southwest), and Candia (southeast). The main entrance of the
park is reached by taking NH 28 north from US 3 in Suncook or south
from US 4 at the Epsom traffic circle, then taking Bear Brook Rd. and
following signs to the park's tollbooth just west of the main developed
recreation facilities near Catamount Pond.

Black Hall Road

This gravel road runs north from the State Park Rd. to the northern
park boundary at River Rd. in Epsom. (The entire road is called River
Rd. on the USGS map.) It is an attractive walk or bike ride with varied terrain and easy grades.

The road (no sign) begins at an orange gate 0.2 mi. west of the
tollbooth, passes through a pine forest, then descends to cross Catamount Brook on a bridge. This marshy waterway carries the outflow
from Catamount Pond to the east on its way to the Suncook River,

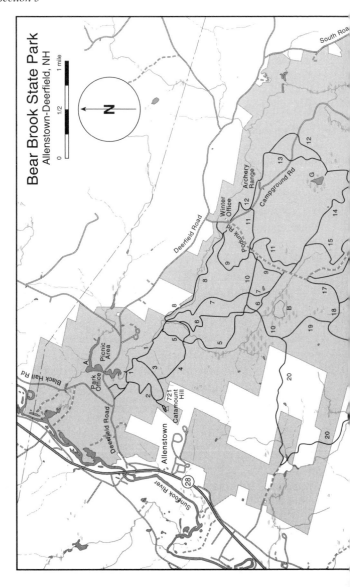

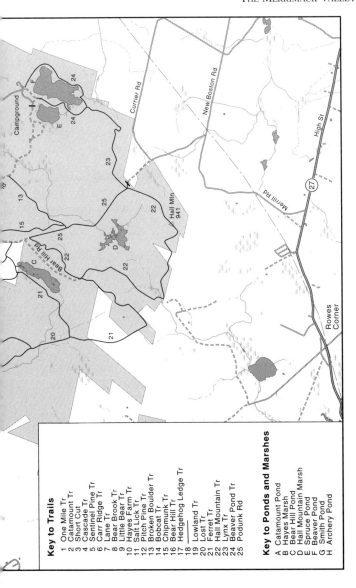

Key to Trails

1 One Mile Tr
2 Catamount Tr
3 Short Cut
4 Cascade Tr
5 Sentinel Pine Tr
6 Carr Ridge Tr
7 Lane Tr
8 Bear Brook Tr
9 Little Bear Tr
10 Hayes Farm Tr
11 Salt Lick Tr
12 Pitch Pine Tr
13 Broken Boulder Tr
14 Bobcat Tr
15 Chipmunk Tr
16 Bear Hill Tr
17 Hedgehog Ledge Tr
18
19 Lowland Tr
20 Lost Tr
21 Ferret Tr
22 Hall Mountain Tr
23 Lynx Tr
24 Beaver Pond Tr
25 Podunk Rd

Key to Ponds and Marshes

A Catamount Pond
B Hayes Marsh
C Bear Hill Pond
D Hall Mountain Marsh
E Spruce Pond
F Beaver Pond
G Smith Pond
H Archery Pond

which lies a short distance west of this point. The road then ascends gradually, passes several unmarked old woods roads, crosses beneath a power line in a semi-open area, and ends at an orange gate at the blue-blazed park boundary and a Snowmobile Route #15 sign.

Black Hall Road (AMC Bear Brook State Park Map)
Distance from State Park Rd. (330')

   to River Rd. (320'): 1.0 mi. (1.6 km.), 30 min.

One Mile Road

This scenic road, one mile in length, connects several of the most popular trails in the northwest corner of the park and allows for numerous possible loop hikes. In winter it is heavily used as a snowmobile trail. It is marked with yellow blazes and is easy to follow.

The road leaves the State Park Rd. just west of the tollbooth and heads southeast through an attractive red pine grove. At 0.2 mi. the road swings left (east) and passes a woods road (right) that is a winter snowmobile access route. Shortly, a trail on the left leads 0.1 mi. to the Bear Brook Trail at the Bear Brook bridge, 0.3 mi. south of the Catamount Pond recreation area. Just a few feet beyond, the Catamount Hill Trail leaves on the right for Catamount Hill and the Cascade Trail. At 0.5 mi. the yellow-blazed, unsigned Shortcut Trail crosses, ascending to the right 0.3 mi. to the Catamount Hill Trail and Cascade Trail, and descending to the left 0.1 mi. to the Bear Brook Trail. One Mile Road crosses a tributary of Bear Brook, then almost immediately passes an unsigned yellow-blazed trail (left) which leads in 25 yd. to the Bear Brook Trail 0.5 mi. east of the Bear Brook bridge. The road enters another red pine grove, passes the junction with the Sentinel Pine Trail on the right at Snowmobile Sign #2, then merges with the Bear Brook Trail coming in from the left, and ends at a turnaround that is 0.1 mi. west of the Lane Trail and Cascade Trail by way of the Bear Brook Trail.

One Mile Road (AMC Bear Brook State Park Map)

Distances from State Park Rd. (330')

- *to* Catamount Hill Trail (340'): 0.3 mi., 10 min.

- *to* Shortcut Trail (350'): 0.5 mi., 15 min.

- *to* Sentinel Pine Trail (330'): 0.9 mi., 25 min.

- *to* Bear Brook Trail (330'): 1.0 mi. (1.6 km.), 30 min.

- *to* Lane Trail and Cascade Trail (330') via Bear Brook Trail: 1.1 mi. (1.8 km.), 35 min.

Catamount Hill Trail

This trail ascends from One Mile Road to the summit of Catamount Hill (721 ft.), the third highest point in Bear Brook State Park. A section of the trail that once formed a loop near the western park entrance was abandoned due to logging activity on private land; the present trail, which is completely on park land, heads south, then east to the western end of the Cascade Trail. There are several interesting views from semi-open ledges near the summit.

The trail leaves One Mile Road, 0.3 mi. east of the tollbooth on State Park Rd. and 0.4 mi. south of the Catamount Pond recreation area by the Bear Brook Trail and Connector Trail. It ascends, passing almost immediately the abandoned section (right). The trail swings left, angles up the slope and passes an east view just beyond some boulder caves. At 0.5 mi. it reaches an excellent northwest outlook toward Mt. Kearsarge and Concord from a small ridge. After a short descent, the Summit Loop Trail is reached. This 0.4-mi. loop leads across semi-open ledges to several attractive southern outlooks surrounding the clearing at the summit of Catamount Hill.

The main trail descends off the ridge and swings left (north-northeast) along the blue-blazed park boundary markers. At 0.9 mi. the Shortcut Trail descends to the left on an old road through a pine forest 0.3 mi. to One Mile Road, then continues briefly as a yellow-blazed trail to Bear Brook Trail, 0.5 mi. from the Catamount Pond recreation area.

From here, the Catamount Trail coincides with the Cascade Trail and descends in an easterly direction, crossing a tributary of Bear Brook on stepping-stones. After a brief ascent on scattered ledges, it reaches a lookout ledge on the left with partial views toward Fort Mtn. and Nottingham Mtn. The two trails descend 0.2 mi. to the Sentinel Pine Trail, then continue through a hemlock grove to a log bridge over Catamount Brook, where the Cascade Trail continues east toward the Carr Ridge Trail, Bear Brook Trail, and Lane Trail.

Catamount Hill Trail (AMC Bear Brook State Park Map)
Distances from One Mile Road (350')

- *to* Summit Loop Trail (650'): 0.6 mi., 300 ft., 25 min.

- *to* Catamount Hill (721') via Summit Loop Trail: 0.8 mi., 400 ft., 35 min.

- *to* Shortcut Trail and Cascade Trail (500'): 0.9 mi., 350 ft. (rev. 150 ft.), 40 min.

- *to* Catamount Brook (450'): 1.6 mi. (2.6 km.), 400 ft. (rev. 50 ft.), 1 hr.

Cascade Trail

This scenic trail connects the Bear Brook Trail with several paths in the northwest corner of the park, allowing numerous circuits. It is named for the small cascades on Catamount Brook, located in a beautiful hemlock grove near the trail's eastern terminus. The western 0.7 mi. of this trail coincides with the Catamount Hill Trail and provides easy access to the summit of Catamount Hill.

The trail leaves the Bear Brook Trail next to the terminus of the Lane Trail, 0.3 mi. from the tollbooth and a short distance east of the east end of One Mile Road. It ascends onto a narrow ridge in a generally south-southwest direction through a mixed pine forest, following Catamount Brook to the right. At 0.1 mi. the Carr Ridge Trail leaves left toward Hayes Marsh, and the Cascade Trail enters a hemlock grove along the brook. At 0.4 mi. the Cascade Trail swings right (west), crosses Catamount Brook on a log bridge, and coincides with the Catamount Hill Trail from here on.

The two trails cross the Sentinel Pine Trail at 0.5 mi., ascend on scattered ledges through a mixed oak forest, and reach the height-of-land, with a partially obscured outlook (right) toward Fort Mtn. and Nottingham Mtn. at 0.7 mi. The trails descend to and cross Bear Brook on stepping-stones, then ascend briefly to the Shortcut Trail, which enters on the right (see the description of the Shortcut Trail under the Catamount Hill Trail). From here, the Catamount Hill Trail continues alone to the Summit Loop Trail and Catamount Hill.

Cascade Trail (AMC Bear Brook State Park Map)
Distances from Bear Brook Trail (350')

- *to* Catamount Brook and Catamount Hill Trail (450'): 0.4 mi., 100 ft., 15 min.
- *to* Sentinel Pine Trail (450'): 0.5 mi., 100 ft., 35 min.
- *to* Shortcut Trail (500'): 1.1 mi. (1.8 km.), 150 ft., 40 min.
- *to* Catamount Hill (721') via Catamount Hill Trail and Summit Loop Trail: 1.6 mi. (2.6 km.), 400 ft., 1 hr.

Bear Brook Trail

This scenic trail follows Bear Brook upstream from the point where it enters Catamount Pond at the recreation area to the Podunk Rd. bridge, just north of the park winter office and Campground Rd. It is marked with yellow blazes and is easy to follow, with the exception of a small recently logged area near Podunk Rd.

The trail leaves the swimming and picnic area and crosses the yellow-blazed footbridge over Bear Brook inlet at the south end of Catamount Pond. The route then crosses Deerfield Rd., winds south through the picnic area (watch for sparse blazes), and passes around the baseball diamond to the footbridge across Bear Brook. At 0.3 mi. the Catamount Trail heads straight uphill, and the Bear Brook Trail turns left up an embankment and parallels the south bank of Bear Brook upstream (left) and One Mile Road (right).

At 0.6 mi. the trail enters as the left branch of a fork, where the unsigned Shortcut Trail ascends right 0.3 mi. to the Cascade Trail and Catamount Hill Trail northeast of Catamount Hill. At 1.0 mi. the Sentinel Pine Trail diverges uphill to the right. The Bear Brook Trail merges left onto One Mile Road, then continues straight ahead onto an old road at a chain-link gate. After crossing Catamount Brook, the trail turns left onto a footpath at a three-way intersection, where the Cascade Trail leaves uphill on the right and the Lane Trail continues straight on the old road.

The Bear Brook Trail then turns right (east) along the south bank of Beaver Brook and passes a beaver dam (left) and then a bridge that crosses the brook to an old road (left). It enters an attractive hemlock forest, then emerges into a recently logged area where much of the trail has been disrupted. If the trail is lost in this area, continue in a generally easterly direction parallel to the brook until Podunk Rd. is reached. The trail itself passes a small bluff overlooking a marshy area, then swings alongside a logging road (Little Bear Trail). At 2.5 mi., a short yellow-blazed trail leaves right and runs 0.1 mi. to a parking area directly across from the park winter office and Campground Rd. The main trail swings left, then right, along the brook and reaches the Podunk Rd. bridge, just north of the park winter office and south of Deerfield Rd.

Bear Brook Trail (AMC Bear Brook State Park Map)
Distances from Catamount Pond Beach

> *to* Catamount Trail (300'): 0.3 mi., 10 min.

> *to* Shortcut Trail (300'): 0.6 mi., 20 min.

> *to* Sentinel Pine Trail (300'): 1.0 mi., 30 min.

> *to* Lane Trail and Cascade Trail (320'): 1.1 mi., 35 min.

> *to* Little Bear Trail (350'): 2.5 mi., 1 hr. 15 min.

> *to* Podunk Rd. (350'): 2.6 mi. (4.2 km.), 1 hr. 20 min.

Lost Trail

This old road heads southwest from the Hayes Farm Trail and Low-land Trail to Dodge Rd., the unofficial western entrance to the park, then turns east to end at the Ferret Trail south of Bear Hill Pond. It forms two sides of a 5.6-mi. triangular snowmobile loop that is nor-mally entered from Dodge Rd. Though less popular for hiking than the more central trails, it offers solitude and several scenic areas, par-ticularly near the Old Reservoir in the southwestern corner of the park. It passes in and out of the park several times, and with a few exceptions is easy to follow.

The road leaves the western terminus of the Hayes Farm Trail and the northern terminus of the Lowland Trail (Snowmobile Sign A) and ascends gradually onto a small ridge, leaving the state park at the blue-blazed boundary. It passes several frog ponds, re-enters the park where an old woods road leaves left, descends for 0.1 mi., and then turns left onto a dirt road (in the reverse direction, turn right here onto an orange-blazed road). In another 0.1 mi. the trail crosses a tributary of Boat Meadow Brook on a bridge, then turns left onto another dirt road (in the reverse direction turn right, following orange blazes and snowmobile markers). In another 0.2 mi., the small parking area at the Dodge Rd. trailhead is reached. To reach this point by automobile, leave NH 28 0.7 mi. south of the main park access road; take a left onto unsigned but paved River Rd., which parallels NH 28 for 0.8 mi.; then turn left onto Dodge Rd. (sign). In 0.4 mi. the road becomes rough dirt and may be impassable for automobiles beyond this point. In another 0.4 mi. it reaches the trailhead at a fork (no sign).

The Lost Trail continues by turning sharp left at the fork and fol-lowing the dirt road in an east-southeast direction. It passes an old gated woods road (right), crosses the tributary of Boat Meadow Brook, and re-enters the state park (blue-blazed boundary). After passing a large open gravel pit and field (right), the route passes sev-eral unmarked roads, leaves and re-enters the park, and passes a swampy area (right). At 1.0 mi. from Dodge Rd. it reaches the west-ern end of the Old Reservoir (right) in an attractive hemlock and pine grove next to a small clearing where illegal camping has occurred. The road swings left, follows the northern shore of the reservoir, then crosses a bridge over an inlet brook at its eastern end next to a beaver lodge (right). Shortly the route passes alongside Boat Meadow Brook in a marshy area (right), bears left at a fork, passes by several swampy sections, and reaches the southern terminus of the Lowland Trail (left) at Snowmobile Sign C.

The Lost Trail continues straight here, crosses a tributary brook and then Boat Meadow Brook, passes through several wet and swampy areas, and ends at the Ferret Trail (Snowmobile Sign #12), 0.4 mi. south of Bear Hill Pond.

Lost Trail (AMC Bear Brook State Park Map)

Distances from Hayes Farm Trail and Lowland Trail, northern terminus (500')

   to Dodge Rd. trailhead (350'): 1.5 mi., 45 min.

   to Old Reservoir campground (450'): 2.5 mi., 1 hr. 15 min.

   to Lowland Trail, southern terminus (500'): 3.8 mi., 1 hr. 55 min.

   to Ferret Trail (550'): 4.2 mi. (6.8 km.), 2 hr. 5 min.

Lowland Trail

This old road is used primarily as a snowmobile trail in winter and is part of a 5.6-mi. triangular loop originating from Dodge Rd. at the southwestern end of the park. It connects the Hayes Farms Trail south of Hayes Marsh with the Lost Trail near Bear Hill Pond, thus linking the trails in the center of the park with those in the southern part. The grades are gentle and the road is easy to follow.

The trail begins at Snowmobile Sign A, at the junction of the Lost Trail (north terminus) with the Hayes Farm Trail, 1.0 mi. from Podunk Rd. and 1.5 mi. from Dodge Rd. It heads in a generally southeast direction, bypasses several wet sections, crosses a stream, and at 0.7 mi. reaches an unmarked road (left) at Snowmobile Sign B which leads 0.2 mi. to the Hedgehog Ledge Trail, 0.5 mi. south of Podunk Rd.

The Lowland Trail ascends gradually by a switchback, enters a pine grove, passes a small frog pond (left), descends through several wet areas, and ends at the Lost Trail (south terminus) at Snowmobile Sign C, 0.5 mi. west of the Ferret Trail and 1.3 mi. east of the Old Reservoir.

Lowland Trail (AMC Bear Brook State Park Map)

Distance from Hayes Farm Trail and Lost Trail, north terminus (350')

   to Lost Trail, south terminus (500'): 1.8 mi. (2.9 km.), 55 min.

Sentinel Pine Trail

This trail connects the Bear Brook Trail at a point 1.0 mi. east of the Catamount Pond recreation area with the Hayes Farm Trail a short distance north of Hayes Marsh. It passes though attractive pine forests and by a small upland marsh.

It leaves the Bear Brook Trail at Snowmobile Sign #2 and ascends gradually on an old road through red pines, then white pines, in a southerly direction. At 0.3 mi., the road crosses the Cascade Trail and descends gradually to Catamount Brook, which it crosses on a small bridge. It enters a mixed oak forest and ascends a small ridge angling left (east), with an attractive small marsh to the right. At 1.2 mi. it reaches the height-of-land, descends into a white pine forest, swings left, and crosses the yellow-blazed Carr Ridge Trail at 1.3 mi. After a brief descent, it ends at the Hayes Farm Trail (Snowmobile Sign #3), 0.5 mi. west of Hayes Field and Podunk Rd.

Sentinel Pine Trail (AMC Bear Brook State Park Map)

Distances from Bear Brook Trail (300')

   to Cascade Trail (450'): 0.3 mi., 150 ft., 15 min.

   to height-of-land (500'): 1.2 mi., 200 ft., 40 min.

   to Carr Ridge Trail (500'): 1.3 mi., 200 ft., 45 min.

   to Hayes Farm Trail (500'): 1.4 mi. (2.3 km.), 200 ft., 50 min.

Carr Ridge Trail

Carr Ridge is a minor subsidiary ridge extending northwest from Hayes Marsh to the ravine of Catamount Brook just east of Catamount Hill. The trail traverses this ridge through a wide variety of forests with interesting vistas of several natural features. It links the Lane Trail, 0.3 mi. west of Podunk Rd. near Hayes Marsh to the Cascade Trail, thus providing access to Catamount Hill and the Catamount Pond recreation area in the northwest corner of the park. It is well marked with yellow blazes.

Leaving the Lane Trail, the Carr Ridge Trail heads west, skirting the northern end of Hayes Marsh in a pine forest. It swings right (northwest) and ascends Carr Ridge, crossing the Hayes Farm Trail at 0.3 mi. and the Sentinel Pine Trail at 0.4 mi. It becomes level on the ridge at 0.6 mi. in a mixed oak forest, then descends with minor ups and downs through small stands of white pine. It passes several large glacial erratic boulders in a gully, then ascends briefly and swings right onto a small ridge before descending into a pine and hemlock forest, where it meets the Cascade Trail at a point overlooking Catamount Brook.

Carr Ridge Trail (AMC Bear Brook State Park Map)

Distances from Lane Trail (500')

  to Sentinel Pine Trail (500'): 0.4 mi., 10 min.

  to Cascade Trail (400'): 1.4 mi. (2.3 km.), 45 min.

Hayes Marsh Trail

This scenic woods road connects Podunk Rd. with the Lost Trail and Lowland Trail just southwest of Hayes Marsh, a beautiful open wetland through which the Catamount Brook passes on its way to Bear Brook and the Suncook River. The trail skirts open meadows and the western edge of the marsh with its fine views, attracting mountain bikers in summer and snowmobilers and cross-country skiers in the winter. The grades are gentle and the trail is easy to follow.

The trail leaves Podunk Rd. (Snowmobile Sign #6), 0.5 mi. south of the park winter office on Campground Rd., and ascends gradually, passing the Little Bear Trail (which has cross-country ski trail markers) almost immediately. The Hayes Marsh Trail passes an unmarked road (left) that leads to the east end of an open meadow, and the Lane Trail leaves on the right at 0.4 mi. at Snowmobile Sign #5 and runs to Bear Brook Trail and the northwest region of the park. The Hayes Marsh Trail ascends into a pine grove and reaches the Sentinel Pine Trail, which enters on the right at Snowmobile Sign #3. The Hayes Marsh Trail now swings left (south) and descends gradually, passing the unsigned yellow-blazed Carr Ridge Trail at 0.7 mi., and reaches the west end of Hayes Marsh along an aqueduct wall over Catamount Brook at 0.8 mi. The view overlooking this wide watery expanse is one of the finest in the park. The old road continues generally south into a pine grove (Snowmobile Sign #4), passes a small frog pond (left), and ends at the northern terminus of the Lost Trail and the Lowland Trail (Snowmobile Sign A).

Hayes Marsh Trail (AMC Bear Brook State Park Map)
Distances from Podunk Rd. (510')

   to Sentinel Pine Trail (500'): 0.5 mi., 15 min.

   to Lost Trail and Lowland Trail (500'): 1.1 mi. (1.8 km.), 35 min.

Lane Trail
This attractive woods road leads from Hayes Field at Podunk Rd. west over a small ridge to the Bear Brook Trail and Cascade Trail, 1.1 mi. east of the Catamount Pond recreation area. Although the trail follows a woods road for its entire length, it is poorly signed and should be followed with care.

The trail follows an unmarked road that leaves Podunk Rd. 0.8 mi. south of Campground Rd. and the park winter office and follows the northern edge of Hayes Field. Almost immediately it passes the Little Bear Trail (right), an unmarked cross-country ski trail. At 0.2 mi., it leaves the field at its northwest corner and enters a pine forest. The trail passes the Carr Ridge Trail (left) at 0.3 mi., then ascends gradually to a beautiful open field, which it traverses on the southwest side. After crossing the Hayes Farm Trail at 0.5 mi., the trail re-enters the woods, ascends gradually to the height-of-land, then descends past several unmarked trails (use care to identify the proper route). The trail makes a wide swing to the right, then turns left at the bottom of the hill in a fine pine and hemlock forest and ends at the Bear Brook Trail and Cascade Trail. Continue straight on the Bear Brook Trail for the Catamount Pond recreation area.

Lane Trail (AMC Bear Brook State Park Map)
Distances from Podunk Rd. at Hayes Field (500')

- *to* Hayes Farm Trail (500'): 0.5 mi., 15 min.
- *to* Bear Brook Trail and Cascade Trail (320'): 1.5 mi. (2.4 km.), 45 min.

Bear Hill Trail

Bear Hill (835 ft.) is the second highest hill in the park and is the site of a former fire tower located in a pine and oak forest; at present there are no views. The trail leads from Podunk Rd. over Bear Hill and down to the Ferret Trail, just south of Podunk Rd. It is poorly marked in the section east of the top of Bear Hill but is not difficult to follow.

From Podunk Rd., just east of the trailhead for the Hedgehog Ledge Trail, the Bear Hill Trail ascends gradually on an old road marked with yellow blazes, which runs in a generally southeast direction through a pine and beech forest. It passes through several hemlock groves, through which Podunk Rd. may be seen to the left. At 0.8 mi. the trail meets another old road that ascends from the left from Podunk Rd. The trail turns to the right onto this road and ascends 0.2 mi. to the fire tower remains at the summit of Bear Hill.

To continue on the trail, backtrack a short distance, then make a sharp right (which is a left for one ascending toward the summit) onto an old road at a double blaze, and descend gradually to the Ferret

Trail, an unsigned road. From here it is 0.2 mi. south (right) to the eastern terminus of the Hedgehog Ledge Trail and 0.2 mi. north (left) to Podunk Rd.

Bear Hill Trail (AMC Bear Brook State Park Map)
Distances from Podunk Rd. (600')

- *to* Bear Hill (835'): 1.0 mi., 250 ft., 40 min.
- *to* Ferret Trail (700'): 1.3 mi. (2.1 km.), 250 ft. (rev. 150 ft.), 45 min.

Hedgehog Ledge Trail

The Hedgehog Ledges are an interesting series of rock outcroppings and erratic boulders that extend down the southern slope of Bear Hill. The Hedgehog Ledge Trail leads from Podunk Rd. past these ledges to the Ferret Trail south of Podunk Rd. It also provides access to the Lowland Trail and the Hayes Marsh region by a short woods road not shown on the park map.

The trail leaves Podunk Rd. at a small parking area 1.3 mi. south of Deerfield Rd., and descends south on an old woods road past stone walls in a small clearing (left) to a junction at 0.5 mi. Here the short woods road that is not shown on the park map continues 0.3 mi. straight ahead to the Lowland Trail at Snowmobile Sign #B, while the Hedgehog Trail turns left (signs). Soon the trail ascends along the south slope of Bear Hill past large boulders and along the base of multiple rock outcrops in an oak forest. At 1.1 mi., the trail emerges onto a small ridge in a mixed pine and oak forest, then passes blue boundary blazes and a semi-open marsh (right) before ending at the Ferret Trail, 0.4 mi. south of Podunk Rd.

Hedgehog Ledge Trail (AMC Bear Brook State Park Map)
Distances from Podunk Rd. (600')

- *to* Lowland Trail (550') via old road: 0.8 mi. (1.3 km.), 25 min.
- *to* Ferret Trail (700'): 1.3 mi. (2.1 km.), 40 min.

Bobcat Trail

This attractive trail connects Podunk Rd. opposite Hayes Field with the Broken Boulder Trail, 0.2 mi. south of the Smith Pond Shelter. It follows an old road that runs east with gentle grades, for much of its length through a mixed pine forest.

It leaves Podunk Rd. at a chain-link gate opposite Hayes Field (Cross-Country Ski Sign #9), 0.8 mi. south of Campground Rd. and the park winter office. It passes through an attractive pine plantation and reaches the Salt Lick Trail (left) at 0.1 mi. and the Chipmunk Trail on the right at Cross-Country Ski Sign #14 at 0.3 mi. At 0.9 mi. the trail swings sharp left off the old road to bypass a short swampy section, then zigzags back to rejoin the road, which it follows past a swampy area to end at the Broken Boulder Trail (Cross-Country Ski Sign #7).

Bobcat Trail (AMC Bear Brook State Park Map)

Distance from Podunk Rd. (500')

   to Broken Boulder Trail (500'): 1.5 mi. (2.4 km.), 45 min.

Little Bear Trail

Due to recent logging operations, the northern section of this trail has been temporarily obliterated. It now leaves Hayes Field and follows a circuitous course north to the park winter office by either the Bear Brook Trail (which has also recently been disrupted) or a new logging road. It should be followed with care, and is best hiked in a south-to-north direction due to poor signage and blazing at its northern end.

The trail leaves the gravel road in Hayes Field on a cross-country ski trail approximately 60 yd. west of Podunk Rd., and heads north through a pine forest. The trail swings left, crosses the Hayes Farm Trail at 0.3 mi., and continues straight past a green gate onto an old road. Almost immediately, the route turns right onto a trail (sign) and bears left at a fork. The trail descends gradually, zigzagging through a section with blowdowns (use care in skirting around this area) until the route merges right onto a logging road (arrow) in a recently logged area. The route follows the logging road in an easterly direction through a clearing and begins to parallel the Bear Brook Trail (left). From here, the Bear Brook Trail may be followed 0.1 mi. to Podunk Rd. at the bridge over Bear Brook, or the yellow-blazed cross-country ski trail may be followed to the right uphill 0.1 mi. to a parking area directly across from the park winter office at the intersection of Podunk Rd. and Campground Rd. Allow extra time due to the obstacles and the logging disruption mentioned.

Little Bear Trail (AMC Bear Brook State Park Map)
Distances from Hayes Field (500')

  to logging road (450'): 1.0 mi., 30 min.

  to Podunk Rd. and park winter office (400'): 1.4 mi. (2.3 km.), 40 min.

Salt Lick Trail

This attractive walk leads from the Pitch Pine Trail, 0.3 mi. east of the park winter office, to the Bobcat Trail, 0.1 mi. east of Podunk Rd. and 0.2 mi. west of the Chipmunk Trail. It heads generally south by wide zigzags, occasionally touching the east edge of Podunk Rd. along the way. Due to recent logging activity, it is probably best to approach this trail directly from Campground Rd.

The Salt Lick Trail leaves the Pitch Pine Trail on a cross-country ski trail next to a quarry entrance (Cross-Country Ski Sign #2) and crosses Campground Rd. almost immediately, then descends into a pine forest and turns sharp right onto an old road that ascends gradually to Podunk Rd. opposite a cross-country ski trail entrance. The trail now turns sharp left onto another old road, continues south making several sharp turns, passes a marshy area (left), and ends at the Bobcat Trail next to a beautiful red pine grove.

Salt Lick Trail (AMC Bear Brook State Park Map)
Distances from Pitch Pine Trail near Campground Rd. (450')

  to Podunk Rd. opposite cross-country ski trail (500'): 0.5 mi., 15 min.

  to Bobcat Trail (500'): 1.3 mi. (2.1 km.), 40 min.

Pitch Pine Trail

This trail runs east from the park winter office on Podunk Rd. through the Archery Range to the Broken Boulder Trail at its northern terminus. It then swings south, crosses Campground Rd., and ends at the Broken Boulder Trail, just north of Smith Pond. Due to recent logging activity near its beginning and the potential danger for hikers within the archery range during shooting season, the trail can be recommended only from the northern terminus of the Broken Boulder Trail toward Smith Pond.

The recommended part of the trail (westbound) leaves the Broken Boulder Trail just north of Smith Pond (Cross-Country Ski Sign #6) and follows an old road north 0.4 mi. to Campground Rd. (Cross-Country Ski Sign #5). It crosses the road diagonally right, passes a recent skidder road shortly thereafter, then swings left (west) and descends gradually along the side of a small ridge to the Broken Boulder Trail at its northern terminus.

Pitch Pine Trail (AMC Bear Brook State Park Map)
Distances from Broken Boulder Trail near Smith Pond (500')

- *to* Campground Rd. (450'): 0.4 mi., 10 min.
- *to* northern terminus of Broken Boulder Trail (400'): 0.8 mi. (1.3 km.), 25 min.

Chipmunk Trail

This trail parallels Podunk Rd. from the Bobcat Trail to the Broken Boulder Trail near its southern terminus. Due to recent and extensive logging activity, it cannot be recommended south of Spruce Pond Rd. The northern half, however, is scenic with several interesting natural and historic features.

The trail leaves the Bobcat Trail (Cross-Country Ski Sign #14) and heads in a southeast direction through a pine forest. At 0.2 mi., it passes a stone wall and a Forest Demonstration Area (left), crosses a small stream, enters a hardwood forest, and passes the nineteenth-century Leavitt Family burial ground (right) as the trail ascends gradually. The route zigzags through a hemlock grove, reaches a small height-of-land, and descends gradually to Spruce Pond Rd. (Cross-Country Ski Sign #13), just 0.1 mi. east of Podunk Rd. From here the Chipmunk Trail has been virtually obliterated by logging activity. To reach the Broken Boulder Trail, turn right (southwest) onto Spruce Pond Rd., then left (southeast) onto Podunk Rd., and walk 1.0 mi. to the old road and trail sign on the left.

Chipmunk Trail (AMC Bear Brook State Park Map)
Distances from Bobcat Trail (550')

- *to* Leavitt Family burial ground (550'): 0.4 mi., 10 min.
- *to* Spruce Pond Rd. (600'): 1.0 mi. (1.6 km.), 35 min.
- *to* Broken Boulder Trail (500') via Spruce Pond Rd. and Podunk Rd.: 2.1 mi. (3.4 km.), 1 hr. 5 min.

Broken Boulder Trail

This scenic trail follows old roads from the Pitch Pine Trail just east of the archery range, crosses Campground Rd., then continues south past Smith Pond Shelter and Spruce Pond Rd., ending at Podunk Rd. midway between Spruce Pond Rd. and the gated eastern entrance off Currier Rd. It passes through fine pine and hemlock forests, passing by Smith Pond, Broken Boulder itself (located on Spruce Pond Rd.), and the ruins of an old mill on Bear Brook. With its strategic location, bisecting the eastern half of the park, it makes many loop hikes possible.

The trail leaves the Pitch Pine Trail and descends gradually, crossing a small stream on a bridge, then ascends to cross Campground Rd. at 0.3 mi. It continues south on an old road (Cross-Country Ski Sign #4) with views through the trees toward Smith Pond (right) until it reaches the southeast terminus of the Pitch Pine Trail (left, Cross-Country Ski Sign #6) at 0.6 mi. In a short distance, an unmarked road leaves right and runs 0.1 mi. to the Smith Pond Shelter with its beautiful views of Smith Pond and the surrounding marshlands.

At 1.0 mi. the Bobcat Trail leaves right (Cross-Country Ski Sign #7) for Podunk Rd. at Hayes Field. The Broken Boulder Trail enters a fine pine and hemlock forest, crosses a small bridge, and at 1.4 mi. turns left (east) onto Spruce Pond Rd. (Cross-Country Ski Sign #10). In a short distance, Broken Boulder (a large erratic split by frost action) is passed, and the trail turns right (south) off of Spruce Pond Rd. onto an old road (Cross-Country Ski Sign #11) and re-enters the woods. The road passes through a wet and swampy section, crosses several small streams, then ascends gradually by the remains of an old mill on Bear Brook (left). The trail climbs a small embankment, merges left onto a logging road in a recently logged area, and continues straight through a large clearing past the Chipmunk Trail (right) at 2.3 mi. just before reaching Podunk Rd. at granite boulder barriers.

Broken Boulder Trail (AMC Bear Brook State Park Map)
Distances from Pitch Pine Trail (400')

   to southern terminus of Pitch Pine Trail (500'): 0.6 mi., 20 min.

   to Spruce Pond Rd. (500'): 1.4 mi., 45 min.

   to Podunk Rd. (600'): 2.4 mi. (3.9 km.), 1 hr. 20 min.

Hall Mountain Trail

This varied trail swings through the southeast corner of the park, crossing over Hall Mtn. (941 ft.), an ill-defined ridge with several semi-open viewpoints whose summit is the highest point in the park. The trail runs in a clockwise direction from Podunk Rd., 0.1 mi. west of the gated entrance off Currier Rd. It climbs south, then west, over Hall Mtn., then descends to a beaver bog and continues north to Podunk Rd., 1.4 mi. west of the trail's origin. Extra time should be allowed on the less well-defined sections of the trail.

It leaves Podunk Rd. opposite the Lynx Trail (Snowmobile Sign #18) and descends gradually on an old road (Snowmobile Sign #17) in a southerly direction past several stone walls. It enters a fork as the left branch (no sign); in the opposite direction, bear right at the fork.

It ascends gradually past a recently logged area (right) on the northern slope of Hall Mtn. After passing a large old elm (right), the grade eases as the road passes a stone wall, descends, swings sharp right (west), and ascends to the high point of Hall Mtn. on a semi-open ridge at 1.0 mi. There are several viewpoints to the south from attractive quartz ledges on the left that are partly covered with oaks, pines, and blueberry bushes.

The trail continues along the ridge briefly, then descends on a path marked by Snowmobile Sign #16 (left), leaves the park and shortly re-enters it (blue boundary blazes) in a hemlock grove. The route passes a beaver bog near a beaver lodge and dam (right) in a wet area, turns sharp right (north) onto a boardwalk, and follows an old road through a beech forest.

At 2.8 mi. the trail turns right onto the Ferret Trail (Snowmobile Sign #15) and coincides with it for 0.1 mi. through a recently logged area. At a double blaze (right) marked by orange ribbons, the route leaves the Ferret Trail and runs downhill on a circuitous and faded pathway (often difficult to follow). As an alternative, inexperienced hikers may prefer to follow Bear Hill Rd. north through the 4-H Camp to Podunk Rd. During the summer season, however, the park management requests that hikers use the Hall Mountain Trail to Podunk Rd. if possible.

After 0.9 mi. of zigzag descent (watch carefully for yellow blazes and orange ribbons), a stone wall is passed (left) and the trail merges with an old grassy road that leads directly to Podunk Rd., 0.1 mi. east of Bear Hill Rd. and 0.4 mi. west of the Broken Boulder Trail.

Hall Mountain Trail (AMC Bear Brook State Park Map)
Distances from Podunk Rd. at Snowmobile Sign #17 (750')

>   *to* Hall Mtn. (941'): 1.0 mi., 200 ft., 35 min.

>   *to* Ferret Trail and Bear Hill Rd. (750'): 2.8 mi., 1 hr. 15 min.

>   *to* Podunk Rd. (700'): 3.7 mi. (6.0 km.), 1 hr. 45 min.

Ferret Trail

This trail loops in a counter-clockwise direction around Bear Hill Pond in the southeastern corner of the park, passing through oak forests and hemlock groves and near open marshes. Bear Hill Pond is extremely attractive, particularly along its western and northern shores. Park management requests that during the summer season hikers should not use Bear Hill Rd. through the 4-H Camp; this section may be bypassed on the Hall Mountain Trail (see trail description), which begins on Podunk Rd. 0.1 mi. east of Bear Hill Rd.

The Ferret Trail begins at the automobile turnaround on Podunk Rd. where the Bear Hill Rd. (Snowmobile Sign #9) leaves to the south through an orange gate. The route ascends along this road 0.3 mi. to the 4-H Camp and its cabins, then turns left onto a gravel driveway by Channell Hall (left). It swings right, then left, and follows the dirt road past the camp's cabins (right) overlooking the pond. The trail passes a silo (right), cuts left across a field, and enters a grassy road (Snowmobile Sign #14) just before the Hall Mountain Trail (the preferred summer route) comes in on the left from Podunk Rd.

The Ferret Trail merges with the Hall Mountain Trail and continues straight ahead through a recently logged area until it reaches a junction (Snowmobile Sign #15) at 0.8 mi., where the Hall Mountain Trail turns left toward Hall Mtn. From there the route continues on the grassy road (Snowmobile Route 15S) through an oak forest and is easier to follow.

One mile later, after passing the park boundary blazes and an old stone wall, the road reaches a T intersection (Snowmobile Sign #13) at an old grassy road lined with stone walls. The trail turns right (west) here, passes more park boundary markers, and descends gradually. It passes another grassy road (left) at 2.5 mi., where Snowmobile Route 15S leaves the trail, and in another 0.2 mi. reaches a junction (Snowmobile Sign #12) where the unsigned Lost Trail continues straight ahead toward the Lowland Trail, Hayes Marsh, and points west.

The Ferret Trail turns sharp right (north) here onto an old road in a pine and hemlock grove and ascends gradually. It crosses several streams on small bridges, the largest being the outlet brook flowing from Bear Hill Pond. After attaining a small height-of-land, the road descends through an attractive section with marshlands to the left and Bear Hill Pond to the right. The road crosses a small culverted inlet stream, and at 3.7 mi. reaches the yellow-blazed Hedgehog Ledge Trail (left). In less than 0.1 mi. an unmarked road (right) leads in 200 yd. to a beautiful view of Bear Hill Pond from a rocky promontory on its northwest shore. The main route crosses another culverted stream, ascends gradually, and in 0.1 mi. reaches an unsigned and unblazed road (left), which is the Bear Hill Trail. The Ferret Trail ascends a short distance over a small oak ridge and descends to Podunk Rd. at Snowmobile Sign #8, 0.1 mi. west of the trail's origin.

Ferret Trail (AMC Bear Brook State Park Map)
Distances from Podunk Rd. at Snowmobile Sign #9 (700')

- *to* Hall Mountain Trail (750'): 0.8 mi., 25 min.
- *to* Lost Trail (550'): 2.7 mi., 1 hr. 20 min.
- *to* Hedgehog Ledge Trail (700'): 3.7 mi., 1 hr. 55 min.
- *to* northwest shore of Bear Hill Pond (650') via short spur: 3.9 mi., 2 hr.
- *to* Bear Hill Trail (700'): 3.9 mi., 2 hr.
- *to* Podunk Rd. at Snowmobile Sign #8 (700'): 4.1 mi. (6.6 km.), 2 hr. 5 min.

Lynx Trail

This trail follows old roads over rolling terrain, connecting the southern end of Beaver Pond with Podunk Rd. near its gated east entrance off Currier Rd. It leaves the Beaver Pond Trail at a three-way intersection (Snowmobile Sign #19) 0.9 mi. south of the campground store, and ascends gradually south on an old road through several logged clearings. At 0.4 mi. the trail turns sharp right (signs) onto an overgrown old road. (The road straight ahead continues as a snowmobile route 0.2 mi. to Currier Rd.)

The trail turns sharp right, then left, and soon reaches a height-of-land. It descends into a mixed hemlock forest, passing a rocky outcropping (right) and a marshy wetland area (right). It passes through a corduroy section in a wet area and ascends gradually past two stone walls to Podunk Rd. at Snowmobile Sign #18, 0.1 mi. west of the gated entrance to Currier Rd. and diagonally across from the Hall Mountain Trail at Snowmobile Sign #17 under a set of utility lines.

Lynx Trail (AMC Bear Brook State Park Map)
Distance from Beaver Pond Trail (500′)

   to Podunk Rd. at Hall Mountain Trail (750′): 1.3 mi. (2.1 km.),
      250 ft., 45 min.

Beaver Pond Trail

This easily followed, scenic loop may be used to explore the interesting and varied terrain and ecology of Spruce Pond and Beaver Pond, and also as an access to the Hall Mtn. region from Beaver Pond Campground. The easiest parking access during the warmer months is in the vicinity of the campground store near the end of Campground Rd.; there is limited parking at Beaver Pond Beach and at the southern end of the campground, where the trail begins. In winter it is necessary to walk the 2.9 mi. on Campground Rd. (also used as a snowmobile trail) from the park winter office, on Podunk Rd. just south of Deerfield Rd. To reach the trailhead, walk south from the campground store on a paved road past campsite #64 onto an old road marked with Snowmobile Sign #20. At 0.2 mi. from the store, the road bears right (arrow and yellow blazes) where there is limited parking on the left.

   The trail heads south on an old road between Spruce Pond (right) and Beaver Pond (left). The route bears left at a fork, then passes a side path to Spruce Pond (right) in a beautiful oak, birch, and hemlock grove. It shortly passes a side path to Beaver Pond (left) and at 0.6 mi. crosses a scenic boardwalk and bridge (dedicated to the Indiana Fire Crew 1995), and continues through a marsh of cattails, leatherleaf, and maples. The trail passes a log bench (left), swings left (east), crosses a boardwalk through a swampy area, and at 0.9 mi. reaches a three-way intersection where the Lynx Trail (Snowmobile Sign #19) leaves right toward the Hall Mountain Trail.

The trail now makes a left turn, then a right turn onto a path along the south shore of Beaver Pond. It follows the southern and then the eastern shoreline of the pond until it reaches a hemlock grove, where it turns sharp right, crosses an outlet stream on a small bridge, then swings left along a small cove. The trail passes through a marshy area and swings away from the pond again, until it turns left onto an old road along the north shore of the pond at 1.7 mi. The trail crosses the Beaver Pond Beach toward a campground road at a steel barrier; from here it is 0.3 mi. back to the campground store on the paved road.

Beaver Pond Trail (AMC Bear Brook State Park Map)

Distances from campground store (500')

- *to* Spruce Pond (500'): 0.4 mi., 10 min.
- *to* Lynx Trail (500'): 0.9 mi., 25 min.
- *to* Beaver Pond Beach (490'): 1.7 mi., 50 min.
- *to* campground store (500') via complete loop: 2.0 mi. (3.2 km.), 1 hr.

OAK HILL

Oak Hill (990 ft.) is a long ridge running east and west, located in Loudon and Concord. On the summit is a high fire tower that affords expansive views stretching from Monadnock to Mt. Washington in clear weather, and there are several other viewpoints with less sweeping views (but views unobstructed by the several communications towers in the vicinity of the fire tower). Oak Hill stands in the middle of a fairly large (for this part of the state) area that is almost completely undeveloped (except as stated at the summit), covered with beautiful woods where only the ever-present stone walls and a few cellar holes remind the visitor that Oak Hill was once almost entirely open pasture and farm land. Today deer and coyotes are common residents. The easiest access is by the road to the summit and fire tower; this road is normally closed to public vehicular travel but open to pedestrians and bicyclists. The city of Concord owns a large area on the western slopes—abandoned farmland taken over for unpaid taxes—and manages it as a conservation and public recreation area administered by the Concord Conservation Trust. A network of trails has been established in this area. Refer to the USGS Penacook and Loudon quadrangles.

Oak Hill Summit Road

This road, usually closed to automobiles, provides an easy and very popular hike to the fire tower and its views. From I-93 at the end of the Exit 16 eastern off-ramp, go almost straight up a short, steep hill on Shawmut St., then bear left at 0.7 mi. as Shawmut St. becomes Oak Hill Rd. at the junction with Appleton St. Pass Turtletown Pond and continue up the road, with an occasional glimpse up to the white quartzite south ledge. The summit road (gated) is on the left, 4.0 mi. from the Exit 16 off-ramp, just before the height-of-land on Oak Hill Rd. There is a hanging sign for the fire tower here, giving a mileage exactly double the actual distance. Park carefully along the roadside, avoiding No Parking areas—particularly the entrance to the road itself. Distances to the tower are shown by red disks on trees at 0.1-mi. intervals on the road.

Easy to moderate ascents alternate with long level sections, and at 0.6 mi. the road comes to a fork where a woods road diverges to the right headed north toward Loudon's School St., used as a snowmobile route to Canterbury. On the main road at this fork a large cellar hole is located on the right, opposite an old former millpond that has reverted to a swamp. At a small rise about 100 yd. before this fork is reached, a beaten path diverges to the left (for an ascending hiker) uphill from the road through an opening in the stone wall that lines the road; this path winds through the woods with minor ups and downs for 0.4 mi. to the white quartzite south ledge mentioned above, where there is a fine view out over Concord to the hills and mountains of southwestern New Hampshire, including Monadnock. The road continues to alternate moderate ascents and flat sections until it reaches the summit and fire tower.

Oak Hill Summit Road (USGS Penacook and Loudon quads)
Distance from Oak Hill Rd. (568')

> *to* summit of Oak Hill (990'): 1.3 mi. (2.0 km.), 450 ft., 50 min.

Oak Hill Trails

This network of trails on the western part of Oak Hill, maintained by the Concord Conservation Trust, passes two outlooks and traverses interesting woods, and is connected to the summit and fire tower by an unofficial trail across a strip of private land. Walks of low to moderate strenuousness of virtually any length can be selected, with loop hikes including a visit to the summit running in the range of 4 to 5 mi. Trails are marked by yellow plastic strips nailed to trees. There are presently two trailheads on Shaker Rd., reached from the end of the eastern off-ramp of I-93's Exit 16 by turning left on Mountain Rd., then bearing right on Shaker Rd. in 0.5 mi. The south trailhead is 2.0 mi. from the Exit 16 off-ramp, and the north trailhead is 0.5 mi. beyond. Neither trailhead is obvious, but with a little searching both can be found fairly readily. Distances to various points are generally shorter from the north trailhead, but if the Vista is included the south trailhead generally provides shorter distances. Trail maps are usually available in boxes a short distance up the trail from the road.

The *Lower Trail* leaves the north trailhead; it passes junctions with the north leg of the Upper Trail on the left at 0.2 mi., the south leg of the Upper Trail on the left at 0.3 mi., and the Vista Trail on the left at 0.5 mi. It reaches the south trailhead at 0.6 mi.

The *Upper Trail* climbs from the north junction with the Lower Trail, passing the junction on the right with the Ledges Trail in 25 yd., to the junction with the Dancing Bear Trail (straight ahead) at 0.3 mi., where it turns right, climbs, runs level, and then descends. It crosses the Ledges Trail at 0.7 mi. and continues to the south junction with the Lower Trail at 0.8 mi.

The *Vista Trail* leaves the Lower Trail 0.2 mi. from the south trailhead, passes the Ledges Trail on the left at 0.1 mi., climbs to a rocky knob with a fine view toward Mt. Kearsarge at 0.2 mi., then descends to rejoin the Ledges Trail at 0.3 mi.

The *Ledges Trail* leaves the Vista Trail 0.3 mi. from the south trailhead, and at 0.1 mi. the Vista Trail rejoins on the right. At 0.2 mi. the Ledges Trail crosses the southern leg of the Upper Trail, and at 0.4 mi. it ends on the northern leg of the Upper Trail 25 yd. above the junction with the Lower Trail.

The *Dancing Bear Trail* leaves the Upper Trail 0.5 mi. from the north trailhead and climbs over a low knoll into a sag; at 0.3 mi., as the trail begins to climb again, the lower end of the Swope Slope Trail diverges left. The Dancing Bear Trail continues to a four-way junction at 0.6 mi., where it ends. Here the Krupa Loop goes straight ahead and to the right, while on the left a short path leads down to Swope Slope in 0.1 mi.

The *Krupa Loop* begins at the four-way junction with the Dancing Bear Trail and the short connecting path to Swope Slope, 1.1 mi. from the north trailhead. Following it in a clockwise direction, it goes straight ahead from the end of the Dancing Bear Trail. At 0.1 mi., where the unofficial trail to the summit of Oak Hill continues straight ahead and the Swope Slope Trail enters on the left, the Krupa Loop turns right and swings through a rocky area, returning to the four-way junction at 0.7 mi.

The *Swope Slope Trail* diverges left from the Dancing Bear Trail 0.8 mi. from the north trailhead and runs 0.4 mi. to Swope Slope, a cleared area with views to the north. Here the short trail from the four-way junction enters on the right. The Swope Slope Trail continues to join the Krupa Loop at 0.6 mi.

The unofficial trail to the summit of Oak Hill, 0.6 mi. long, continues straight where the Swope Slope Trail enters on the left and the Krupa Loop turns right. It is not blazed but is fairly well beaten and can be followed readily if care is exercised. It runs across a fairly level area then, after a short climb, bears left and descends slightly through a stone wall. It then climbs again, curling around to the north side of the summit. It enters a cleared area and ascends it (the footway may be obscure in this area but the route is obvious), reaching the summit area at a communications tower clearing a short distance from the fire tower.

Section *4*

The Lakes Region

South of the White Mtns. and east of the natural central dividing line formed by the Merrimack River and its northern extension, the Pemigewasset River, the terrain consists of a multitude of medium and small mountains and hills, many with interesting views. But the dominating feature is the fine collection of lakes and ponds generously scattered among the hills, including Lake Winnipesaukee, New Hampshire's largest lake, and numerous smaller lakes, of which Squam Lake is the most prominent. For the purposes of this book the Lakes Region is restricted to the area east of the Pemigewasset River, though in tourist publications the Lakes Region includes some areas to the west, notably Newfound Lake. The unifying theme of the hills and mountains covered in this section is that views usually include a significant lake, most often either Winnipesaukee or Squam. The mountains with trails described here include Green Mtn. in Effingham south of Ossipee Lake, the Squam Range and the Rattlesnakes north of Squam Lake, Red Hill between Squam Lake and Lake Winnipesaukee, the Ossipee Range east of Lake Winnipesaukee, the Belknap Range and Mt. Major west of Lake Winnipesaukee, and Devils Den Mtn. in New Durham south of Lake Winnipesaukee.

Green Mountain

The Squam Range and the Rattlesnakes

Red Hill

Ossipee Mountains

The Belknap Range and Mt. Major

The Belknap Range and Mt. Major (cont.)

GREEN MOUNTAIN

Green Mtn. (1884 ft.) is an isolated small mountain in the town of Effingham. The state owns 15 acres on the summit, where there is a 61-ft. fire tower. The views are excellent and extensive in all directions—the White Mtns., particularly the Sandwich Range over Ossipee Lake, are seen from an unusual and interesting perspective—but the high tower must be climbed to obtain any significant views. Refer to the USGS Freedom quadrangle. In addition to the firewarden's trail on the north side of the mountain, now called the High Watch Trail, there are also two trails on the south side, the Dearborn Trail and Libby Road Trail, that make a loop hike possible. For information concerning conservation efforts on Green Mtn., contact the Green Mtn. Conservation Group, PO Box 95, South Effingham, NH 03882.

High Watch Trail

From the western junction of NH 25 and NH 153 (northbound) near Effingham Falls, go south on Green Mtn. Rd. for 1.2 mi., then turn left on a gravel road (sign: "Green Mt. Fire Tower") and follow it for 0.2

mi. to a T intersection with a paved road, High Watch Rd. Turn left here and follow High Watch Rd. At 1.2 mi., just past the Lakeview Neurorehabilitation Center, the road becomes rough gravel and continues another 0.2 mi. to a crossroads in the woods (sign: "Green Mt. Fire Tower"). Park here. This trail is shown accurately on the USGS Freedom quadrangle.

The High Watch Trail follows the road to the right (south), passing a High Watch Preserve sign. The old woods road that the trail uses is moderately steep and severely eroded in places. It runs toward the fence of the Lakeview Center's parking area and then climbs across a service road that runs to a fenced-in building on the left at 0.4 mi. Soon it bears left at a fork where the road to the right is becoming overgrown. At 0.9 mi. the grade becomes easy for a while, then climbs more steeply again until it swings to the left and becomes progressively less steep until it reaches the summit and its fire tower.

Green Mountain Trail (USGS Freedom quad)
Distance from crossroads on High Watch Rd. (740')

> *to* summit of Green Mtn. (1884'): 1.4 mi. (2.2 km.), 1150 ft., 1 hr. 15 min.

Dearborn Trail

This recently opened trail ascends Green Mtn. from the southeast. It is not shown on the USGS Freedom quadrangle, though its approximate route up the ridge northeast of Salmon Brook is easily identified. It is probably the most attractive trail on Green Mtn. due to the light use it has received and the ledgy, wooded terrain it passes through, but because of the light use the footway is not well established and the blazes must be followed with care. In one section the destruction of trees caused by the January 1998 ice storm may cause this part of the trail to become somewhat overgrown by low vegetation in midsummer, making it even more necessary to follow the markings with care. To make a loop hike, it is recommended that you ascend by this trail and descend by the Libby Road Trail.

The trailhead for the Dearborn Trail is on Hobbs Rd. From NH 153 on the north edge of Effingham village, at a junction where there is a historical marker for the "First Normal School in New Hampshire," follow Hobbs Rd. for 1.3 mi.; the last 0.2 mi. is rough and has not been plowed in winter. The trailhead is in a field at the height-of-land opposite a house that was under construction in 1998. There is a trail sign at the back edge of the field. To reach the trailhead for the Libby Road Trail from this trailhead, follow Hobbs Rd. (not passable for most cars) west to the junction with Old Pound Rd. (passable for cars) at 0.4 mi., then continue straight on Libby Rd. (no sign, not passable for most cars) to a woods road with a green gate on the right at 1.0 mi.

From the trailhead, the Dearborn Trail follows an old woods road uphill. It passes a property boundary line at 0.7 mi., where it narrows to a footpath, and then climbs through a section of large pines which permit glimpses across the valley. At 0.9 mi. there is a split boulder to the right of the trail that looks as if it had been sliced into three pieces with a knife. At 1.1 mi. the trail reaches a shoulder where it runs level for a short distance, then swings right and climbs moderately past a yellow-blazed property boundary and continues to ascend below a rocky ridge-crest to the left of the trail. It becomes less steep and winds through woods with ledges, crosses the blue-blazed state land boundary, and reaches the summit.

Dearborn Trail (USGS Freedom quad)
Distances from Hobbs Rd. (550')

- *to* summit of Green Mtn. (1884'): 1.4 mi. (2.3 km.), 1350 ft., 1 hr. 25 min.

- *to* starting point by complete loop via Libby Road Trail, Libby Rd., and Hobbs Rd.: 4.3 mi. (6.9 km.), 1450 ft., 2 hr. 55 min.

Libby Road Trail

This trail is a woods road currently used by the firewarden to ascend the mountain in an ATV. It has some loose rock footing and is not a particularly attractive trail, but it is easy to follow and makes possible a loop hike in combination with the Dearborn Trail. It is accurately shown on the USGS Freedom quadrangle. From NH 153 in Center Effingham opposite the Baptist church, take Town House Rd. east for 1.8 mi., then turn right on Libby Rd. (sign: "Green Mt. Fire Tower") and follow it for 0.5 mi. to a woods road with a green gate on the left (sign: "Green Mt. Fire Tower"). Libby Rd. is rough but passable to this point in most cars. To reach the trailhead for the Dearborn Trail from this trailhead, follow Libby Rd. (not passable for most cars) east to the junction with Old Pound Rd. (passable for cars) at 0.7 mi., then continue straight on Hobbs Rd. (no sign; not passable for most cars) to a field on the left at 1.0 mi.

The trail follows the woods road past the gate, passing a cabin (left) at 0.2 mi. and reaching a small brook at 0.7 mi. At 0.9 mi. the trail swings to the right away from the brook and climbs to a hairpin turn to the right at 1.6 mi. From here the trail climbs past the firewarden's cabin to the summit and tower. To find this trail from the summit, descend to the front of the firewarden's cabin; the woods road can be seen clearly from there.

Libby Road Trail (USGS Freedom quad)
Distance from Libby Rd. (720')

   to summit of Green Mtn. (1884'): 1.8 mi. (2.9 km.), 1150 ft., 1 hr. 30 min.

THE SQUAM RANGE AND THE RATTLESNAKES

The Squam Range begins at Sandwich Notch across from Mt. Israel and runs roughly southwest toward Holderness. This area is almost entirely private property, open to day hikers by the gracious permission of the landowners, but camping is not permitted. Its peaks, from northeast to southwest, are an unnamed knob (2218 ft.), Mt. Double-head (2158 ft.), Mt. Squam (2223 ft.), Mt. Percival (2212 ft.), a knob sometimes called the Sawtooth (2260 ft.) that is the actual high point of the range, Mt. Morgan (2220 ft.), Mt. Webster (2076 ft.), Mt. Livermore (1500 ft.), and Cotton Mtn. (1270 ft.). The Crawford-Ridgepole Trail crosses over or near all of these summits except for Cotton Mtn., and several trails ascend the ridge from NH 113; curiously, the Sawtooth, the high point of the range, is bypassed by the trail. By far the most popular hike on the range, often fairly crowded, is the loop over Mts. Morgan and Percival, which offer superb views south over the lake and hill country and north to the higher mountains; the rest of the range is lightly visited and the trails, including the Crawford-Ridgepole Trail, often require some care to follow, though the rewards of pleasant walks to several excellent viewpoints are great.

The Rattlesnakes—West Rattlesnake (1260 ft.) and East Rattlesnake (1289 ft.)—are a pair of hills that rise just across the highway from Mt. Morgan and Mt. Percival and offer excellent lake views for little effort. West Rattlesnake has fine views to the south and west from its southwest cliff. East Rattlesnake has a more limited but still excellent view over Squam Lake. Five Finger Point, which lies southeast of the Rattlesnakes and has a perimeter trail connected to the Rattlesnakes' trail network, offers attractive lakeside walking on undeveloped rocky shores.

The area containing these trails is shown on the USGS Squam Mtn. and Holderness quadrangles, though the Crawford-Ridgepole Trail up to the southeast summit of Cotton Mtn. is not shown, and the Old Highway is shown but not titled. The Squam Lakes Association (SLA), which maintains most of the trails on Squam Range, publishes Bradford Washburn's detailed map of the Squam Range (scale 1:15,000) and a trail guide to the paths they maintain, both of which can be ordered from the SLA, PO Box 204, Holderness, NH 03245 (603-968-7336). The Washburn map, although offering much greater detail than any other map, also covers the Rattlesnakes but omits the southwestern end of the Squam Range. However, the SLA trail guide has a map that, while not nearly as detailed as the Washburn map, covers the southwest end of the Squam Range (and also Red Hill) to an extent that will probably be adequate for the great majority of hikers. The AMC Crawford Notch–Sandwich Range map (map #3 in the *AMC White Mountain Guide*) also covers most of the Squam Range (and also the Rattlesnakes), but omits approximately the same part of the Squam Range as the Washburn map.

Crawford-Ridgepole Trail

This trail follows the backbone of the Squam Range from Sandwich Notch Rd. to the south knob of Cotton Mtn. Except for the very popular segment between Mt. Percival and Mt. Morgan, the trail is used infrequently, despite fine views in the Squam-Doublehead section.

The trail starts on the Sandwich Notch Rd. 0.5 mi. beyond Beede Falls (Cow Cave) and 2.0 mi. south of the power line along the Beebe River. From the road (sign) it ascends steeply, passes southeast of the summit of an unnamed wooded peak (2218 ft.), and continues along the ridge across a saddle to Doublehead Mtn. (2158 ft.), where there is a good view north just before the summit of East Doublehead. At 1.9 mi., 100 yd. beyond the summit of East Doublehead, the trail bears right and descends where the Doublehead Trail diverges left to NH 113. There is a very fine viewpoint, well worth the side trip, on the Doublehead Trail 0.1 mi. from this junction. After passing over West Doublehead, where there is an outlook to the north, the Crawford-Ridgepole Trail continues along the ridge, much of the way over ledges which are slippery when wet. It crosses the east summit of Mt. Squam (2223 ft.), where there is a fine view, at 3.0 mi. The trail continues to the Mount Percival Trail and Mt. Percival's excellent views at 4.4 mi., passes just west of the actual high point of the range (sometimes called the Sawtooth, it can be reached by a short but thick bushwhack and has a good view), and continues to a junction with the Mount Morgan Trail at 5.2 mi. Here the Mount Morgan Trail leads to the right 90 yd. to a fork; the left branch (almost straight ahead) leads another 50 yd. to a cliff-top viewpoint, while the right branch leads 50 yd. to the true summit of Mt. Morgan, where there is an interesting view north.

From this junction the Crawford-Ridgepole Trail and the Mount Morgan Trail coincide, descending a set of steps. Shortly a spur path branches right, ascends a ladder, and climbs about 100 yd. through a boulder cave to the cliff-top viewpoint. The main trail descends to a junction at 5.6 mi. where the Mount Morgan Trail continues its descent to NH 113, while the Crawford-Ridgepole Trail turns right for Mt. Webster. At 7.2 mi. a spur path leads left 50 yd. to the summit of Mt. Webster, and at 7.5 mi. an unmarked spur leads left a few steps to the beautiful east outlook.

The trail continues past the junction with the Old Mountain Road at 9.6 mi. and climbs to the summit of Mt. Livermore (view) at 10.0 mi. Coinciding with the Prescott Trail, it descends west from Mt. Livermore along a stone wall, then turns left on an old carriage road and descends by switchbacks. At 10.3 mi. the Prescott Trail branches left. The Crawford-Ridgepole Trail crosses two tiny streams near a low pass, then climbs through a rocky area in a beautiful hemlock grove to a south spur of Cotton Mtn. Here the Crawford-Ridgepole Trail ends, since the Science Center of New Hampshire has closed the former connector to its trails because it requires an admission fee for use of its trails. From the spur of Cotton Mtn., descent can be made by following the yellow blazes of the former Cotton Mountain Trail down to the edge of the large gravel pit and thence to NH 113 near the Old Highway trailhead. This old trail has been somewhat disrupted by logging but can be followed downhill fairly readily, though ascent by this route is not recommended.

Crawford-Ridgepole Trail (USGS Squam Range and Holderness quads)

Distances from Sandwich Notch Rd. (1220')

- *to* East Doublehead summit (2158'): 1.9 mi., 1150 ft. (rev. 200 ft.), 1 hr. 30 min.

- *to* Mt. Squam, east summit (2223'): 3.0 mi., 1450 ft. (rev. 250 ft.), 2 hr. 15 min.

- *to* Mt. Percival summit (2212'): 4.4 mi., 1700 ft. (rev. 250 ft.), 3 hr. 5 min.

- *to* upper junction with Mount Morgan Trail (2200'): 5.2 mi., 1800 ft. (rev. 100 ft.), 3 hr. 30 min.

- *to* Mt. Livermore summit (1500'): 10.0 mi., 2300 ft. (rev. 1000 ft.), 6 hr. 10 min.

- *to* spur of Cotton Mtn. (1210'): 11.3 mi. (18.1 km.), 2600 ft. (rev. 600 ft.), 6 hr. 55 min.

Doublehead Trail

This trail provides access to a ledge high on Doublehead Mtn. that provides one of the finest views in the Squam Range. It begins on NH 113 at a point 3.5 mi. southwest of Center Sandwich, following a gravel road (part of the old Holderness–Center Sandwich highway) that diverges right (west) at an angle past an old cemetery and a residence. Most vehicles should park near NH 113, taking care not to block any roads.

Continue on the old highway. The trail proper leaves the old highway on the right 1.0 mi. from NH 113 and follows a logging road that bears to the right through a clearing. At 1.5 mi. the trail turns left onto a skidder road and enters an overgrown logged area where the footway is poorly defined and blazes must be followed with care. In another 100 yd. the trail turns sharp right (arrow) across a small brook, follows another skidder road, and joins a small brook. At the top of a steep pitch it turns sharp left and soon crosses a stone wall, where it re-enters mature woods. It ascends steeply up the valley of a small brook, then swings right and climbs to a ledge at 2.3 mi. with excellent views to the south. It then turns left off the ledge and climbs to the Crawford-Ridgepole Trail 80 yd. west of the summit of East Doublehead.

Doublehead Trail (USGS Squam Range quad)
Distance from NH 113 (720')

> *to* Crawford-Ridgepole Trail (2120'): 2.4 mi. (3.9 km.), 1450 ft.,
> 1 hr. 55 min.

Mount Percival Trail

This trail provides access to the fine views and interesting boulder caves on Mt. Percival, and in combination with the Mount Morgan and Crawford-Ridgepole trails offers one of the most popular and scenic loop hikes on the southern fringe of the White Mtns. It begins on the north side of NH 113, 0.3 mi. northeast of the Mount Morgan Trail parking area (which is usually the best place to park).

It follows a logging road past a gate to an old clearing, then bears left into the woods, passes a stone wall, bears left through another old clearing (arrow), and passes several more stone walls. After a short ascent, the trail turns right (east) and traverses the south slope of Mt. Percival for 0.1 mi. The trail becomes steep at 1.6 mi., climbing past a fine view of Squam Lake to the summit, where it joins the Crawford-Ridgepole Trail. Just below the summit a side path diverges left and ascends very roughly and strenuously through a boulder cave, then rejoins the main path just below the summit.

Mount Percival Trail (USGS Squam Range quad)
Distances from NH 113 (800')

> *to* to Mt. Percival summit (2212'): 1.9 mi. (3.1 km.), 1450 ft., 1 hr. 40 min.

> *for* loop over Mts. Percival and Morgan via Mount Percival, Crawford–Ridgepole, and Mount Morgan trails: 4.8 mi. (7.7 km.), 1550 ft., 3 hr. 10 min.

Mount Morgan Trail

This trail leaves the west side of NH 113, 0.5 mi. northeast of its junction with Pinehurst Rd. (the road that leads to Rockywold and Deephaven camps). From a small clearing (parking), the trail follows a logging road, turning left off it almost immediately. The trail bears right at a fork and soon begins the steeper ascent of the southeast slope of the mountain. At 1.7 mi. the Crawford-Ridgepole Trail enters left from Mt. Webster, and the two trails coincide, passing a spur path that branches left, ascends a ladder, and climbs about 100 yd. through a boulder cave to the cliff-top viewpoint. After climbing a set of steps, the trails soon reach a junction where the Crawford-Ridgepole Trail diverges right for Mt. Percival. Here the Mount Morgan Trail leads left to the cliff-top viewpoint; partway along, a short spur leaves it on the right and runs to the true summit.

Mount Morgan Trail (USGS Squam Range quad)
Distance from NH 113 (800')

> *to* Mt. Morgan summit (2220'): 2.1 mi. (3.4 km.), 1450 ft., 1 hr. 30 min.

Old Highway

This trail, used for access to the lower ends of the Prescott Trail and Old Mountain Road, continues straight where NH 113 turns right 1.3 mi. northeast of Holderness and 0.2 mi. beyond a gravel pit where parking is available on the shoulder of NH 113. A century ago, the old road followed by this trail was part of the main highway between Holderness and Center Sandwich. It leaves NH 113 at the same point as a paved driveway. The Prescott Trail diverges left (north) at the height-of-land at 0.9 mi., 100 yd. beyond the Prescott Cemetery, and the Old Mountain Road diverges left at an acute angle at 1.1 mi. and runs near the edge of a large field. The Old Highway continues past a sugarhouse to a locked gate at the edge of a paved road that runs to NH 113 (no parking here).

Old Highway (USGS Squam Range and Holderness quads)
Distances from NH 113 (585')

> *to* Prescott Trail (900'): 0.9 mi., 300 ft., 35 min.

to paved road (750'): 1.4 mi. (2.2 km.), 300 ft. (rev. 150 ft.), 50 min.

Prescott Trail

This trail to Mt. Livermore (1500 ft.) turns left off the Old Highway at the height-of-land 0.9 mi. from NH 113, 100 yd. beyond the Prescott cemetery. It follows a logging road for 0.2 mi., turns sharp left off it and ascends gradually, then turns right uphill at 0.3 mi. The trail now climbs by switchbacks over a low ridge and descends gradually to the Crawford-Ridgepole Trail, which enters left at 1.0 mi. From this point the two trails ascend together via switchbacks. Just below the summit they turn sharp right and ascend steeply to the summit, where there is a view over Squam Lake.

Descending, the Crawford-Ridgepole Trail heading south and the Prescott Trail leave the summit together, turn sharp right (west) and descend along an old stone wall, then turn left onto an old bridle trail. After 0.4 mi. the Crawford-Ridgepole Trail leaves on the right.

Prescott Trail (USGS Squam Range quad)
Distances from Old Highway Trail (900')

- *to* Crawford-Ridgepole Trail (1200'): 1.0 mi., 300 ft., 40 min.
- *to* summit of Mt. Livermore (1500'): 1.4 mi. (2.2 km.), 600 ft., 1 hr.

Distance from NH 113 (585')

- *for* loop over Mt. Livermore (1500') via Old Highway, Prescott Trail, Crawford-Ridgepole Trail, Old Mountain Road, and Old Highway: 4.5 mi. (7.2 km.), 1000 ft., 2 hr. 45 min.

Old Mountain Road

This trail leaves the Old Highway Trail 1.1 mi. from its western end at NH 113, and ascends on an old road to the Crawford-Ridgepole Trail at the low point between Mt. Livermore and Mt. Webster. The old road continues on from here descending to the north, but this section is not an official trail.

Old Mountain Road (USGS Squam Range quad)
Distance from Old Highway (800')

>   *to* Crawford-Ridgepole Trail (1300'): 0.7 mi. (1.1 km.), 500 ft., 35 min.

Rattlesnake Paths

The *Old Bridle Path* is the easiest route to the West Rattlesnake outlooks. A very short and easy route to an excellent viewpoint, it receives very heavy use. It leaves NH 113 between Center Sandwich and Holderness, 0.5 mi. northeast of the junction with Pinehurst Rd. (the road to Rockywold and Deephaven camps) and about 70 yd. southwest of the entrance to the Mount Morgan Trail (where there is a small parking area). It follows an old cart road 0.9 mi. (40 min.) to the cliffs near the summit. Descending, this trail begins slightly northwest of the summit cliffs.

The *Ramsey Trail* is a much steeper route to West Rattlesnake. It leaves Pinehurst Rd. 0.7 mi. from NH 113 and 90 yd. east of the entrance to Rockywold and Deephaven camps, along with the Undercut Trail (sign), which has another entrance almost opposite the camp entrance. In 0.1 mi. there is a crossroads, where the Ramsey Trail takes a sharp right and climbs steeply 0.4 mi. to a point just north of the summit cliffs, joining the Old Bridle Path (no sign at top). Left at the crossroads is the alternate route 0.1 mi. to Pinehurst Rd.; the *Undercut Trail* continues straight ahead from the crossroads and runs 0.9 mi. (follow markings very carefully) to NH 113 0.1 mi. west of the Old Bridle Path parking area.

The *Pasture Trail* leads to West Rattlesnake from Pinehurst Rd. 0.9 mi. from NH 113. Park in the small area to the right before the first gate. The trailhead is 100 yd. east of the gate. Start on a road to the left, then turn right past Pinehurst Farm buildings. At 0.2 mi. the East Rattlesnake and Five Finger Point trails diverge right, and in 15 yd. the Pasture Trail bears left where the Col Trail continues straight ahead. The cliffs are reached at 0.6 mi. from the gate after a moderate ascent.

The *Col Trail* continues straight where the Pasture Trail bears left 0.2 mi. from the gate on Pinehurst Rd. In 0.3 mi. it joins the Ridge Trail, follows it right for 30 yd., then turns left (sign, "Saddle"), passes over the height-of-land, and descends (follow with care) to the edge of a beaver swamp. It enters an old road and turns left, then bears right and reaches a gravel road 0.7 mi. from the Ridge Trail junction. This trailhead is reached in 0.2 mi. from NH 113 at a point 0.3 mi. east of the Holderness-Sandwich town line.

The *Ridge Trail* connects West and East Rattlesnake. It begins just northeast of the cliffs of West Rattlesnake and descends gradually. At 0.4 mi. the Col Trail comes in from the right, and just beyond leaves again to the left. The Ridge Trail ascends, and the East Rattlesnake Trail enters right at 0.8 mi. The Ridge Trail reaches the outlook ledge at 0.9 mi. and continues to the summit and the Butterworth Trail at 1.0 mi.

The *East Rattlesnake Trail* branches right from the Pasture Trail 0.2 mi. from the gate. In 25 yd. the Five Finger Point Trail continues straight ahead. The East Rattlesnake Trail turns left and ascends steadily 0.4 mi. to the Ridge Trail, 0.1 mi. west of the East Rattlesnake outlook. The *Five Finger Point Trail* runs on a slight downgrade for 0.7 mi. to a loop path 1.3 mi. long that circles around the edge of Five Finger Point, with several interesting viewpoints and attractive small beaches where swimming is permitted (no lifeguards).

The *Butterworth Trail* leads to East Rattlesnake from Metcalf Rd., which leaves NH 113 0.7 mi. east of the Holderness-Sandwich town line. The trail leaves Metcalf Rd. on the right 0.5 mi. from NH 113 and climbs moderately 0.7 mi. to the summit. The East Rattlesnake viewpoint is 0.1 mi. farther via the Ridge Trail.

RED HILL

Red Hill (2030 ft.) and its ledgy northern spur, Eagle Cliff (1410 ft.), rise between Squam Lake and Lake Winnipesaukee. The summit of Red Hill (which has a fire tower) offers excellent views in all directions for very modest effort; Eagle Cliff offers interesting but much less extensive views and a somewhat more challenging trail to ascend.

Red Hill Trail

In Center Harbor at the junction of NH 25 and NH 25B, go northwest on Bean Rd. for 1.4 mi., turn right (east) and follow Sibley Rd. (sign for fire lookout) for 1.1 mi., then turn left and continue 0.1 mi. and park on the side of the road. The trail, an old jeep road, soon makes a sharp right turn uphill and crosses a brook. At 0.4 mi. it swings left around a cellar hole and enters the old firewarden's road to the summit. At 1.0 mi. there is a piped spring left. The Eagle Cliff Trail enters on the left just before the fire tower and firewarden's cabin on the summit of Red Hill.

Red Hill Trail (USGS Center Sandwich and Center Harbor quads)
Distance from parking area (680')

> *to* Red Hill summit (2030'): 1.7 mi. (2.7 km.), 1350 ft., 1 hr. 30 min.

Eagle Cliff Trail

This trail ascends Red Hill via Eagle Cliff, which has fine views but may be hazardous in wet or icy conditions. From the junction of NH 25 and NH 25B in Center Harbor, follow Bean Rd. for 5.2 mi. to a turnout at the edge of Squam Lake, about 0.3 mi. north of the Moultonborough-Sandwich town line. The trail is well marked but there is no trail sign at the beginning, which is difficult to see from the road: it is a path through a ditch in a thicket, 200 yd. south of the lakeside turnout, 50 yd. north of a high hedge, and directly opposite a "Traffic Turning and Entering" sign.

The trail climbs through an overgrown field and enters the woods. It ascends on a well-beaten path, becoming steep and rough as it gets well up on the ledge, and reaches the main viewpoint on Eagle Cliff at 0.6 mi. From the upper ledge, the trail enters the woods and continues along the ridge toward the fire tower on Red Hill. It crosses a knoll and descends sharply to a small pass at 1.0 mi., where the Teedie Trail enters right.

Teedie Trail. This path descends in 0.6 mi. to a gravel driveway next to a private tennis court on Bean Rd. at the Moultonborough-Sandwich town line, about 0.3 mi. south of the beginning of the Eagle Cliff Trail. It should be considered as a way of avoiding the descent over the Eagle Cliff ledges in adverse conditions.

The Eagle Cliff Trail crosses another knoll and ascends steadily through a mixture of young growth in cutover areas and mature woods, and about a quarter-mile below the summit it enters an area burned over by a fire set by an arsonist in April 1990. It finally levels out and meets the Red Hill Trail just below the summit of Red Hill. Descending, it diverges right from the Red Hill Trail (jeep road) just below the firewarden's cabin (sign).

Eagle Cliff Trail (USGS Center Sandwich quad)
Distances from Bean Rd. (580')

  to Eagle Cliff viewpoint (1270'): 0.6 mi., 700 ft., 40 min.

  to Red Hill fire tower (2030'): 2.6 mi. (4.1 km.), 1650 ft. (rev. 200 ft.), 2 hr. 10 min.

OSSIPEE MOUNTAINS

These mountains, located just northeast of Lake Winnipesaukee, occupy a nearly circular tract about 9 mi. in diameter. They are the result of an unusual geological formation called a ring dike, where magma wells up into a circular fracture in the earth's crust. The range shelters beautiful Dan Hole Pond on its southeast edge. Mt. Shaw (2990 ft.), the highest of the Ossipees, affords excellent views toward the White Mtns. and other mountains to the east from its cleared summit; it can be ascended by a trail from NH 171. A southern shoulder called Black Snout (2803 ft.) offers excellent views to the south and west, particularly over Lake Winnipesaukee. Bald Knob (1801 ft.) is a rocky promontory that also offers excellent views across Lake Winnipesaukee to the mountains beyond. See the USGS Melvin Village quadrangle, and for other parts of the Ossipee Range the Tuftonboro, Ossipee Lake, and Tamworth quadrangles, which corner near the center of the Ossipee Mtns. The Melvin Village and Tamworth quadrangles show the locations of many of the old carriage roads of the Plant Estate, which is now operated as a commercial tourist attraction called Castle in the Clouds. These old roads are used for horseback riding in summer and snowmobiling in winter. There are no regularly maintained hiking trails on the range, but the two trails described below can be followed fairly well by experienced, observant hikers. Other paths have been cut from time to time and may be encountered, but these are not usually marked and cleared well enough to be followed by hikers who are not familiar with them.

Mount Shaw Trail

This trail (no sign) begins as a woods road on the north side of NH 171, 3.9 mi. east of the junction of NH 109 and NH 171, 3.8 mi. west of Tuftonboro, and 9.7 mi. west of the junction of NH 171 and NH 28 in Ossipee. The trailhead is just east of the bridge over Fields Brook and nearly opposite Sodom Rd. (the road from NH 171 to Melvin Village). The trail is fairly easy to follow, but since it is not officially maintained it cannot be recommended for inexperienced hikers. It must be followed very carefully because it is blazed irregularly in dark red, which is sometimes difficult to see. In addition, it is overgrown in places and has suffered much blowdown recently, which may cause some trail-finding problems from time to time.

The trail follows the dirt road north 0.3 mi. to a hemlock grove (left), where there is a cascade on the left. The trail detours above the stream around a washout, then bears left and follows the stream. It reaches a fork at 0.7 mi., where it bears right, then keeps right after passing through an old logging camp clearing. At 0.9 mi. it bears left on an old road and goes through a deep cut, then bears right. The trail again bears left at 1.1 mi., then leaves the road on the right at 1.4 mi. It follows the east bank of Fields Brook and then crosses it, and bears right at a cairn. It recrosses to the east bank at 1.8 mi. and climbs steeply out of the ravine to join an old carriage road at 2.5 mi., where it turns right and passes a side trail at 2.7 mi. that leads right 0.3 mi. to an open knob with a good view out over Lake Winnipesaukee to the west and south. (This knob is often referred to as Black Snout, but it is not the peak labeled Black Snout Mtn. on maps.) The Mount Shaw Trail continues on the carriage road and reaches the summit at 3.5 mi., where there are excellent views especially to the north and east.

Mount Shaw Trail (USGS Melvin Village quad)

Distance from NH 171 (680')

> *to* Mt. Shaw summit (2990'): 3.5 mi. (5.6 km.), 2300 ft., 2 hr. 50 min.

Bald Knob Trail

This trail (no sign) begins on NH 171 at the Moultonborough-Tuftonboro town line, about 0.6 mi. west of the Mt. Shaw trailhead at the Fields Brook bridge. There may or may not be trail signs; No Trespassing signs traditionally have not been intended to keep hikers out, and this path receives fairly heavy use. Follow the dirt road into the overgrown gravel pit. This is the most difficult part of the trail to follow; you may have to search around to find it. In general one should bear left at junctions, and particularly avoid a footpath to the right at a fork, taking the dirt road that bears left instead. However, once out of the gravel pit and into the woods, the trail is very well beaten and easy to follow.

The trail ascends steeply over rough and eroded terrain, reaching the first ledge at 0.7 mi. It passes more ledges with excellent vistas and then goes into the woods again, runs through an area with a number of boulders, and heads generally north, ascending at a less steep grade. The trail then turns west, scrambles up through a wide V in the rock, and enters an old carriage road turnaround before reaching Bald Knob with its fine views of Lake Winnipesaukee.

It is possible to follow old carriage roads all the way from Bald Knob to the Mount Shaw Trail; the trip is an easy woods walk with no views and few interesting features, but it does make a fairly long loop hike possible. Continuing from the summit turnaround, the road runs to a junction with another road at a hairpin turn on the latter; take the right (uphill) branch. The road crosses a brook on a bridge at 2.4 mi. and enters a T intersection at 3.7 mi.; take the road to the right here. The Mount Shaw Trail enters this road at 4.7 mi., 0.2 mi. below the spur road to Black Snout and 1.0 mi. below the summit of Mt. Shaw.

Bald Knob Trail (USGS Melvin Village quad)

Distances from NH 171 (700')

to Bald Knob (1801'): 1.1 mi. (1.7 km.), 1100 ft., 1 hr. 5 min.

to Mt. Shaw (2990') via carriage roads: 6.8 mi. (10.9 km.), 2500 ft., 4 hr. 40 min.

THE BELKNAP RANGE AND MT. MAJOR

The Belknap Mtns. are a prominent range west of Lake Winnipesaukee in the towns of Gilford, Gilmanton, and Alton. The range and the county in which it rises were named for Jeremy Belknap (1744–1796), author of the first comprehensive history of New Hampshire and a member of one of the early (1784) scientific expeditions to Mt. Washington (though Belknap himself did not reach the summit). The principal peaks on the main ridge, from north to south, are Mt. Rowe (1690 ft.), Gunstock Mtn. (2250 ft.), Belknap Mtn. (2382 ft.), and Piper Mtn. (2044 ft.). A fire tower on Belknap and the cleared summit of Gunstock, as well as numerous scattered ledges on all the peaks, provide fine views of Lake Winnipesaukee, the Ossipee and Sandwich ranges, and Mt. Washington. Principal trailheads are located at the Gunstock Recreation Area (east side) and Belknap Carriage Rd. (west side). The East Gilford Trail also ascends from the east. Paths along the ridge connect all four summits. Mt. Major (1786 ft.), which has excellent views over Lake Winnipesaukee, is located in Alton, east of the main Belknap Mtns. A long, lumpy ridge runs east from Belknap Mtn. to Mt. Major, consisting of Straightback Mtn. (1910 ft.) and several other humps that are officially nameless but have been given local names by the Boy Scouts: Mt. Klem (2001 ft.), Mt. Mack (1945 ft.), and Mt. Anna (1670 ft.). The jewel of this range is Round Pond, a beautiful and secluded mountain pond lying at the foot of Mt. Klem, just south of the main ridgecrest, at an elevation of 1652 ft. Refer to the USGS West Alton and Laconia quadrangles.

Public and quasi-public organizations own most of the peaks and much of the slopes of the Belknap Mtns. In general, camping and fires are prohibited in this area. The public ownership includes Belknap County (the Gunstock Recreation Area), the state of New Hampshire (Belknap Mountain State Forest), and the town of Gilford. The Griswold Hidden Valley Scout Reservation, owned by the Daniel Webster Council Boy Scouts of America, includes much of the land to the south of the eastern ridge and a considerable portion of the ridge itself, including most of Round Pond (the western shore is part of Belknap Mountain State Forest) and Mts. Klem, Mack, and Anna. A major network of trails has been developed in this reservation, of which the ones on and near the ridgecrest, described below, are open to public use. The trails near the main camp area are not open to the general public without advance permission. A volunteer organization, the Belknap Range Trail Tenders (BRATTs), has recently been established to assume primary responsibility for the maintenance of trails on the Belknap Range; for information on trail maintenance activities contact Hal Graham, 1204 New Hampton Rd., Sanbornton, NH 03268 (603-286-3506).

The Gunstock Recreation Area is a four-season recreation area off NH 11A, operated by Belknap County. It includes a major downhill ski area located on Mt. Rowe and Gunstock Mtn. and a large campground. Ellacoya State Beach on Lake Winnipesaukee is nearby. The chairlift on Gunstock Mtn. operates on weekends and holidays in summer. The ski trails can be used to ascend Gunstock Mtn. and Mt. Rowe, and there is also an extensive network of cross-country ski trails, many of which are available as multi-use trails during the non-winter months. A trail map is available at the information center.

The Belknap Carriage Rd., which provides access to all the trails on the west side of the Belknap Range, is reached by leaving NH 11A at Gilford village and following Belknap Mountain Rd. south, bearing left at 0.8 mi. and right at 1.4 mi. At 2.4 mi. the Belknap Carriage Rd. forks left and leads in 1.5 mi. to a parking area. Various relatively easy loop hikes may be made from this trailhead. For the Green, Red, and Blue trails, follow the road up to the firewarden's garage (signs on wall). The White Trail is a short distance down the road.

Blue Trail

This trail runs from the Belknap Carriage Rd. to the summit of Belknap Mtn. It follows the extension of the carriage road past the garage and the junctions with the Red and Green trails, descends slightly to cross a brook, then diverges right and climbs to the Belknap-Gunstock col at 0.6 mi. Here the orange-blazed Overlook Trail continues straight and the white-blazed Saddle Trail turns left for Gunstock Mtn. The Blue Trail, now coinciding with the Belknap Range Trail, turns right and climbs, passing an outlook to Gunstock Mtn. at 0.7 mi. and an excellent outlook across Lake Winnipesaukee to the Sandwich Range (and Mt. Washington in clear weather) at 0.8 mi., and continues to the summit.

Blue Trail (USGS Laconia and West Alton quads)
Distances from Belknap Carriage Rd. parking area (1670')

   to Belknap-Gunstock col (2000'): 0.6 mi., 350 ft., 30 min.

   to Belknap Mtn. summit (2382'): 1.1 mi., 700 ft., 55 min.

Green Trail

The Green Trail, which starts at the end of the Belknap Carriage Rd., is the shortest route to Belknap Mtn. but is rather steep with ledges that are slippery when wet, particularly when descending. It leaves the carriage road extension behind the garage and ascends on a service road, crossing a telephone line. It continues to climb, passes a well, and reaches the tower at the summit.

Green Trail (USGS Laconia and West Alton quads)
Distance from Belknap Carriage Rd. parking area (1670')

   to Belknap Mtn. summit (2382'): 0.7 mi. (1.1 km.), 700 ft., 40 min.

Red Trail

This trail, less steep and more scenic than the Green Trail but some-what rough in parts, climbs from the Belknap Carriage Rd. to the summit of Belknap Mtn. It leaves the carriage road extension just beyond the Green Trail junction, climbs past a good outlook to the west at 0.5 mi., and continues to the summit.

Red Trail (USGS Laconia and West Alton quads)
Distance from Belknap Carriage Rd. parking area (1670')

   to Belknap Mtn. summit (2382'): 0.8 mi. (1.3 km.), 700 ft., 45 min.

White Trail

This white-blazed trail ascends to the summit of Belknap Mtn. via the Belknap-Piper col. It begins on the Belknap Carriage Rd. 0.1 mi. below the parking area, just below the highest bridge. It ascends to the Belknap-Piper col at 0.4 mi., where the Old Piper Trail goes right to

Piper Mtn. The White Trail turns left here and scrambles up a ledge to an outlook south and west. In a short distance a side trail runs right 30 yd. to an excellent outlook to the east. The White Trail continues to climb to the junction with the East Gilford Trail, which enters from the right on the ledges. The two trails, which also coincide with the Belknap Range Trail in this segment, ascend together to the summit and its fire tower.

White Trail (USGS Laconia and West Alton quads)

Distance from Belknap Carriage Rd. parking area (1670')

   to Belknap Mtn. summit (2382'): 1.1 mi. (1.7 km.), 750 ft., 55 min.

Old Piper Trail

This trail, currently faintly blazed in blue but slated to be reblazed in orange, leaves the White Trail in the Belknap-Piper col. In 30 yd. it passes a junction on the left with the blue-blazed Piper Link, which leads to the Belknap Range Trail at the bottom of the Boulder Trail. It climbs, passing two sections where alternate routes briefly diverge and then rejoin, and the well-defined trail ends at 0.4 mi. at a rocky knob in the Piper Mtn. blueberry fields where a rock throne has been constructed on top of the ledge. The true summit of Piper Mtn. is 0.2 mi. farther south and can be reached by beaten paths starting at a large cairn at the far end of the throne-capped ledge. The footway is somewhat difficult to follow, but the route is fairly obvious in clear weather; in fog, however, this could be an extremely confusing area, very easy to get lost in.

Old Piper Trail (USGS Laconia quad)

Distance from Belknap-Piper col (1800')

   to throne on false summit of Piper Mtn. (2030'): 0.4 mi. (0.7 km.), 250 ft., 20 min.

Ridge Trail

This white-blazed trail, a segment of the Belknap Range Trail, runs from the main parking lot at the Gunstock Recreation Area to the summit of Mt. Rowe, then continues along the ridge to the summit of Gunstock Mtn. The first part was formerly known as the Try-Me Trail. It starts on a gated paved road 100 yd. north of the main base lodge and follows the road uphill. At 0.3 mi. it turns left onto a gravel service road and climbs fairly steeply to a communications tower at 0.8 mi., near the flat summit of Mt. Rowe. The trail continues to the left on a woods road along the nearly level ridge with excellent views. Take care to stay on the blazed route, avoiding side roads and beaten paths. Shortly after some smooth ledges the trail turns left off the road, runs into a small ravine, and then climbs up into blueberry patches. It comes within sight of a ski trail and turns right, staying to the right of (above) the ski trail as it climbs through patches of woods and open places. At 1.7 mi. it joins another road (sign). Turn left and cross over snowmaking pipes to a ski trail, then turn right up the ski trail (which is also the Flintlock Trail) on a service road, continuing on the ski trail when the road swings off to the left. The ski trail curves around to the left and climbs to the summit.

Ridge Trail (USGS Laconia and West Alton quads)

Distances from Gunstock Recreation Area parking lot (930')

- *to* summit of Mt. Rowe (1690'): 0.8 mi., 750 ft., 45 min.
- *to* summit of Gunstock Mtn. (2250'): 2.4 mi. (3.9 km.), 1550 ft., 2 hr.

Flintlock Trail

This trail uses ski trails to ascend Gunstock Mtn. from the Gunstock Recreation Area main parking lot. Start by aiming for a large stone fireplace on the lower part of the slopes. This trail (no sign) follows a service road that curves upward to the right and crosses under the chairlift. The Ridge Trail enters from the right at 1.0 mi., and the trails coincide to the summit of Gunstock Mtn., always keeping to the right on ski trails. Descending, keep to the left edge of the ski trails until the Ridge Trail enters (sign), then bear right on the service road.

Flintlock Trail (USGS Laconia and West Alton quads)

Distance from Gunstock Recreation Area parking area (930')

> *to* summit of Gunstock Mtn. (2250'): 1.7 mi. (2.7 km.), 1300 ft., 1 hr. 30 min.

Brook Trail

This trail, blazed in yellow, is the most direct hiking trail from the Gunstock Recreation Area to the summit of Gunstock Mtn. It is rather steep and rough in places. Start by aiming for a large stone fireplace on the lower part of the slopes. This trail (sign) goes to the right of the fireplace and follows the left edge of a ski trail for about 50 yd., then enters the woods and crosses a brook, follows the bank of the brook, and crosses another ski trail. After re-entering the woods, it crosses and quickly recrosses a brook, and soon begins to climb away from the brook as it ascends in the valley. At 0.5 mi. it crosses another ski trail and climbs, steeply at times, until it meets a stone wall, turns left along it, and soon reaches another ski trail at 1.2 mi. It crosses this trail and ascends along the left edge to the junction with yet another ski trail, which it immediately crosses, entering the woods over snowmaking pipes. It then climbs to a junction with the Saddle Trail on the ridgecrest at 1.5 mi., where it turns right. From here it is a segment of the Belknap Range Trail. The trail scrambles up a short steep section, then turns left and climbs more gradually, passing two memorial stones and a picnic table and soon reaching the summit.

Brook Trail (USGS Laconia and West Alton quads)

Distance from Gunstock Recreation Area parking area (930')

> *to* summit of Gunstock Mtn. (2250'): 1.7 mi. (2.7 km.), 1300 ft., 1 hr. 30 min.

Saddle Trail

This very short white-blazed trail, also a segment in the Belknap Range Trail, connects the col between Belknap Mtn. and Gunstock Mtn. with the Brook Trail. Leaving the junction with the Overlook Trail and the Blue Trail in the col, it crosses the flat sag and climbs moderately to the junction where the Brook Trail enters on the right.

Saddle Trail (USGS Laconia quad)

Distance from Belknap-Gunstock col (2000')

   to Brook Trail junction (2100'): 0.1 mi. (0.2 km.), 100 ft., 5 min.

Round Pond Trail

This trail is a multi-use trail of the Gunstock Recreation Area trail system, running from the main ski area parking lot to Round Pond. In addition to providing access to Round Pond from the recreation area, it connects with the Overlook Trail, the East Gilford Trail, and the Belknap Range Trail (both at the beginning and near Round Pond), making possible a great variety of loop hikes from several trailheads.

There are two ways of starting out from the ski area parking lot. One route follows the access road back past the last of the maintenance buildings, then turns right on the Cobble Mountain Trail (#5). After 70 yd. turn right onto the Maple Trail (#9). After 0.3 mi. turn right at a T intersection for 50 yd., then turn sharp left at the fork where the other access route bears right. The second access route can be found by passing through a gate under a hanging sign ("Cobble Mountain Stables"), then going to the left of the base building of the Pistol chairlift and following a woods road signed "Connector" (#15). In 0.3 mi. from the gate with the hanging sign, this trail reaches the fork (its first significant junction) and turns sharp right where the first route bears left.

The trail, still a well-defined woods road, climbs to the top of a rise where it crosses a stone wall, bears right uphill on the better road at a fork, and crosses another stone wall. At 0.9 mi. the Oak Trail (#7) diverges right. At 1.0 mi. the woods road turns sharp left at the edge of a small field; it is possible (and easier, though this is not the signed route) to continue straight along the edge of the field and pick up the continuation of this trail—the other (southern) end of the Oak Trail (#7)—next to a bridge over a small brook. The Maple Trail continues along the road about 100 yd. to a T intersection, where another trail (#8) enters on the left and continues across the field to the bridge, where it meets the Oak Trail (#7). In the opposite direction, you have the option of following the edge of the field to the Maple Trail (#9) at its sharp turn, or crossing the field to the other trail (#8), then immediately turning left on the Maple Trail (#9).

From the field, the Round Pond Trail follows the Oak Trail (#7) across the bridge and into the woods, then 30 yd. from the bridge it diverges left onto a footpath (sign). From this point it is marked mostly by black diamonds inscribed "B20." It crosses a stone wall, a small brook, a larger brook with a plank bridge at 1.4 mi., and another small brook. It then enters an old woods road and follows it to the right, then turns left off the end of the road just as it reaches the edge of a swamp. It climbs rather steeply for a short distance, then levels off and reaches the East Gilford Trail at 1.8 mi. Here it turns right and coincides with the East Gilford Trail for 0.3 mi., then leaves it on the left (sign) and runs with minor ups and downs to a woods road at 2.3 mi. It follows this woods road to the left across a brook, and 20 yd. past the brook it turns sharp right on another woods road. (By continuing straight ahead on the first woods road, one can reach the East Gilford Trail in 0.6 mi. at the fork 0.4 mi. from its trailhead.) At 3.0 mi., just before the Round Pond Trail reaches the height-of-land, the blue-blazed Belknap Range Trail enters on the right and diverges on the left 30 yd. farther on. The Round Pond Trail then descends moderately to a beautiful secluded spot on the shore of Round Pond.

Round Pond Trail (USGS West Alton quad)

Distances from Gunstock Recreation Area parking lot (930')

- *to* northern junction with Oak Trail #7 (1100'): 0.9 mi., 200 ft., 35 min.

- *to* lower junction with East Gilford Trail (1200'): 1.8 mi., 400 ft., 1 hr. 5 min.

- *to* Belknap Range Trail (1680'): 3.0 mi., 1000 ft., 2 hr.

- *to* Round Pond (1652'): 3.1 mi. (5.4 km.), 1000 ft., 2 hr. 5 min.

Overlook Trail

This new trail, blazed in orange, connects the main parking lot at the Gunstock Recreation Area with the col between Belknap Mtn. and Gunstock Mtn., providing a convenient route to either peak and offering a fine viewpoint along the way. It is also the easiest and most convenient route for ascending either mountain in winter (when the Belknap Carriage Rd. is not open), since it has easier grades than the Brook Trail and does not cross any downhill ski trails. It was opened in November 1998, carefully located to avoid as much as possible steep areas that are vulnerable to damage by erosion.

It leaves the main parking area by following the Round Pond Trail (#9, see above), with which it coincides to the first (northern) junction with the Oak Trail (#7) at 0.9 mi. Here it turns right onto the Oak Trail (#7) and follows this trail for 0.3 mi. to a point just past a hairpin turn. Here the Overlook Trail diverges right, immediately descends across a branch of Poorfarm Brook, and begins to climb. Constantly winding about to avoid any steep grades, it ascends to the upper edge of a steep slope and, at 1.7 mi. from the parking area, reaches open ledges covered with low juniper bushes where there is a fine outlook to the east across the valley. The trail re-enters the woods, descends through a dip, and resumes the climb. At 2.1 mi. it crosses a small brook that falls in tiny needles of water over a five-foot vertical ledge to the left. After crossing more small brooks the grade becomes easier, then steeper again as the trail enters the main ravine below the ridgecrest. At 2.9 mi. it reaches the col between Belknap Mtn. and Gunstock Mtn. For Gunstock Mtn. turn right on the white-blazed Saddle Trail to the yellow-blazed Brook Trail. For Belknap Mtn. turn left on the blue-blazed Blue Trail. Straight ahead is the Blue Trail to the upper end of the Belknap Carriage Rd.

Overlook Trail (USGS West Alton quad)

Distances from Gunstock Recreation Area parking area (930')

- *to* Oak Trail (#7) junction (1100'): 0.9 mi., 200 ft., 35 min.

- *to* divergence from Oak Trail (1150'): 1.2 mi., 250 ft., 45 min.

- *to* overlook (1560'): 1.7 mi., 650 ft., 1 hr. 10 min.

- *to* Belknap Mtn.–Gunstock Mtn. col (2000'): 2.9 mi. (4.7 km.), 1100 ft., 2 hr.

- *to* Belknap Mtn. summit (2382') via Blue Trail: 3.4 mi. (5.5 km.), 1500 ft., 2 hr. 25 min.

- *to* Gunstock Mtn. summit (2250') via Saddle Trail and Brook Trail: 3.3 mi. (5.3 km.), 1350 ft., 2 hr. 20 min.

East Gilford Trail

This trail, perhaps the most attractive on the Belknap Range, is also sometimes referred to as the Yellow Trail since it has yellow blazes. To reach it, turn right off NH 11A at a point 1.7 mi. south of the Gunstock Recreation Area road onto Bickford Rd., then turn left on Wood Rd. and park near the junction (or—as is recommended by the Gilford police—at the bridge across the small brook in the sag on Bickford Rd.). Do not under any circumstances park near the house at the end of Wood Rd.

The trail (sign) follows a cart track that diverges left at a telephone pole before reaching the white house at the end of the road. It circles around to the right and bears right at a fork at 0.4 mi. (The left branch here immediately crosses the brook and runs 0.6 mi. to a junction with the Round Pond Trail 0.8 mi. below Round Pond.) At 0.5 mi. the multi-use Round Pond Trail (marked B20) from the Gunstock Recreation Area to Round Pond enters on the right, and at 0.7 mi. it diverges on the left. The trail soon begins to climb more steeply, and at 1.1 mi. it passes to the left of an interesting rock formation where nearly perfectly rectangular blocks of rock have been riven from a ledge by frost action. The trail winds back and forth, angling up the ledgy face of the mountain, and views begin to appear. At 1.6 mi., just above an excellent outlook over Lake Winnipesaukee, the blue-blazed Boulder Trail (part of the Belknap Range Trail) enters on the left (sign). Now coinciding with the Belknap Range Trail, the East Gilford Trail continues across ledges and through patches of woods at a moderate grade and joins the White Trail, which enters from the left at 1.9 mi. The two trails coincide, passing a communications shed and tower and reaching the summit at 2.1 mi.

East Gilford Trail (USGS West Alton quad)
Distances from junction of Bickford Rd. and Wood Rd. (1070')

   to   junction with Boulder Trail (2100'): 1.6 mi., 1050 ft., 1 hr. 20 min.

   to   summit of Belknap Mtn. (2382'): 2.1 mi. (3.3 km.), 1300 ft., 1 hr. 40 min.

Piper Link

This trail links the col between Belknap Mtn. and Piper Mtn. with the lower end of the Boulder Trail (a part of the Belknap Range Trail), giving convenient access to the fine ledges on the east side of Mt. Belknap from the Belknap Carriage Rd. It leaves the Old Piper Trail 30 yd. south of its junction with the White Trail and descends to a small brook and crosses it, then descends fairly steeply on a rocky slope with loose footing, where the woods were severely damaged by the January 1998 ice storm. At 0.4 mi. it reaches the bottom of the descent and swings left uphill, and at 0.5 mi. it passes a ledge with a good view up to Piper Mtn. It now crosses a minor ridge and descends easily with occasional small ascents to a junction with the Belknap Range Trail at the foot of the segment called the Boulder Trail. This junction is well signed. Turn left uphill to ascend Belknap Mtn., or bear right for Round Pond, Mt. Major, or other objectives between those two places.

Piper Link (USGS Laconia and West Alton quads)
Distance from Belknap-Piper col (1800')

> *to* Boulder Trail junction (1550'): 1.0 mi. (1.6 km.), 100 ft. (rev. 350 ft.), 35 min.

Boulder Trail

This trail, a segment of the Belknap Range Trail, ascends the steep east ledges of Mt. Belknap. The trail footway is not well established in several places, and the markings must be looked for and followed with great care. Beginning where the Piper Link enters the Belknap Range Trail at the foot of the east ledges, it climbs over a slope of loose talus blocks and up ledges with partial but ever-improving views, meeting the East Gilford Trail (sign) just above an excellent outlook ledge on that trail. The two trails ascend together, soon joined by the White Trail, to the summit of Belknap Mtn.

Boulder Trail (USGS West Alton quad)
Distances from Piper Link junction (1550')

> *to* East Gilford Trail junction (2100'): 0.4 mi. (0.6 km.), 550 ft., 30 min.

> *to* summit of Belknap Mtn. (2382') via East Gilford Trail: 0.8 mi. (1.3 km.), 850 ft., 50 min.

Round Pond Woods Road

Although on private land and not a maintained trail, this clear, easily followed woods road is the shortest route to beautiful Round Pond. It also provides access to (or a convenient exit from) points on the ridge between Belknap Mtn. and Mt. Major. It begins on a side road, the middle of three roads (and the only one of the three not paved at the start) that turn right off NH 11A about 2.2 mi. south of the access road to the Gunstock Recreation Area and 0.4 mi. south of Bickford Rd. (the access road to the East Gilford Trail). The trailhead is in a small parking spot on the left where the woods road diverges from the side road 0.2 mi. from NH 11A.

The road soon reaches the lower edge of a field; there are views as the road passes the upper part of this field. At a fork at 0.4 mi., take the right branch that runs across the bottom of the upper field. (The left branch runs along the left edge of this field parallel to a stone wall and ends in 250 yd. at the top of the field, from which there are fine views to the north.) The road climbs at a moderate grade to the height-of-land at 1.0 mi., then continues with slight ups and downs to a junction at 1.2 mi. where the blue-blazed Belknap Range Trail (sign: "Mt. Belknap") enters on the right. The road continues as part of the Belknap Range Trail, extending almost to the summit of Mt. Mack.

Round Pond Woods Road (USGS West Alton quad)
Distance from side road off NH 11A (1200')

   to Belknap Range Trail (1670'): 1.2 mi. (1.9 km.), 500 ft., 50 min.

Mount Klem Loop

This trail runs from the shore of Round Pond to a point just east of the summit of Mt. Mack, missing the wooded, viewless summit of Mt. Klem by about 100 yd. and 50 ft. of elevation. It is a much longer and more strenuous but much more scenic alternative to the Belknap Range Trail between the two end points. It is marked with red wooden diamonds nailed to trees and is fairly easy to follow, although some care is needed, particularly in the open areas.

The northwestern trailhead is on the Belknap Range Trail, in the section where the trail is a woods road running near the edge of the pond, 0.1 mi. east of the point where the Belknap Range Trail enters the woods road and 0.1 mi. west of the Boy Scout camping area. At this junction it is marked only by two red wooden diamonds (no sign); the diamonds are facing toward a westbound hiker; eastbound, the trail diverges on the left just after the woods road begins to climb away from the edge of the pond. The southeastern trailhead, which is amply signed, is on a ledge just east of the summit of Mt. Mack.

Leaving the shore of Round Pond, the trail climbs steadily through a dense coniferous forest, then levels and passes through a small sag. It then climbs more easily, crossing a stone wall and ascending to a ledgy area where it swings to the left, descending slightly, then ascends slightly across another ledgy outcrop. It now descends slightly through a shallow, flat sag, and runs on contour as it curls around the north end of Mt. Klem somewhat below the true summit at 0.6 mi. At 0.8 mi. it passes a cleared outlook to the northeast and swings right, then runs almost level for some distance. Finally it begins to descend and crosses an open area with views at 1.0 mi. It descends across another ledgy spot with a view into a sag at 1.3 mi., then climbs up to a rocky knob, crosses a small dip, and climbs to its southeastern junction with the Belknap Range Trail near the summit of Mt. Mack.

Mount Klem Loop (USGS West Alton quad)
Distance from Round Pond (1652')

 to Mt. Mack (1945'): 1.6 mi. (2.5 km.), 550 ft., 1 hr. 5 min.

Mount Major Trail

Mt. Major offers views that are among the best in southern New Hampshire for the effort required, but the upper ledges are steep and dangerous in wet or icy conditions. These dangerous ledges and the easy accessibility of the mountain have combined to produce a number of serious injuries, particularly in late fall and winter when ice is present. In such conditions the unofficial alternative route mentioned below is probably safer, and it may also be a better choice for the descent at other times—as well as providing good views from the open west ridge that are not duplicated by the main trail.

This trail begins at a parking area (large sign) on NH 11, 4.2 mi. north of Alton Bay and 1.7 mi. north of the junction of NH 11 with NH 11D. The trail follows a lumber road west, ascending a steep, severely eroded section where several alternate roads diverge and rejoin; the road farthest to the right (ascending) offers slightly better footing than the others. At the top of this steep section, at 0.3 mi., the road becomes nearly level and smooth. At 0.7 mi. the Mt. Major Trail diverges sharp left on a path marked with dark-blue paint. It climbs steeply through second growth and over ledges, with some steep scrambles near the top. At several points there are one or more alternate paths, all of which rejoin and lead to the summit. The summit, with the ruins of a stone hut, is reached at 1.5 mi. This is also the eastern terminus of the Belknap Range Trail.

For the alternate route, continue on the lumber road past where the primary trail leaves it. There are several diverging roads along this route but none of them is nearly as clear and obvious as the correct route. At 1.2 mi. the road appears to end, but a lesser woods road bears right toward a small brook, crosses it, and continues to climb, with loose footing on some severely eroded sections. At 1.6 mi. it swings left away from the edge of the valley and climbs to the col between Mt. Major and Straightback Mtn. at 1.9 mi., where it meets the Belknap Range Trail. Here the two trails, coinciding, turn left and climb mostly over open ledges with good views to the summit at 2.4 mi. Descent by this route is made somewhat difficult by the fact that the path is not well marked on the ledges, but in clear weather the route—directly toward Straightback Mtn.—is fairly obvious, and the path becomes evident in the woods just above the trail junction in the col. Turn right onto the woods road here; the rest of the route is unmistakable.

Mount Major Trail (USGS West Alton quad)

Distances from NH 11 (650')

- *to* Mt. Major summit (1786') via primary route: 1.5 mi. (2.4 km.), 1150 ft., 1 hr. 20 min.

- *to* Mt. Major summit (1786') via alternate route: 2.4 mi. (3.8 km.), 1150 ft., 1 hr. 45 min.

- *to* starting point via complete loop: 3.9 mi. (6.2 km.), 1150 ft., 2 hr. 30 min.

Belknap Range Trail

This trail (at least in theory) extends from the Gunstock Recreation Area to the summit of Mt. Major, using all or part of several other trails along the way. Sections of this trail, even between Mt. Belknap and Mt. Major, have existed in some form for a number of years, but only very recently has it been possible for the average hiker to have any hope of following large segments of this route. Much of the trail between the Gunstock Recreation Area and Mt. Anna is easy to follow, and the rest requires only reasonable care. Between Mt. Anna and Mt. Major following some parts of this trail requires a substantial amount of care, though considering the constant improvement of this trail as a whole in the last few years, significant improvement in the less well-defined sections may be hoped for in the near future. In the next few years, also, the entire route may be uniformly blazed, possibly in white.

Leaving the Gunstock Recreation Area main parking lot, the Belknap Range Trail follows the Ridge Trail over Mt. Rowe to the summit of Gunstock Mtn. at 2.4 mi. It then descends on the Brook Trail and Saddle Trail to the Belknap-Gunstock col at 2.8 mi., and follows the Blue Trail to the summit of Belknap Mtn. at 3.3 mi. It then descends on the combined Boulder Trail, East Gilford Trail, and Old Piper Trail, following the Boulder Trail as the others diverge and becoming quite steep until it reaches the sag where the Piper Link enters on the right at 4.1 mi.

From here on, the Belknap Range Trail, which is mostly blazed in blue, no longer coincides with other trails. It climbs over several small humps and through the sags between them, then climbs with two short steep pitches up a larger hump. It then runs along the north side of the ridge with minor ups and downs, and meets the Round Pond Trail coming up from the left (north) at 4.9 mi. It turns right on this trail, then diverges left off it in 30 yd. (From this junction, the Round Pond Trail descends gradually 0.1 mi. to a secluded spot at the shore of the pond.) The Belknap Range Trail ascends easily over a knoll, descends and crosses a moist flat sag, and then, with the pond in sight on the right, swings left, climbing briefly to the Round Pond Woods Road at 5.2 mi. To the left it is 1.2 mi. to a side road 0.2 mi. from NH 11A. The Belknap Range Trail follows the road to the right, passing a side path on the right leading to the pond and then descending to the edge of the pond. The Mount Klem Loop, a longer and more scenic alternate route between Round Pond and Mt. Mack, diverges left at 5.4 mi., just after the road begins to climb gradually away from the pond. Then the road swings away from the pond and at 5.5 mi. enters a small clearing among the pines—an outpost campsite of the Hidden Valley Reservation. (To the right at this campsite, a trail marked by red wooden diamonds continues near the pond, crosses an inlet brook in 100 yd., and reaches a junction in another 100 yd. Here this trail continues straight ahead to Hidden Valley, while a branch trail turns left and climbs 0.2 mi. to rejoin the Belknap Range Trail 0.3 mi. above the campsite.)

From the campsite, the Belknap Range Trail continues straight ahead (away from the pond) on the woods road. At 5.8 mi. the branch trail enters on the right, and the Belknap Range Trail continues to climb, passing a ledge with a wide view south and west to the Uncanoonuc Mtns., Crotched Mtn., the Pack Monadnocks, and Monadnock at 6.0 mi. It crosses over the ledgy summit of Mt. Mack, passing a communications tower and an apparently defunct windmill, and reaches the junction with the Mount Klem Loop just beyond at 6.1 mi. From this junction the trail turns right but soon swings back to the left and descends at easy to moderate grades. In all it descends over 500 feet—the last part with several minor ups and downs—until it reaches its low point at a mossy brook at 6.8 mi. It begins to climb a bit, crossing a stone wall that is the Gilford-Gilmanton town line, and then climbs more seriously, although descending briefly at one point to cross a brook, to the flat ledgy summit of Mt. Anna, where views are restricted. At 7.5 mi., in the flat summit area, a trail junction is reached; the trails to the right and straight ahead descend toward Hidden Valley, while the Belknap Range Trail turns left and starts a mild descent.

At 7.6 mi. the trail reaches the top of a short steep, rocky pitch, then makes numerous small ascents and descents with occasional slightly obscure places. At 8.2 mi. it bears left at a small rock face, and at 8.4 mi. it enters an open ledgy area with views ahead to part of Straightback Mtn. and, higher up, back to Belknap Mtn. The general route across this area is obvious, but it is poorly marked; there is little problem in clear weather, but in fog it could be very difficult to cross this area correctly without following a compass course. The trail climbs to a point just north of the south summit of Straightback Mtn. at 8.7 mi., where it turns sharp left. The various ledges and open areas of this summit repay exploration. The trail now descends, mostly in the woods, often angling to the left. At 9.1 mi. it crosses a ledge with a glimpse of Lake Winnipesaukee, then descends again to the col between Straightback Mtn. and Mt. Major, reaching a trail junction just on the Mt. Major side of the col at 9.3 mi. The path on the left here is the alternate route of the Mount Major Trail, which descends to the parking lot on NH 11 in 1.9 mi. The Belknap Range Trail now ascends the ridge, soon coming into the open and following a poorly marked but fairly obvious route up to the summit of Mt. Major at 9.7 mi., where there are magnificent views and the remains of a stone hut.

Belknap Range Trail (USGS Laconia and West Alton quads)

Distances from Gunstock Recreation Area parking area (930')

- *to* summit of Gunstock Mtn. (2250'): 2.4 mi., 1550 ft. (rev. 200 ft.), 2 hr.

- *to* summit of Belknap Mtn. (2382'): 3.3 mi., 1950 ft. (rev. 250 ft.), 2 hr. 40 min.

- *to* Round Pond Trail junction (1680'): 4.9 mi., 2200 ft. (rev. 950 ft.), 3 hr. 35 min.

- *to* summit of Mt. Mack (1945'): 6.1 mi., 2550 ft. (rev. 100 ft.), 4 hr. 20 min.

- *to* summit of Mt. Anna (1670'): 7.5 mi., 3050 ft. (rev. 750 ft.), 5 hr. 15 min.

- *to* high point on Straightback Mtn. (1880'): 8.7 mi., 3450 ft. (rev. 200 ft.), 6 hr. 5 min.

- *to* summit of Mt. Major (1786'): 9.7 mi. (15.6 km.), 3650 ft. (rev. 300 ft.), 6 hr. 40 min.

DEVILS DEN MOUNTAIN

The summit of this small mountain (1110 ft.) in the town of New Durham is an interesting rock formation with an excellent view of the White Mtns. over Lake Winnipesaukee, with rugged Rattlesnake Island in the foreground. There is no official trail, but the mountain is easy to climb. From New Durham village, off NH 11, take the road to Powder Mill Fish Hatchery and Merrymeeting Lake to a junction where the pavement on the main road ends and North Shore Rd. (which is paved) enters on the right. Follow the dirt road ahead (which is too rough for most ordinary cars), bearing uphill to the right at a fork at 0.8 mi. The road continues at easy grades, then makes a fairly steep and rough descent into a dip where there is a beaver pond on the left at 1.3 mi. The road next ascends to a height-of-land at 1.5 mi., where a woods road turns left (faint arrow on a rock), runs past the end of a stone wall and swings right, then continues to the foot of the summit ledges at 1.8 mi. Here one can go straight up the rock face by means of a short crack with excellent hand- and footholds, or bear left and follow a beaten path that swings around the side of the ledge and climbs it from the back side over easy ledges. Note carefully the ascent route for use on the descent—there is a confusing network of beaten paths on the summit ledges.

Devils Den Mountain (USGS Wolfeboro and Alton quads)

Distance from road junction at northwest end of Merrymeeting Lake (690')

  to summit of Devils Den Mtn. (1110'): 1.9 mi. (3.0 km.), 600 ft. (rev. 150 ft.), 1 hr. 15 min.

Section 5

Southeastern New Hampshire

This section covers the southeastern portion of New Hampshire, extending from the seacoast to the first significant ranges of hills—the Pawtuckaway Mtns., which rise to just short of the 1000-foot level in Nottingham and Deerfield about 25 miles from the Atlantic Ocean, and the Blue Hills, which reach an elevation of 1400 feet in Strafford and Farmington about 30 miles inland.

New Hampshire's coastline totals only 18 miles—the least of any state that has a coastline at all—but it provides a fine variety of scenery and terrain, from rocky headlands to salt marshes to the fine harbor at the mouth of the Piscataqua River, shared between Portsmouth NH and Kittery ME. This harbor and other areas near the Piscataqua were the site of much of New Hampshire's early settlement, and of the renowned shipbuilding industry that developed at Portsmouth in early colonial times, which provided the central symbol of a ship under construction for the state flag. But the two most significant features of the New Hampshire seacoast area are not on the coastline itself: about ten miles out to sea the picturesque Isles of Shoals rise a few dozen feet above the weather-driven surf, while just a few miles inland lies what is perhaps the crown jewel of the area, the 4500-acre tidal estuary called Great Bay, which may well be the most important ecosystem in the state.

Behind the coastal area the land is only rarely flat, being mostly low rolling hills consisting largely of piles of gravel left behind by retreating glaciers. Many of the more prominent hills are drumlins, heaps of gravel usually about a mile long and a quarter-mile wide, oriented parallel to the track of the glacier in a northwest-southeast direction and rising 100 to 150 feet above the surrounding countryside. Perhaps the most prominent and accessible of these hills—as well as one of the most finely formed—is Stratham Hill in Stratham, south of Great Bay. Continuing inland, hills become higher, and some of them are formed by bedrock with occasional rocky outcrops. Eventually the first real ranges—the Pawtuckaways and the Blue Hills—are encountered.

Included in this section are the trail network on the Pawtuckaway Mtns. and near Pawtuckaway Lake in 5535-acre Pawtuckaway State Park, and a number of scattered hills and other natural features that offer interesting walks, including the Isles of Shoals, Odiorne Point State Park, Great Bay, Stratham Hill, Rock Rimmon Hill, Stonehouse Pond, Garrison Hill, Parker Mtn. and Blue Job Mtn. in the Blue Hills Range, and Teneriffe Mountain and Preserve.

Pawtuckaway State Park (cont.)

Teneriffe Mountain and Preserve

ISLES OF SHOALS

This small group of picturesquely rocky, windswept islands lies about ten miles southeast of Portsmouth Harbor, divided between New Hampshire and Maine. Though the islands are generally considered to amount to nine—Duck, Appledore, Smuttynose, Malaga, and Cedar in Maine, and Star, White, Seavey, and Lunging in New Hampshire—there are many other rocks and ledges, and White and Seavey Islands are joined at low tide. Appledore is the largest at 95 acres and rises over 60 ft. above mean sea level, making it also the loftiest of the Isles. Refer to the USGS Isles of Shoals quadrangle.

These islands have a history that is much greater than their small size might suggest, and that history and a general aura of romance have led to the publication of an unusual number of books about them (several of which are available at the Star Island bookstore). Although they had been sighted no later than 1603, it was probably Capt. John Smith's visit to the islands in 1614 that most effectively brought them to the attention of the British seafaring men as a potentially valuable base near highly productive fishing grounds. In early colonial times a very prosperous industry developed around the fisheries, and the Isles became particularly noted for the production of a premium grade of dried fish called dunfish. In 1767 the population of the village of Gosport on Star Island was reported as 284—a fairly large number of inhabitants on a 40-acre island. At the time of the Revolutionary War, however, the islanders were forcibly evacuated because their suspected sympathy with the British could not be tolerated in such a potentially strategic location; most did not return after the war, and the fishing industry slowly declined.

But the Isles were merely entering another era. Thomas Laighton arrived on White Island in 1839 with his family to operate the lighthouse there, and in 1848 he opened a hotel on Appledore. His daughter Celia Laighton Thaxter became a well-known poet throughout New England, adding to the appeal of the place. That hotel no longer exists, but a hotel built on Star Island in the 1870s still stands and has been a home for religious conferences for more than a century.

At present, several of the smaller islands are owned by individuals or families. Duck Island, once used as a bombing target, is now maintained as a sanctuary for waterfowl, and unauthorized visits are not allowed. Appledore and Star, the two largest islands, are owned by the Star Island Corporation, which is composed of representatives of the Unitarian-Universalist and Congregationalist religious groups. Star Island is managed as a home for religious conferences, while Appledore is managed primarily as the site of a marine biology laboratory operated by Cornell University with the cooperation of the University of New Hampshire.

The most convenient access to the Isles of Shoals for the general public at the present time is provided by the Isles of Shoals Steamship Co. (Barker Wharf, 315 Market St., Portsmouth, NH 03801; 800-441-4620, 800-894-5509 in NH; www.islesofshoals.com). They operate a daily cruise during the summer season that provides a three-hour stopover on Star Island, allowing ample time to explore the points of interest on the island, such as the rugged, rocky headlands, Betty Moody's cave (a traprock dike with a cave formed by boulders that have fallen from its sides), the John Smith Monument, and a number of old or historic buildings. A map of Star Island showing all principal points of interest is available at the Barker Wharf office. This stopover cruise is limited to 100 visitors per day, so reservations are highly recommended. Visitors to Star Island should comply with the owners' regulations for use of the island, and be careful to avoid the abundant poison ivy.

ODIORNE POINT STATE PARK

Located in the town of Rye along the edge of the southern part of Portsmouth Harbor, in the area where the Piscataqua River merges into the Atlantic Ocean, Odiorne Point State Park contains the Seacoast Science Museum and offers fine opportunities for walking along the shore in the transition zones between land and water, an area where resident plants and animals must be able to deal with significant regular fluctuations in the salt content of the water as the tides rise and ebb. Once an area of fine summer homes that was taken over by the military during World War II to provide protective fortification for the harbor, it was given to the state after the war to be turned into a park; some of the former Fort Dearborn's gun emplacement earthworks still exist. The park has two entrances from NH 1A, the main one being near the science museum and the secondary one somewhat farther to the north just before the bridge over Berrys Brook. In addition to the shoreline, the area is crisscrossed by old roads and paths that offer a variety of interesting walks, with the longer loops around the area reaching a length of 1.0 mi. to 1.5 mi. depending on the route chosen. Visitors should take care to avoid the plentiful poison ivy. Refer to the USGS Kittery quadrangle.

GREAT BAY

Great Bay is a 4500-acre tidal estuary, the largest inland tidal bay on the east coast of the United States, furnishing an ecosystem that is particularly notable for the constant, rhythmic changes in the conditions that confront resident plants and animals. At low tide much of the bay becomes exposed mud flats, while at high tide most of these flats are covered by water. Numerous rivers and brooks constantly feed the bay with fresh water, while the high tides of the Atlantic, coming twice each day, cause salt water to flow up the Piscataqua River and into the bay. Thus the salinity of the water varies from place to place and is constantly fluctuating with the tides. At low tide, minerals and organisms flow out of the bay and down the Piscataqua to the coastal region. This constant bi-directional flow of nutrients and organisms contributes to the importance of Great Bay as a habitat that nurtures many forms of life, both resident and visitor. The bald eagle is a particularly notable example of the many kinds of wildlife that find a bountiful food supply here.

Hiking opportunities around Great Bay are relatively limited, but there are several areas where visitors can enjoy short, easy walks while learning about this magnificent resource. Poison ivy may be present in these areas and care should be taken to avoid it.

Great Bay National Wildlife Refuge

This area was once occupied mainly by farms with pastures, orchards, and woodlots before it became part of Pease Air Force Base. After the base was closed, the 1054-acre portion on and near Great Bay was turned into a national wildlife refuge. Most of the area is not open to the public; public access is confined to designated trails and this restriction is strictly enforced. At present trails consist of (1) the *Ferry*

Way Trail, about 1.5 mi. long, which runs past a former weapons-storage complex to an old field and apple orchard, then makes a loop out to the edge of the bay and back to the field; and (2) the *Peverly Pond Trail,* a loop about 0.3 mi. long that leads to the shore of Upper Peverly Pond. Other trails may be open, at least on a seasonal basis. To visit Great Bay National Wildlife Refuge, take US 4/NH 16 (the Spaulding Turnpike) to the Pease International Tradeport (Exit 1), then follow "Great Bay Refuge" signs to the parking area. Trail maps are usually available here. Further information can be obtained from the Refuge Manager, Great Bay National Wildlife Refuge, 336 Nimble Hill Rd., Newington, NH 03801 (603-431-7511).

Adams Point

Located on the west shore of the north arm of Great Bay—known as Little Bay—Adams Point is almost directly opposite the less prominent point reached by the Ferry Way Trail in the Great Bay National Wildlife Refuge. The large field and shoreline offer interesting views, including one across Great Bay with two small, photogenically placed islands in the foreground. Adams Point, now almost reverted to nature except for the UNH Jackson Estuarine Laboratory, has at various times supported a farm, a hotel, a brickyard, and a shipyard. The *Evelyn Browne Trail,* about a mile long, makes a loop through the eastern part of the point; another path, also about a mile long, circles the south and west perimeter of the point and connects back into the Evelyn Browne Trail. The shoreline is accessible from this trail at several points. A trail map is usually available at the trailhead, which is reached by following NH 108 south (toward Newmarket) from Durham. At a point 1.1 mi. from the intersection of NH 108 and Main St. in Durham, bear left on Durham Point Rd. After 3.9 mi. on Durham Point Rd., turn left through a gate with a sign for the Jackson Estuarine Laboratory, and proceed for 1.2 mi. past a boat launch area to the parking area at the trailhead.

Sandy Point

Sandy Point, at the southwest corner of Great Bay, offers short inter-
pretive trails and a small but excellent discovery center where many
exhibits help to reveal the importance of Great Bay as a habitat and
ecosystem. It is reached from NH 33, 0.3 mi. west of Stratham Hill
Park (0.4 mi. west of the New Hampshire Technical Institute), by taking Sandy Point Rd. for 1.0 mi., then turning left at a T intersection
and continuing 0.1 mi. to the end of the road.

STRATHAM HILL

Located in Stratham, Stratham Hill (290 ft.) is a textbook example of
a drumlin, a pile of gravel left by the continental glacier. It is about
150 ft. high and a half-mile long by a quarter-mile wide, oriented in
the direction of the glacier's travel—northwest to southeast. There are
good views to the north and east from the summit, and in almost all
directions from the former fire tower, which has an open observation
deck built to replace the cab. Refer to the USGS Newmarket quadrangle. Access is from Stratham Hill Park on NH 33, 0.1 mi. west of the
New Hampshire Technical Institute. Park in the large parking area and
enter the fenced inner area through a gate.

The summit can be reached by a direct trail 0.2 mi. long from the
northwest and by a woods road 0.5 mi. long that makes a gentler
ascent along the southwest slope. The structure of the drumlin is
revealed more clearly from the walk along this road. A loop hike
ascending by the northwest ridge trail and returning by the woods road
is recommended here, but it is equally convenient to ascend and return
by either route or make the loop in the opposite direction. The trail
along the northwest ridge turns left just before the second building on
the left beyond the gate. It ascends a gravel path, and in about 100 yd.
it passes a plaque to the right of the trail that commemorates the spot
where Robert Lincoln, son of Abraham Lincoln, declaimed the Dec-
laration of Independence as a student at Philips Exeter Academy on
July 4, 1860. Just before reaching the summit tower, the path passes a

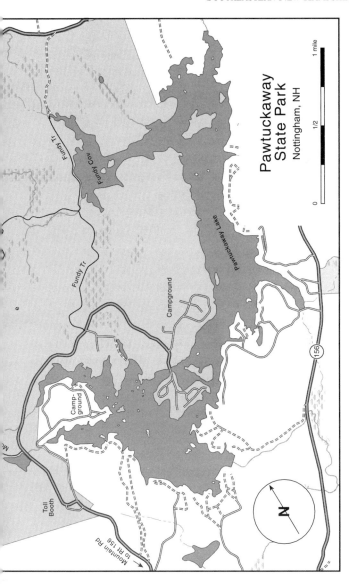

Pawtuckaway
State Park
Nottingham, NH

0   1/2   1 mile

Fundy Tr

Fundy Cov

Fundy Tr

Pawtuckaway Lake

Campground

Campground

156

Toll
Booth

Mountain Rd

to Rt 156

N

circular viewfinder dated 1881 that helps identify visible locations, though some no longer exist and many are no longer visible, at least from ground level. To return via the woods road, continue southeast along the grassy ridge until the unmistakable road swings right into the woods.

In order to use this woods road as an ascent route, its lower end can be reached from the parking area by continuing straight on the path from which the direct trail diverges. At a point just before a gate surrounded by boulders, where the path leads out of the park toward a farmhouse, the summit road turns left.

Stratham Hill (USGS Newmarket quad)
Distances from gate in Stratham Hill Park (160')

- *to* summit of Stratham Hill (290') via northwest ridge: 0.2 mi. (0.4 km.), 130 ft., 10 min.

- *to* starting point (160') via woods road: 0.7 mi. (1.2 km.), 130 ft. (rev. 130 ft.), 25 min.

ROCK RIMMON HILL

This small hill (345 ft.) on the Kingston-Danville town line is unusual for this part of the state because it is formed by a rocky outcrop, with a very steep, south-facing ledge about 150 ft. high. The former fire tower has been removed and the summit has been abused by visitors (litter, much broken glass, etc.), but the outlook across Long Pond to the low, rolling hills stretching southward is one of the few such views available in this area and Rock Rimmon Hill itself is interesting as a rock formation. Refer to the USGS Kingston quadrangle. The easiest access is from a new housing development at the hill's northwest foot. From NH 111A, 2.7 mi. north of its junction with NH 111 near South Danville or 3.5 mi. south of its junction with NH 107 near Fremont, follow Long Pond Rd. east for 0.6 mi., then turn left on Rock Rimmon Rd. and follow it 0.5 mi. to a ⊤ intersection. Turn right here onto Emerald Drive and follow it for 0.7 mi. until the pavement ends where Opal Drive enters on the left. Continue straight about 40 yd. to a crossroads. Most vehicles should park here. The road on the right (south) at this crossroads descends gently, then climbs, becoming steadily rougher, to the summit of Rock Rimmon Hill at 0.4 mi. This crossroads also can be reached from the east, from Kingston village just off NH 125. From the village green, next to the fire station, follow Rock Rimmon Rd. Pavement ends at 1.0 mi., and after the last house at 1.5 mi. the road becomes too rough for most vehicles. The crossroads is reached at 2.1 mi., where the road to the summit is on the left.

Rock Rimmon Hill (USGS Kingston quad)
Distance from Rock Rimmon Rd. (212')

> *to* summit of Rock Rimmon Hill (345'): 0.4 mi. (0.7 km.), 150 ft., 15 min.

PAWTUCKAWAY STATE PARK

The Pawtuckaway Mtns. in Nottingham are a series of three parallel ridges—North Mtn. (995 ft.), Middle Mtn. (845 ft.), and South Mtn. (885 ft.)—all contained within Pawtuckaway State Park (5535 acres), the finest natural area in southeastern New Hampshire. The valley east of North Mtn. contains an extraordinary collection of huge boulders and several other unusual and interesting rock formations, designated as the Boulder Natural Area. While the mountains are small and provide only a few sweeping viewpoints, they offer a variety of rugged, rocky scenery that surpasses even some of the four-thousand-foot peaks of the White Mtns. The trails in Pawtuckaway State Park are covered by the AMC Pawtuckaway State Park Map. Refer also to the USGS Mt. Pawtuckaway quadrangle.

The mountains can be reached from NH 107 between Deerfield and Raymond, 3.2 mi. north of its junction with NH 101 Business Loop, where there is a fire lookout sign. The road, called Reservation Rd., leads east, becoming gravel after 0.9 mi. Bear right at 1.2 mi. and reach a junction at 2.3 mi. From this point the roads make a loop through the heart of the Pawtuckaway Mtns.; the road to the left at this junction, the western branch of the loop (which continues on beyond the north end of the loop for some distance), is known as Round Pond Rd. The eastern branch of the loop, which meets Reservation Rd. 0.2 mi. farther east, is called Tower Rd. These roads are rough and eroded at times, but walking distances to most objectives from the loop are relatively short. The eastern branch of the loop (Tower Rd.) has received the majority of the traffic in the recent past, since the west branch (the southern part of Round Pond Rd.) has sometimes been under more than a foot of water from a beaver flowage near its midpoint, which makes it a problem to pass through either in a car or on foot.

For the trails to the three main mountains, continue on Reservation Rd. to the junction with Tower Rd., then turn left (sign: "Lookout Tower") on Tower Rd. and follow it for 0.8 mi. Here on the left is a small clearing, the former location of the ranger's cabin, where there is a tiny old graveyard in the woods at the edge of the clearing. A few cars can be parked here. The Tower Trail Connector to the Mountain Trail from the main part of the state park enters about 50 yd. beyond here at a small parking area on the right, and the short path to the South Mtn. tower leaves the same parking area on the right in another 50 yd. The Middle Mountain Trail begins about 50 yd. below (south of) the ranger's cabin site. Location #7, where the South Ridge Connector leads to the Shaw Trail and the South Ridge Trail, is 0.2 mi. farther along the road beyond the Tower Trail. The north end of the loop (the junction of Tower Rd. and Round Pond Rd.) is about 1.8 mi. from the junction of Tower Rd. with Reservation Rd. This point (the north end of the loop) also can be reached directly from Reservation Rd. by Round Pond Rd. in about 1.3 mi. when that road is passable. The Boulder Trail to the Boulder Natural Area and North Mtn. begins on Round Pond Rd. 0.4 mi. north of the north loop junction. The other end of the Boulder Trail, which gives access to the boulders and North Mtn. via the Lower Slabs, begins at the edge of Round Pond 0.6 mi. farther along this road (this section may not be passable for ordinary cars).

The easiest road access to the mountains is from the state park off NH 156, but walking distances are much longer—though in winter, when Reservation Rd. is not open, access to some of the trails on the mountains may be more convenient from this side. Reach the trails by following the road toward the swimming beach, passing a tollbooth (fee charged in summer), and then passing a pond on the left. The park furnishes trail maps that are usually available at the visitor center; most trailheads and important junctions are numbered, with small signs that are keyed to locations on the map. The trails in the eastern part of the park are maintained for multiple use, and are particularly favored by trail bikers in summer and snowmobilers in winter. These trails are sometimes muddy in places and offer few long-range views, but they frequently traverse interesting woodlands and pass near extensive swamps. They will probably appeal most to hikers looking for pleasant but not spectacular walks fairly close to home.

Boulder Trail

This scenic short trail runs through the principal boulder field and passes the Lower Slabs as well as several other interesting rock formations. It provides access to the northern terminus of the North Mountain Trail and to Round Pond Rd. at Round Pond (the northern terminus of the South Ridge Trail), and also makes possible several interesting loops in the Round Pond and North Mtn. areas.

The trail leaves Round Pond Rd. at the hairpin turn 0.4 mi. north of Tower Rd. at Location #11 and 0.6 mi. west of Round Pond at Location #9. It descends on an old woods road through a dense hemlock forest, swings right and then left, and meets the northern terminus of the North Mountain Trail in 0.2 mi. at Location #10, in the midst of an impressive boulder field of large moss-covered glacial erratics. Here the trail turns sharp right (east), becoming a footpath, and passes through a stone wall, then skirts the northern side of an attractive open marsh. At 0.5 mi. the trail reaches a clearing at the base of an impressive set of nearly vertical ledges next to the marsh and immediately passes beneath several overhanging boulders (arrow). It passes several slabs and ledges in a hemlock grove (a mecca for local rock climbers) and soon reaches a junction (marked by a trail sign for the Lower Slabs) next to a seasonal stream. Here there is a side path to the left, shown on the park map as a link between the Boulder Trail and Round Pond Rd. just north of Round Pond but no longer officially maintained; it can be followed for about 100 yd. to some interesting rock formations. The main trail passes a beaver dam (right) that partially obstructs the brook connecting the marsh with Round Pond, swings left and then right, and descends to the Round Pond Rd. at the northwest corner of Round Pond at Location #9, directly opposite the northern terminus of the South Ridge Trail.

Boulder Trail (AMC Pawtuckaway State Park Map)
Distances from Round Pond Rd. (450')

to North Mountain Trail (400'): 0.2 mi., 5 min.

to Round Pond Rd. at Round Pond (350') at Location #9: 0.7 mi. (1.1 km.), 20 min.

North Mountain Trail

This recently lengthened trail, which traverses North Mtn. from north to south, is the longest in the park and provides the most scenic trip. Of particular note among the features passed along the way are the collection of large glacial erratic boulders in the valley at the east end of the mountain, and the Devil's Den, a cave formed by the removal of a large fragment of rock by frost action, located in the wild, boulder-strewn eastern promontory. North Mtn. has many interesting and striking vistas along its ridge, and the hemlock groves on the north side of the mountain are among the finest in the park.

The northern end of this trail is on the Boulder Trail near the boulder field at Location #10, 0.2 mi. from Round Pond Rd. via the boulders and 0.5 mi. from Round Pond Rd. at Round Pond (the northern trailhead of the South Ridge Trail) via the Lower Slabs. The southern trailhead is on Reservation Rd., 1.8 mi. east of NH 107 and 0.5 mi. west of Round Pond Rd., at a sharp turn in the road where there is a small area for parking directly opposite the extension of Snowmobile Route 17W. Since the greatest amount of use is on the section between the boulders and the summit of North Mtn., this trail is described in the north-to-south direction.

From the junction at Location #10 the trail climbs at a moderate grade through a beautiful hemlock forest to Dead Pond at 0.6 mi., then turns left and climbs steeply up a boulder-strewn promontory, which is covered with lichens and moss and contains many boulder caves, and soon reaches the Devil's Den (a crevice cave in the rocks to the left of the trail); nearby there is an outlook to the right across Dead Pond. From here the trail angles steeply up the north side of the ridge and, marked with cairns, continues near the ridgecrest to a small col below another set of boulder cliffs. It then climbs by a switchback in beautiful hemlock woods to an excellent outlook to the east (including Middle Mtn. and South Mtn.) on a bluff where there is a large green Public Service Company communications reflector. It then continues along the ridge to the overgrown summit at 1.2 mi. from Location #10. The ledgy summit is marked by a cairn, and there is a limited view west toward Fort Mtn.

The trail continues along the ledgy ridgecrest, descending easily with occasional short ascents, passing through patches of hemlock woods and encountering the blue-blazed park boundary line. At 1.9 mi. the trail reaches the shoulder of the ridge at a rocky outlook next to an old stone fireplace, then begins a steeper decent down the rocky ridge over scattered ledges, passing several easterly views toward Middle Mtn. over a large marshy area. At the foot of the steep section, at 2.2 mi., the trail meets an intersection of roads, of which the better woods road ascends on an angle from the left and continues roughly straight ahead. The North Mountain Bypass follows the section of road that ascends from the left here, and Snowmobile Route 17W also enters here on a woods road from the right. The North Mountain Trail continues on the road nearly straight ahead, coinciding with Snow-mobile Route 17W as it descends gradually, swinging left, then right, and passing an old road that diverges on the right. It crosses a stream near several stone walls, then ascends gradually, passes through a clearing where another old road enters on the right, and continues to Reservation Rd.

North Mountain Trail (AMC Pawtuckaway State Park Map)
Distances from Boulder Trail at Location #10 (400')

- *to* North Mtn. summit (995'): 1.2 mi., 600 ft., 55 min.
- *to* North Mountain Bypass (700'): 2.2 mi., 700 ft. (rev. 400 ft.), 1 hr. 25 min.
- *to* Reservation Rd. (600'): 2.7 mi. (4.3 km.), 700 ft., 1 hr. 40 min.

North Mountain Bypass

This trail mostly follows woods roads, connecting Round Pond Rd. with the North Mountain Trail at the south end of North Mtn., and provides a return route for a loop hike over North Mtn. It is easy to follow for most of its length and has good footing with easy to moderate grades. Since the south end of the loop has the easiest vehicular access, this trail is described as a return route from north to south.

The trail leaves Round Pond Rd. at a point about 0.3 mi. north of its junction with Tower Rd. at Location #11 and about 0.1 mi. south of the southern terminus of the Boulder Trail. It ascends on an old road through pine and hemlock forest, heading generally southwest. It soon bears right onto an old road coming in from the left, then swings sharp right to reach a viewpoint overlooking a large clearing (left). It descends gradually, skirts the north end of a large bog, then ascends gradually through mixed forest. The trail swings left, then right, and at 0.8 mi. it enters another old road (which is also used as a snowmobile trail) and follows it to the right. To the left, this road leads in 0.3 mi. to Round Pond Rd. at a point 0.4 mi. south of Tower Rd. at Location #11 and 0.9 mi. north of Reservation Rd.

The trail swings left, then right twice along a stone wall as it ascends gradually along the southeast slope of North Mtn. After two more bends, it meets the North Mountain Trail 0.5 mi. north of Reservation Rd. and 1.0 mi. south of the summit of North Mtn. Here the North Mountain Trail continues on the road, bearing left and heading south; at this junction Snowmobile Route 17W comes in from the left, coinciding with the North Mountain Trail, and descends straight ahead on another road.

North Mountain Bypass (AMC Pawtuckaway State Park Map)

Distance from Round Pond Rd. (500')

   to North Mountain Trail (700'): 1.4 mi. (2.3 km.), 200 ft., 50 min.

Distance from Reservation Rd. (600')

   to starting point by complete loop via North Mountain Trail, Boulder Trail, and North Mountain Bypass: 4.9 mi. (7.9 km.), 700 ft., 2 hr. 50 min.

South Mountain Tower Trail

Probably the most popular hike in the park, this trail ascends South Mtn. directly from the north and provides access to the fine views from the fire tower and nearby ledges for a modest effort. The extensive views include Mt. Wachusett, Monadnock, Sunapee Mtn., Lovewell Mtn., Mt. Kearsarge, Blue Job Mtn., and Fort Mtn. The trail begins on Tower Rd. 0.8 mi. north of Reservation Rd., just north of Location #6, where the Tower Trail Connector from the Mountain Trail reaches Tower Rd. The trail ascends by switchbacks through a pine grove on a white-blazed trail; in the lower part there is a steep direct route and a less steep route to the left. The trail passes several boulder caves (left) and the grade eases temporarily, then the path ascends granite steps and climbs by switchbacks again to the open ledges near the summit of South Mtn., where the South Ridge Trail is reached.

South Mountain Tower Trail (AMC Pawtuckaway State Park Map)

Distance from Tower Rd. (540')

   to South Mtn. summit (885'): 0.4 mi. (0.6 km.), 350 ft., 25 min.

South Ridge Trail

This trail traverses South Mtn., giving access to its fire tower and far-reaching views. Most hikers approach the mountain from Tower Rd. to the west, although ambitious hikers may wish to approach it from the State Park Rd. to the east via the less-traveled Mountain Trail or Round Pond Trail. The southern terminus of the South Ridge Trail is near the height-of-land on the Mountain Trail (Location #5), 1.8 mi. west of State Park Rd. at Mountain Pond (Location #2) and 0.6 mi. east from Tower Rd. at the trailhead for the South Mountain Tower Trail (Location #6) via the Tower Trail Connector.

   The trail ascends an old road past several stone walls before entering a hemlock grove with several scattered boulders and ledges. At 0.6 mi. it emerges onto semi-open ledges with increasing views to the west and soon arrives at the summit of South Mtn. Here the South Mountain Tower Trail comes up from the north (left). From the top of the lookout tower the views to the west are extensive, running from Mts. Wachusett and Monadnock to Mt. Kearsarge and beyond.

   From the summit, the trail descends northward on a rocky ridge into a hemlock forest with occasional minor ascents, then swings left across the ridgecrest and descends sharply past several interesting rock formations. At 1.0 mi. it swings left, then right, past a beaver pond (left) as the grade eases. The trail continues through a wet area, crosses a small stream next to a small beaver pond (left), and ascends gradually to an old road at Location #8. From here the old road (the South Ridge Connector) leads left 0.2 mi. to Tower Rd. at Location #7, 0.2 mi. north of the trailheads of South Mountain Tower Trail and the Tower Trail Connector. The South Ridge Trail turns right onto this old road and descends along the stream past a cellar hole (right), which is the foundation of an old mill. In a short distance, the western terminus of the Shaw Trail is reached at a dilapidated bridge (right). This trail leads 2.5 mi. to the Fundy Trail at Fundy Cove but should not be attempted during the wet season and only with extreme caution the remainder of the year since one section is often under deep water (see trail description).

The South Ridge Trail continues straight and descends sharply by a series of switchbacks through a hemlock grove, away from the stream and down to the southwest shore of Round Pond. Here it swings left and follows the south shore of the pond with undulating grades to the Round Pond Rd. opposite the Boulder Trail at Location #9.

South Ridge Trail (AMC Pawtuckaway State Park Map)
Distances from Mountain Trail (500')

> *to* South Mtn. summit (885'): 0.6 mi., 400 ft., 30 min.

> *to* South Ridge Connector at Location #8 (480'): 1.3 mi., 450 ft. (rev. 400 ft.), 50 min.

> *to* Shaw Trail (480'): 1.4 mi., 450 ft., 55 min.

> *to* Round Pond Rd. at Location #9 (350'): 2.0 mi. (3.2 km.), 450 ft. (rev. 150 ft.), 1 hr. 10 min.

Middle Mountain Trail

The trail to Middle Mtn. begins on an old woods road that leaves Tower Rd. just south of the site of the old firewarden's camp, a bit over 100 yd. south of the trailhead for the short trail to the South Mtn. tower. The trail rises on the old road at a moderate grade along a stone wall, passes a small pond (right), then turns sharp left and climbs a steep, badly eroded section to reach the upper shoulder of the mountain in a pine grove. From there the trail ascends with gentle grades over the almost imperceptible summit at 0.8 mi., then descends gradually to a ledge overlooking ponds and swamps and affording distant views to the southwest.

Middle Mountain Trail (AMC Pawtuckaway State Park Map)
Distance from Tower Rd. (500')

   to Middle Mtn. outlook (845'): 1.0 mi. (1.6 km.), 350 ft., 40 min.

Mountain Trail

This trail connects State Park Rd. near the main east park entrance off
NH 156 with Tower Rd. just north of its junction with Reservation Rd.
in the western part of the park. It is the major access route from the
eastern park facilities to the hiking areas surrounding North, Middle,
and South Mtns. It is the preferred route for hikers planning to traverse
between the eastern and western sections of the park, because a section of the principal alternative, the Shaw Trail, is often submerged in
several feet of water (see trail description). The Mountain Trail is a
wide woods road for its entire length, easy to follow and often packed
down by snowmobiles during the winter months.

   The trail begins on State Park Rd. at Location #2, 0.4 mi. north of
the tollbooth and main parking area. There is no parking available at
the trailhead; hikers are required to park in the main parking area. The
trail follows an old road along the northern shore of Mountain Pond
in a hemlock forest, coinciding with the Round Pond Trail. The trail
passes the west end of the pond, enters a wet area in a mixed forest,
and at 0.5 mi. turns right at an intersection where the Round Pond
Trail continues straight ahead.

   After the intersection, the trail descends gradually past a stone
wall and small frog pond (right), ascends gradually and crosses a large
brook, parallels a stone wall, then descends again into a hemlock and
pine forest. The trail swings left near a stone wall, crosses a small
stream, then begins to ascend the south flank of South Mtn., which is
seen across a beaver bog (right). At 1.6 mi. the trail reaches the height-
of-land, then descends gradually to the junction with the South Ridge
Trail (right) at Location #5 at 1.8 mi. The trail then swings right by a
frog pond, passes a stone wall, and almost immediately reaches the
Tower Trail Connector (right), which runs north parallel to Tower Rd.

for 0.6 mi. to the South Mountain Tower Trail. Within another 0.1 mi. the trail reaches Tower Rd. just north of its intersection with Reservation Rd. in a small grassy clearing (no sign, limited parking).

Mountain Trail (AMC Pawtuckaway State Park Map)
Distances from State Park Rd. at Location #2 (250')

- *to* Round Pond Trail junction (350'): 0.5 mi., 100 ft., 20 min.
- *to* height-of-land (550'): 1.6 mi., 300 ft., 55 min.
- *to* South Ridge Trail (500'): 1.8 mi., 300 ft., 1 hr.
- *to* Tower Rd. (450'): 1.9 mi. (3.1 km.), 300 ft. (rev. 100 ft.), 1 hr. 5 min.
- *to* South Mtn. (885') via South Ridge Trail: 2.4 mi. (3.9 km.), 700 ft., 1 hr. 35 min.

Round Pond Trail

This trail connects State Park Rd. near the main east entrance with Round Pond Rd., just north of its junction with Reservation Rd. near the west entrance to the park. It is a major access route from the eastern park facilities to the hiking areas surrounding North, Middle, and South Mtns. In winter, it forms the major snowmobile route through the park as it continues north on Round Pond Rd. to Round Pond. In summer, various connecting roads may be used to link the Round Pond Trail with routes up Middle Mtn., North Mtn., and South Mtn. It is a wide woods road for most of its length and easy to follow.

The trail begins at the State Park Rd. (Location #2), 0.4 mi. north of the tollbooth and main parking area. There is no parking available at the trailhead; hikers are required to park in the main parking area. Coinciding with the Mountain Trail, it follows the old woods road along the northern shore of Mountain Pond in a hemlock forest. After passing the west end of the pond, the trail enters a wet area in a mixed forest, and at 0.5 mi. the route continues straight ahead where the Mountain Trail turns right toward South Mtn.

The trail then ascends 0.4 mi. to a height-of-land and descends to a beaver pond with a dam and lodge (right), where the footway may be flooded during the spring. The trail ascends again through wooden gateposts to Location #14, where another old road continues straight and the trail turns right and emerges in an open area with juniper bushes. The trail then descends past an old stone wall and turns sharp left where another old road continues straight. After crossing a gravel road (the southern extension of Tower Rd.) next to a private home, the trail passes yet another old road, and at 1.6 mi. reaches a junction marked by snowmobile signs. (Straight ahead here, Snowmobile Route 17W follows an old road over a small ridge, then down past several stone walls to end at Reservation Rd. in 0.9 mi., directly opposite the southern end of the North Mountain Trail.)

The Round Pond Trail turns right at this junction and descends to an intersection at Location #13 in a small pine grove and clearing, where an old road continues straight 0.1 mi. to the intersection of Tower Rd. and Reservation Rd. Here the main route swings left, then right, descends past a beaver pond (left), and crosses Reservation Rd. next to the outlet of the pond at 2.0 mi., 0.1 mi. west of its junction with Tower Rd. and 0.1 mi. east of its junction with Round Pond Rd. The trail ascends an old road, swings left past an old cellar hole, runs through a pine plantation, and ends at the Round Pond Rd., about 75 yd. north of its junction with Reservation Rd. and 2.2 mi. south of Round Pond.

Round Pond Trail (AMC Pawtuckaway State Park Map)
Distances from State Park Rd. at Location #2 (250')

  to Mountain Trail junction (350'): 0.5 mi., 100 ft., 20 min.

  to height-of-land (450'): 0.9 mi., 200 ft., 35 min.

  to Reservation Rd. (450'): 2.0 mi., 250 ft., 1 hr. 10 min.

  to Round Pond Rd. (450'): 2.2 mi. (3.5 km.), 250 ft., 1 hr. 15 min.

to Round Pond (350') via Round Pond Rd.: 4.4 mi. (7.1 km.), 500 ft. (rev. 250 ft.), 2 hr. 25 min.

Fundy Trail

This scenic trail connects the State Park Rd. with the boat launch parking area at the northern tip of the northwest arm of Fundy Cove on Lake Pawtuckaway, reached in just over 0.5 mi. by a good gravel road from Deerfield Rd. (There are plans to create a new trail from this location east along the northern shore of Lake Pawtuckaway toward Nottingham Square.) The Fundy Trail is easy to follow with gentle grades and mostly dry footing, passing Burnham's Marsh, Fundy Cove on Lake Pawtuckaway, and the remnants of a nineteenth-century farming community. There is ample opportunity to observe waterfowl and other birds, particularly during the migration season. This marshy lowland contrasts sharply with the small but rugged rocky hills of the western section of the park, and this trail affords an ideal walk for young families, though hikers should be well prepared during mosquito season. The trail leaves the State Park Rd. at Location #3, 1.4 mi. north of the entrance tollbooth and 1.0 mi. north of the trailhead for the Round Pond Trail and Mountain Trail. Parking is available across the road in the group picnic and camping area. Please do not block the trail entrance.

The trail follows a gravel road north between two wooden stakes, turns left onto an old road (arrow), passes through a small clearing, and enters a pine and hemlock forest. The trail crosses a small stream on a snowmobile bridge and follows the western shore of Burnham's Marsh (right), where waterfowl and other birds may be readily observed. The trail curves several times, crosses a stream that runs through a culvert, then enters the woods and passes the northwest corner of Burnham's Marsh just before reaching the southwest shore of Fundy Cove. This quiet and sheltered area is connected by a narrow passage to the main body of Lake Pawtuckaway, which dominates the eastern boundary of Pawtuckaway State Park. There are many views across the cove toward the northern side of the lake.

The trail enters an attractive hemlock forest, crosses an outlet brook on a snowmobile bridge next to a beaver bog and dam (left), and reaches the eastern terminus of the unmaintained Shaw Trail (left) at Location #4. If conditions allow (a section is frequently flooded), the Shaw Trail affords access to the western trail network near Round Pond and South Mtn. (see trail description). The Fundy Trail continues straight along the western shore of Fundy Cove, past numerous unmarked old roads. Soon several old stone walls, cellar holes, and unmarked paths are visible on both sides of the trail. This marks the site of an early farming community that flourished over 150 years ago. The trail bears away from the lake into the forest past several other stone walls and unmarked paths, crosses a bridge over an inlet to the north arm of Fundy Cove, and reaches the boat launch parking area.

Fundy Trail (AMC Pawtuckaway State Park Map)
Distances from State Park Rd. (250')

- *to* Shaw Trail (250'): 1.0 mi., 30 min.
- *to* boat launch (250'): 1.7 mi. (2.7 km.), 50 min.

Shaw Trail

This trail (not officially maintained at present) connects the Fundy Trail near the southwest corner of Fundy Cove with the South Ridge Trail south of Round Pond. It is fairly easy to follow except for an extremely wet section through a swamp near its eastern terminus which may be under several feet of water. For this reason, the trail cannot be recommended except in mid-winter when the marsh is completely frozen and the route is well packed by snowmobiles. It begins at Location #4 on the Fundy Trail, 1.0 mi. north of the State Park Rd. and 0.7 mi. south of the boat launch parking area.

The trail follows an old road west, first along the north side of a beaver swamp (left), then along the south side of an open marsh (right). At 0.4 mi. it passes through a stone wall and crosses an outlet brook that emerges from a beaver pond (right) and flows into a flooded beaver swamp (left). Shortly beyond here, the trail reaches a flooded marshy area which may be very wet and often impassable. During the dry season, a faint path to the right may be used to bypass this short wet section. Please use utmost care when fording this potentially dangerous flooded area. Extra time should be allowed to make this crossing.

The wet section ends approximately 100 yd. directly to the west, at a white blaze where the old road re-enters the forest. From here, the route is safe and easy to follow. The trail swings sharp left (south), crosses an outlet stream along the western shore of the large beaver bog (left), passes two large glacial erratics, crosses a small stream, and at 1.0 mi. makes a 180° hairpin turn to the right (north). In another 0.3 mi., the trail swings left (west) and maintains this general direction for the remainder of its course. It passes a small frog pond (left), descends into a hemlock forest with several wet areas, passes a stone wall, crosses a stream, then swings right and ascends an ill-defined ridge skirting several wet areas. The trail makes several left turns past stone walls, crosses another small stream, swings right near the height-of-land on the northern slope of South Mtn., and descends gradually to cross a partially collapsed bridge over a small brook just before ending at the South Ridge Trail. From here, it is 0.1 mi. south to the South Ridge Connector leading to Tower Rd. and 0.5 mi. north to Round Pond Rd. and the Boulder Trail at the western end of Round Pond.

Shaw Trail (AMC Pawtuckaway State Park Map)
Distances from Fundy Trail (250')

   to the hazardous swamp crossing (260'): 0.4 mi., 0 ft., 10 min.

   to South Ridge Trail (480'): 2.5 mi. (4.0 km.), 250 ft., 1 hr. 25 min.

STONEHOUSE POND

This small, attractive pond in the town of Barrington is dominated by a prow-like ledge that rises about 150 ft. from the water's edge on the southwest shore, forming an unusual and picturesque combination of rock and water. There are interesting views from the top of the ledge down to the pond and out across nearby hills. Refer to the USGS Barrington quadrangle. Access is by means of a side road to a public boat launch (marked with a sign for the boat launch) that leaves US 202/NH 9 2.0 mi. west of the point where these routes divide west of Barrington village, or 3.2 mi. east of where they join US 4 in Northwood. The road to the boat launch is rough and muddy and may not be passable all the way for most vehicles, but the total distance from US 202/NH 9 to the boat launch at the pond's outlet brook is only about 0.3 mi. There is a good view of the Stonehouse from ledges near the launching area. There are no official, marked paths around the pond, but beginning on the far side of the outlet brook there are several beaten paths just above the shoreline that can be followed fairly easily in a clockwise direction to the foot of the Stonehouse, where a steep path ascends a gully and continues across ledges through sparse woods to the summit and the viewpoints down to the pond. The easiest route of return is back along the ascent route, but it is also possible (and quite interesting) to complete the circuit of the pond. The paths on this route are less well beaten, and on the descent from the Stonehouse to the shore of the pond one must use care to stay back from the ledges that drop toward the pond. On reaching the pond, one will encounter the swampy western arm of the pond, with much evidence of beaver activity. It is possible to cross this arm (though probably not with dry feet), but it is better to continue around the periphery of the arm through open woods and return from there along the shore to the boat launch area. From the boat launch to the Stonehouse and back—either by retracing the ascent route or by continuing around the pond—is roughly 0.5 mi.

GARRISON HILL

This small hill (290 ft.) on the Dover-Rollinsford town line boasts what is probably the most elaborate observation tower in New Hampshire, which provides excellent views of southeastern New Hampshire and southwestern Maine. The Pawtuckaways and Blue Hills are prominent, and Mt. Washington can be seen in clear weather, particularly during the months when it has a snow cap. The tower can be reached very easily (during daylight hours) by driving up Abbey Sawyer Memorial Highway, which leaves NH 16 north of the center of Dover and just south of Wentworth-Douglass Hospital. It is also possible to make a short but brisk ascent on foot. Take Old Rollinsford Rd., which runs between the hospital on the north and a group of professional buildings on the south. Vehicle travel ends in a short distance at a gate. Continue on the road for about 0.2 mi., then ascend one of several steep, rough beaten paths on the trails of an abandoned ski area, reaching the summit in another 0.2 mi.

BLUE HILLS RANGE

The Blue Hills are a small but prominent range of hills in the towns of Strafford and Farmington, consisting of (from east to west) Evans Mtn. (1232 ft.), Parker Mtn. (1410 ft.), Mack Mtn. (1170 ft.), Blue Job Mtn. (1357 ft.), Nubble Mtn. (1030 ft.), Hussey Mtn. (1204 ft.), and Chesley Mtn. (1035 ft.). Trails on Parker Mtn. and Blue Job Mtn. offer interesting walks; the best views in the range are obtained from the fire tower on Blue Job Mtn.

Blue Job Mountain Trails

Blue Job Mtn. (1357 ft.) is located in Farmington near the Strafford town line. There are excellent views from the fire tower on the summit. Refer to the USGS Baxter Lake quadrangle. There are several paths on the mountain, including a shaded foot trail and a jeep trail through semi-open former blueberry fields to the summit. In addition to these trails, there is also a beaten path that runs north to the currently active blueberry fields on the north shoulder of the mountain; this path should be noted and avoided by hikers attempting to follow one of the two trails described here. These trails begin on First Crown Point Rd., 5.5 mi. from NH 202A, just past the height-of-land at a point where there are two gates close together on the right (east) side of the road. First Crown Point Rd. leaves NH 202A 5.3 mi. east of its junction with NH 126 in Center Strafford, or 2.8 mi. west of its junction with NH 202 near Rochester.

The main trail to the summit and fire tower begins at the right-hand gate and climbs a rocky path to a point just east of the summit where there is a ledge with a restricted view to the right; here the trail swings left and climbs the last pitch to the summit. The jeep road is better used to descend the mountain because it is easier to follow in that direction (converging rather than diverging at forks) and because it offers good views from several open areas that are more easily appreciated by hikers facing out from the mountain. It leaves the summit roughly southwest at first, then swings left and descends to the right of a communications tower with a shed; at the base of the mountain it meets another jeep road, which it follows left to the trail-head. To ascend by this jeep road, start from the left-hand gate, avoid a right fork after a short distance that leads back to the main trail, and in about 0.1 mi. turn sharp right (uphill) on another road. At a fork in an open area with the previously mentioned communications tower and shed straight ahead, take the left road, which is the less obvious one at this point. (If the right fork is taken by mistake, this jeep road can be rejoined directly behind the tower and shed.) The jeep road climbs to the left of the tower, then swings to the right behind it and continues to the summit.

Blue Job Mountain (USGS Baxter Lake quad)

Distances from First Crown Point Rd. (990')

to Blue Job Mtn. summit (1357'): 0.5 mi. (0.8 km.), 350 ft., 25 min.

to starting point via jeep road: 1.1 mi. (1.7 km.), 350 ft., 45 min.

Parker Mountain Trails

Parker Mtn. (1410 ft.) in the town of Strafford is a long, fairly flat-topped ridge running southwest to northeast, with gentle slopes on the northwest but steep ones on the southeast. Refer to the USGS Parker Mtn. quadrangle. The main trail, the Spencer Smith Trail, ascends from the east (NH 126) and follows the ridgecrest to the summit. It is also possible to make a loop via the Mooers Loop Trail, the Link Trail, and the Spencer Smith Trail; this loop is better done in the sequence mentioned, since the Link Trail is somewhat obscure on the ledges just under the ridgecrest, but the route in this direction is obvious even if the trail is lost. In addition to the trails mentioned here, there are others connected to the summer camps on the ponds at the northwest foot of the mountain.

The Spencer Smith Trail begins at a wide turnout on NH 126 just south of its height-of-land, 7.4 mi. south of its junction with NH 28 in Center Barnstead and 2.5 mi. north of the northern junction with NH 202A in Center Strafford. The two trailheads for the Mooers Loop Trail are located 0.2 mi. and 1.1 mi. south of the trailhead for the Spencer Smith Trail; the southern trailhead is located in a field just south of a white farmhouse and opposite a brick house, marked by a Mooers Loop Trail signpost and a plaque for the Strafford Town Forest mounted on a large rock.

The ridgecrest route, the Spencer Smith Trail, passes a gate and follows a red-blazed woods road uphill. At 0.3 mi. several very short unmarked side paths lead left to a ledge with good views to the south, with nearby Blue Job Mtn. just barely visible to the far left—perhaps the best outlook on the trail. The old woods road continues to climb fairly steeply, rather eroded with less than ideal footing, until it reaches the shoulder of the ridge at 0.4 mi. From there on it follows the ledgy ridgecrest with generally easy grades. At 0.8 mi. it crosses an open ledgy area with views through and over trees, where there is a crudely built stone enclosure. Here the blue-blazed Link Trail enters from the south. The Spencer Smith Trail continues across ledges and through minor sags, passing a sparsely blazed path that runs off to the north. At 1.1 mi. the trail reaches the true summit, where there is a large cairn under a pine tree with a small spruce intertwined and a ledge with old inscriptions nearby. From here a path continues to the northwest, descending across several ledges that provide glimpses through the trees, tantalizing a hiker with the unfulfilled promise of wide views.

To make a loop hike via the Mooers Loop Trail and the Link Trail in the recommended direction, follow the wide gravel shoulder of NH 126 downhill for 0.2 mi. from the trailhead for the Spencer Smith Trail, then follow a woods road, marked with a trail sign, that runs along the base of the steep southeast slope of Parker Mtn. for 0.6 mi. to a junction with the Link Trail (sign). The Link Trail, blazed in blue, ascends at a moderate grade for 0.6 mi. to a ledge 0.3 mi. southeast of the true summit. Blazing is adequate but there is little footway in many places, so the blazes must be followed with care. At the ridgecrest ledges one can go left to the true summit or right to return to NH 126. (Beyond the junction with the Link Trail, the Mooers Loop Trail climbs briefly on the woods road, then diverges left and follows a route with adequate red blazes but little footway—follow with care. The trail swings back toward NH 126, enters another woods road, and passes a route that leaves on the right, profusely blazed in white but not cleared, which runs around the south shore of a small unnamed pond. The Mooers Loop Trail, now mostly blazed in white, descends across a wet sag at the end of the pond, passes through some ruins of an old farm, then diverges left off the woods road to climb over a small knoll, descend past a small old cemetery, and cross a field to NH 126.)

Parker Mountain Trails (USGS Parker Mtn. quad)
Distance from NH 126 (907')

   to summit of Parker Mtn. (1410') via Spencer Smith Trail: 1.1
        mi. (1.8 km.), 500 ft., 50 min.

Distances from NH 126 (907')

> *to* summit of Parker Mtn. (1410') via Mooers Loop Trail, Link Trail, and Spencer Smith Trail: 1.6 mi. (2.5 km.), 600 ft., 1 hr. 5 min.

> *to* starting point by complete loop via Spencer Smith Trail: 2.7 mi. (4.4 km.), 600 ft., 1 hr. 40 min.

TENERIFFE MOUNTAIN AND PRESERVE

Teneriffe Mtn. (1090') is located in the town of Milton, about 2.5 mi. from the Maine border. Its open summit affords fine views, including Mt. Washington in good weather. Refer to the USGS Farmington quadrangle. The Nature Conservancy owns a substantial reservation on the slopes of Teneriffe's eastern knob, purchased to protect the habitat of a rare plant, but this preserve does not include the summit of either of Teneriffe's peaks. The preserve has a trail system which provides an interesting woods walk but no sweeping views. Teneriffe Mtn. itself has no official trails, but experienced hikers can make the ascent by means of a series of snowmobile and ATV trails.

Mount Teneriffe Preserve

The trailhead for the Mt. Teneriffe Preserve trail system is reached by starting from NH 75 at a point 1.0 mi. west of its interchange with NH 16 or 2.4 mi. west of its junction with NH 153 at the south edge of Farmington village. Follow Governor's Rd. for 2.2 mi., then turn right on Teneriffe Mtn. Rd. (no sign) and follow it for 1.6 mi. to a crossroads next to a cemetery. Turn right here onto Mountain Rd. and continue 0.9 mi. to a small parking area (sign) on the left just past the height-of-land. A short distance along the main trail (the Ledge Trail), there is a register box where trail maps are usually available.

After 0.1 mi. the trail swings left where both ends of the short (0.2 mi.) Spur Loop Trail diverge on the right. The main trail crosses a shallow gully at the foot of ledges, ascends easily to a boulder and a restricted outlook to the east on the right of the trail, then descends easily along the foot of a steep, rocky slope. At 0.3 mi. the Back Mountain Trail diverges left (uphill), and at 0.4 mi. the Ledge Trail ends in a grassy area. Here the Back Mountain Trail turns sharp left and runs through the woods for 0.1 mi., then enters a woods road and follows it (in the opposite direction, turn right off the end of the woods road). After 0.3 mi. on the woods road, the trail turns sharp left off it and climbs easily up toward the ridge. This section is adequately marked with Nature Conservancy trail markers nailed to trees but must be followed carefully due to lack of an evident footway in some places. The trail crosses a stone wall and turns left before reaching a second wall, then runs between the two walls. When the wall on the left ends, the trail swings left, then turns right and climbs slightly, and crosses a small grassy opening. It then turns left and descends to the junction with the Ledge Trail.

Mount Teneriffe Preserve Trails (USGS Farmington quad)

Distance from parking area (900')

> *to* starting point via complete circuit of all trails: 2.0 mi. (3.2 km.), 300 ft., 1 hr. 10 min.

Teneriffe Mountain

The obvious easy route to the summit of Teneriffe Mtn. via the open slopes from the height-of-land on Mountain Rd., just above the Nature Conservancy trailhead, is not open to the public. The following route is not difficult to follow, but since there are few useful markings and no signs at intersections it cannot be recommended for inexperienced hikers. The route starts with a snowmobile trail that leaves Teneriffe Mtn. Rd. 1.0 mi. east of Governor's Rd. (see directions above for Mt. Teneriffe Preserve), in a sag at the foot of a fairly steep hill. The trail is a cable-gated woods road with a snowmobilers' sign for "Evergreen Valley" and "Milton 3 Ponds." Follow the woods road over a rise and down across a wet sag with a bridge over a small brook in the middle. The trail then begins to climb, crosses two new bridges a few yards apart in another wet area, and enters a recently logged area where the road improves greatly. After crossing the height-of-land and descending, the snowmobile trail diverges right, and a crossroads is soon reached; the road on the right is no more than a vehicle track, while the route to Teneriffe Mtn. follows a clearer old road that diverges sharp left and descends easily through a small logging clearing to a sag. Here it crosses two wet spots, then climbs briefly, swings right, and runs south, contouring along the west side of Teneriffe Mtn. with minor ups and downs. Just when it seems that the mountain surely must have been passed, an ATV track diverges left at a right angle at a minor height-of-land and climbs to the summit, where there are good views. Views to the east and north, including Mt. Washington, can be obtained by continuing about 50 yd. east to the top of an open slope. The distance of the route is about 2 mi.

Appendix

Accident Report

Your Name_____**Date** _____**TIme**_____

DESCRIPTION OF LOST OR INJURED PERSON:

Name_____**Age/Sex:** _____

Address: _____**Hair:** _____

_____**Fac. Hair** _____

Phone: _____

REPORTING PERSON:

Name _____**Phone:** _____

Address _____

WHAT HAPPENED:

_____

_____

_____

_____

_____

POINT LAST SEEN:

Car Description _____**Date** _____

Car Location _____

Itinerary _____

WEARING (color/style/size):

Jacket _____Shirt _____

Shorts/Pants _____Hat/Gloves _____

Glasses _____Pack _____

Footgear _____Crampons _____

CARRYING (color/style/size/quantity):

Map _____Sleeping Bag _____

Tent/Bivy _____Rain/Windgear _____

Flashlight/Batts _____Extra Clothing _____

Food/Water _____Ski Poles/Ice Axe _____

Experience _____

Physical/Mental Conditions _____

ESSENTIAL PATIENT EXAMINATION

PROBLEM AREAS/INJURIES

❏ Head   ❏ Neck   ❏ Shoulders   ❏ Chest
❏ Abdomen   ❏ Back   ❏ Pelvis

❏ Left Upper Leg   ❏ Left Lower Leg   ❏ Left Foot
❏ Right Upper Leg   ❏ Right Lower Leg   ❏ Right Foot

❏ Left Arm   ❏ Left Hand   ❏ Right Arm   ❏ Right Hand

Chief Complaint and Plan

_____

_____

_____

Problem 2 and Plan

_____

_____

_____

Problem 3 and Plan

_____

_____

_____

BACKGROUND INFORMATION

Allergies _____

Medication _____

Previous Injury/Illness _____

Last 24hr food/water intake _____

Medical Conditions/Other _____

_____

FOR BACK, CHEST, OR ABDOMINAL PAIN, DETERMINE:

History _____

Duration _____

Intensity _____**Changing +/-** _____

VITAL SIGNS

TIME	LEVEL OF CONSCIOUSNESS	BREATHING RATE	PULSE	BLOOD PRESSURE	SKIN	PUPILS
ESSENTIAL				**HELPFUL**		

NOTES

DATE/TIME	WEATHER/LOCATION AND FINDINGS	ACTION TAKEN

Index

Boldface denotes hiking trails. Trails with an asterisk
are mentioned in the text but are not fully described.

About the
Appalachian Mountain Club

Begin a New Adventure!

Join the Appalachian Mountain Club, the oldest and largest outdoor recreation club in the United States. Since 1876, the Appalachian Mountain Club has helped people experience the majesty and solitude of the Northeast outdoors. Our mission is to promote the protection, enjoyment, and wise use of the mountains, rivers, and trails of the Northeast.

Members enjoy discounts on all AMC programs, facilities, and books.

Outdoor Adventure Programs

We offer more than 100 workshops on hiking, canoeing, cross-country skiing, biking, and rock climbing as well as guided trips for hikers, canoers, and skiers.

Facilities: Mountain Huts and Visitor Centers

The AMC maintains backcountry huts in the White Mountains of New Hampshire and visitor centers throughout the Northeast, from Maine to New Jersey.

Books and Maps

Guides and maps to the mountains, streams, and forests of the Northeast—from Maine to North Carolina—and outdoor skill books from backcountry experts on topics from winter camping to fly fishing. Call 1-800-AMC-HILL to request a complete catalog.

The Appalachian Mountain Club
5 Joy Street
Boston, MA 02108
617-523-0636

Find us on the web at www.outdoors.org to order books, make reservations, learn about our workshops, or join the club.